THE CONSCIENCE OF A LIBERAL

BOOKS BY CHESTER BOWLES

The Conscience of a Liberal

The Coming Political Breakthrough

Ideas, People and Peace

American Politics in a Revolutionary World

Africa's Challenge to America

The New Dimensions of Peace

Ambassador's Report

Tomorrow Without Fear

THE CONSCIENCE OF A LIBERAL

CHESTER BOWLES

Selected Writings and Speeches

Introduced and Edited by

HENRY STEELE COMMAGER

HARPER & ROW, PUBLISHERS

New York, Evanston, and London

To D. S. B.

Let My Country Awake

Where the mind is without fear and the head is held high;
Where knowledge is free;
Where the world has not been broken up into fragments by narrow
* domestic walls;*
Where words come out from the depth of truth;
Where tireless striving stretches its arms toward perfection;
Where the clear stream of reason has not lost its way into the dreary
* desert sand of dead habit;*
Where the mind is led forward by thee into ever-widening thought
* and action—*
Into that heaven of freedom, my Father, let my country awake.

from "Gitanjali" by Rabindranath Tagore
A Tagore Reader, *by Ameya Chakravarty, The Macmillan Company*

CONTENTS

ix

SECTION II • PATTERNS OF ECONOMIC ASSISTANCE

SECTION III • THE DEVELOPING CONTINENTS

Asia

BOOK II: REALIZING THE AMERICAN DREAM

SECTION I • TOWARD A MORE ABUNDANT SOCIETY

SECTION II • RESPONSIBLE STATE GOVERNMENTS: KEY TO DECENTRALIZATION

SECTION III · *FREE MEN AND FREE MINDS*

INTRODUCTION

WE are witnessing in our day a revolution comparable to that brought on by the Renaissance and the discovery of the New World in the fifteenth and sixteenth centuries—a revolution so prodigious that it seems to shake the very globe itself. A half-hundred new nations swim over the historical horizon; hundreds of millions of men and women, long neglected and condemned, breathe the air of freedom, raise their heads and their hearts, and demand recognition.

Great new power complexes emerge to challenge the older centers of power in the West: China, India, Latin America, the Arab World, and in the not too distant future, Africa. What it all means is a massive shift in the historical center of gravity from the Atlantic to the Pacific, from the Northern Hemispheres to the Southern, from the European to the non-European world, from the white world to the colored.

Three quarters of the globe is in revolt against the European quarter—and we of America are, of course, part of the European quarter. But when we contemplate this immense revolt we are struck at once by its paradoxical character. For it is a revolt against the West carried on with the tools, the institutions, and the ideas forged by the West over the past five centuries. It is carried on with the instruments of science and technology; it is inspired by Western ideas of change and of progress; it is channeled through that extraordinary Western invention, nationalism.

And here is a second great paradox, that while the instruments of technology and science that are now remaking the non-European world are cosmopolitan and even universal, the political instrument of nationalism is, by contrast, parochial and particularist. All of those instruments which look to a social, cultural and humanitarian revolution are unifying; all of those pressures which look to political revolution are divisive.

This non-European world, now in the throes of a massive revolution, is engaged in an attempt to catch up with the European world by one great convulsive leap; to close in a single generation the gap of centuries that has separated Asia and Africa and most of Latin America from the standards of living that the European world has so long enjoyed.

Can the new nations really win through to independence and reform without loosing the furies of racial, religious, and ideological warfare? We are, all of us, wittingly or unwittingly, in a desperate race—a race between those hopeful and benevolent forces making for unity, prosperity and progress, and those tragic and malevolent forces making for fragmentation, war and destruction.

Will the pressures for independence from the West prove stronger, in the end, than the pressure to enlist the aid of the West? Will the drive for political separatism prove more powerful than the drive for cooperation and combination? Will the dread forces of action through violent revolution impede and frustrate the long processes of progress by evolution?

These are the nightmare questions that haunt the minds of statesmen in every country on the globe.

The West itself is responsible for most of these problems, familiar with them, and required to cope with them. The shape of the future depends on the wisdom, the imagination, and the generosity which the West displays in this crisis of history.

Here the United States occupies what may be called a most-favored nation position. While most of the nations of Europe carved out empires in Asia and Africa, and exploited the peoples of these continents for their own profit, the United States, by great good fortune, managed to avoid both imperialism and colonialism, at least outside of the Americas.

Americans can, then, go to the peoples of what used to be called the "dark" continents, with clean hands. Not only this, but the American people have a longer tradition of self-government, a longer tradition of freedom, and a longer tradition of general public enlightenment than any other people, and these are the things that now inspire the hope and excite the enthusiasm of the peoples of Asia and Africa.

With our wealth, our resources of intelligence and skill, our experience with self-government, our capital of good will, and our immunity from most of the tragic forces of history, we are in a better position to help the new nations of the globe than is any other Western people.

There are difficulties, to be sure, and we should not ignore them. Thus isolation nourished a tradition of non-responsibility; thus immunity from the orthodox manifestations of imperialism conditioned us against even the most enlightened colonialism, and made it difficult for us to understand the problems of many of our Old World associates, while our sometimes sanctimonious repudiation of imperialism laid us open to the charge of hypocrisy in our treatment of the Indian and the Negro. Even our affluence is something of a handicap, for it not only exposes us to envy and suspicion from less fortunate nations, but tends to persuade us to believe that there is really nothing that power cannot do or money cannot buy.

Yet, clearly, the United States holds a central position and plays a decisive role in the postwar world. Because alone of the great nations she emerged from the War rich and powerful, with resources, skills, and political and administrative machinery unimpaired, she alone was in position to seize leadership at a critical moment in history.

It is sobering now to contemplate what might have happened to the Western world—indeed to the whole of the world—had not the New World, in the words of Churchill, "stepped forth to the rescue and liberation of the Old." Had the United States not formulated the Marshall Plan and given Marshall aid; had she not subsidized the rehabilitation of the war-ravaged nations of Western Europe until they were able to take care of themselves; had she not launched and maintained the Berlin air-lift—psychologically a turning point in recent history; had she not prepared to move into the void left by Britain in the Near East; had she not responded sharply and decisively to the crisis in Korea; had she not been able and ready to defend many of the beleaguered peoples of the world all through the nineteen-fifties, the contours of history would have been very different from those which we now discern.

Whatever the future may hold for the United States, none can deny that during this critical decade or so of history she rose to the challenge of events and, by her wisdom, her resources, and her courage, made it possible for the Western world to survive and gather strength for the tasks that lay ahead.

It took Britain a hundred years to learn to be a world power, and perhaps no other Old World nation has ever learned—not Spain, or France, or Germany or Russia or, for that matter, Japan. What is astonishing is that the United States discovered in herself an immense capacity for open-mindedness, and an immense resourcefulness.

Consider what she has learned in less than twenty years!

That the world is *really* one world, that no nation is an island unto itself, and that we share some measure of responsibility for the misfortunes, the failures, the crises, the welfare, of every people.

That the European world, the white world, the Christian world, is not assigned a favored place in the cosmic scheme.

That the world is not to be divided neatly into two opposing camps—ours and the Russian—but is in fact fragmented into many foci of power, and that any strategy based on the notion of Two Worlds is bound to fail.

That we cannot impose our will on other nations, not even on those that are weak, and that we cannot expect other peoples to adopt—or even to approve—our own notions of economics and politics.

That we must not attempt to pressure neutrals into taking sides, but accept and understand neutralism.

That we must work through international organizations and co-operate with other nations—even with rival nations—in the important tasks of aid and rehabilitation.

That economic, social, and cultural aid is far more effective than military aid in almost every situation.

That there are limits to power, even to atomic power, and that for the most part military power carries within itself its own limitations.

That all of us are involved in foreign policy, and that our involvement, as a people, is a total involvement. That there is no peace in our time; that trouble and crisis are normal; and that there is no immunity for the United States from the crises that have for so long afflicted the peoples of the earth.

Most of these things we take for granted now, but they represent the most remarkable advance in sophistication in the whole history of our foreign relations, perhaps in the whole of our history.

*   *   *

ONE of the interesting features of this new enterprise in which we are all so inextricably involved, is the emergence of a new kind of public servant—the international public servant who moves freely from continent to continent, who is as familiar with the problems of India, Bolivia, the Congo and Taiwan as earlier statesmen were with the problems of Massachusetts, Alabama, Minnesota and Oregon; who considers himself not exclusively the spokesman of a particular interest, or economy, or political system, but of the interests of man.

There are antecedents to be sure, especially in the eighteenth century: a Benjamin Thompson who served with equal effectiveness as President of the Royal Institute of London and Prime Minister of Bavaria, or an Andreas Bernstorff who moved easily from the Courts of the German states to the Court of Denmark; a Voltaire, a Condorcet, a Franklin, a Thomas Paine—large spirits who thought of themselves as servants of humanity. But in most parts of the world modern nationalism put an end to all of this.

Now the international scholar, the international scientist, the international statesman who serves his own country by serving others, is once again coming to the fore. A Nansen in Norway, a Spaak in Belgium, a Jean Monnet in France, a Churchill in Britain, a Hammarskjöld, a Myrdal, a Boyd-Orr, a U Thant, a Madame Pandit, a Charles Malik, an Eleanor Roosevelt, a Stevenson—this is the new breed of men and women who provide leadership for the new world that is shaping up before our eyes.

What are the characteristics of this new kind of public servant? First, he is able to emancipate himself from the preconceptions and limitations of parochial nationalism and enter sympathetically into the minds of distant peoples and nations; to accept, instinctively and not just intellectually, the equality of all races and nations; to appreciate interests, habits, mores, cultures, far removed from those in which he was nurtured.

Second, he is not limited by his identification with his own past, or even with his present, but is able to appreciate those great currents of history and of science that are so implacably remaking the world. He is prepared to work with those currents that are sweeping away the last vestiges of imperialism and colonialism and of the exploitation of one race and one continent by another. He is able to see, objectively though never indifferently, the place of his own nation in the new kaleidoscopic pattern that is forming throughout the globe.

Third, he understands that history and politics form a seamless web whose strands stretch from every village and hamlet and city to every other, from country to country and from continent to continent. He knows that isolation, intellectual and moral as well as economic and political, is a thing of the past: that what happens in Burma or the Congo concerns the citizen of Connecticut and of Yorkshire; that all of us are involved in the great enterprise of providing food, medicine, tools, machinery, schools, libraries, hospitals, universities, for those peoples who do not have them. He knows that freedom, too, is a seamless web, that whatsoever we do to the least among us we do to the whole of mankind, and that the test of freedom and of democracy is the willingness to give it practical effect at home as well as to champion it abroad.

Fourth, he is, for all this idealism, a man of affairs, a practical administrator, hard-headed and tough-minded, and—if he is to survive—thick-skinned as well. He needs experience with day-by-day problems of administration; he needs to understand that eloquence and magnanimous gestures are no substitutes for getting on with the job and showing results.

There is no better example of this kind of international public servant than Chester Bowles.

"As a college senior, in 1924, I determined to spend my life in government," Mr. Bowles has written, and he tells us, too—it is an illuminating observation—that he was one of only three or four members of the class of 1924 at Yale for whom a public career held any interest. Circumstances frustrated this early ambition, but did not eradicate it; when war came to America in 1941, Mr. Bowles moved eagerly from private to public enterprise, and it is to public enterprise that he has devoted his energies and his talents for the past two decades.

Four climacterics stand out sharply in Mr. Bowles' career. The first came with the call for public service during the war. First as Price Administrator under President Roosevelt, and later as special assistant to Trygve Lie in the United Nations, Mr. Bowles learned some hard lessons in politics and administration, and was launched upon those world travels which have made him a familiar figure in every continent and almost every country, and which prepared him for conceiving early in 1947 his remarkable paper anticipating the Marshall Plan, which I have included in this collection.

The second climacteric was his election as Governor of Connecticut. That post brought home to him, in daily and familiar fashion, the importance of grass-roots democracy and grass-roots liberalism. It made clear, too, the relation of local to national and even to world affairs. It gave him the habit of address to the people of farm and village and factory and office which has since enabled him to achieve a rapport with the most miscellaneous of audiences in many lands.

The third climacteric came with his appointment as Ambassador to India. This introduced him to another civilization and another world, and it rounded out his education as an international public servant. It is a mark of Mr. Bowles' flexibility that he was able to adapt himself to this position, and to the Indian intellectual and social climate, with extraordinary skill, and to set the tone which has been so successfully maintained by American spokesmen at New Delhi since his ambassadorship.

It made him, too, of all American public figures, the one most knowledgeable about India and her neighbors, the mediator between India and the United States at a time when India was growing into the first rank of world powers and was easily the first of free Asian powers.

The fourth climacteric came in 1960 in the second year of a term as Congressman from Connecticut when Mr. Bowles was chosen first as foreign policy adviser to Senator Kennedy and then as chairman of the Platform Committee of the Democratic National Convention.

From that vantage point he drafted most of the foreign policy planks of the Democratic platform, the civil rights plank, and many of the economic sections as well. In regard to that platform, two features stand out: one is that it is the most liberal platform, both domestically and in its world-wide implications, ever endorsed by the Democratic party; the second is that it was adopted by the convention amid general enthusiasm and with a minimum of controversy.

For that achievement Mr. Bowles deserves no small measure of credit. And it was Mr. Bowles' good fortune to see these platform policies endorsed by the electorate and accepted, in substantial part, by the new Administration which he first served as Under Secretary of State and now serves as the President's Special Representative and Adviser on African, Asian, and Latin-American Affairs. His is a substantial empire, and he presides over it with good sense, good humor, good will and good results.

During twenty years of public service Mr. Bowles has been continuously articulate. In these years he has written no less than seven books setting forth his philosophy of domestic and—particularly—of foreign policy. There is probably no other man in American public life who has spent more time and energy talking foreign policy to the American people over the past decade. In forty-one states, at scores of universities, before Democratic and Republican audiences alike, he has shown an extraordinary capacity to communicate.

As a result, a veritable torrent of articles and addresses has flowed from his indefatigable mind, some of them essays designed for learned journals, some of them persuasive arguments directed to members of Congress or to those who formulate foreign policy, some of them quasi-official reports, some of them occasional or ceremonial addresses, and some of them simply ad-lib statements given without any notes at all.

We present here a representative selection of his papers and addresses that have not heretofore appeared in book form.

My first instinct was to begin with Mr. Bowles' entry into public service as Federal Price Administrator in 1943 when he took charge of a gigantic and chaos-ridden agency, performed a miracle of administrative surgery, and refashioned the Office of Price Administration into a hard-driving, efficient, streamlined obstacle to inflation.

In reviewing this wartime material, however, I have concluded that—despite a consistent strand of postwar consciousness and vision—much of its contents is dated by the period. As a result, I have chosen to begin this volume with the attainment of peace and Mr. Bowles' writings of the postwar era.

I have divided these papers into two broad groupings: those that confront the many faces of foreign affairs; and those dealing largely with the domestic scene.

As Mr. Bowles' contribution is most recently in the realm of foreign policy, it is proper that this category should make up the bulk of the papers. The foreign policy papers are in turn subdivided into appropriate sections dealing with the general issues, questions of economic development, the problems of the "new." nations of Asia, Africa, and Latin America, and those special and insistent problems of defense against the Communist challenge that glare at us from every quarter of the globe.

The domestic selections are also subdivided into appropriate sections dealing with the economics of our society, the responsibilities of state government, and the pervasive problem of civil liberties and civil rights.

The division is a concession to convenience rather than an acknowledgment of disparate interests. A reading of these papers, in the order in which they are printed, brings home to us the consistency and the philosophical unity which have animated Mr. Bowles from the beginnings of his entry into public life.

In putting this material together I have had Mr. Bowles' permission to edit and shorten some of the pieces. I have used the privilege freely. In doing so, however, I have tried to stress certain essential themes which Mr. Bowles has developed over the years and which he treats in varying contexts.

Some of Mr. Bowles' thinking over the past two decades is now embodied in national policies and legislation. More of it occupies today the center of our national debate. And some, too, points to decisions we have not yet faced—but must if we are to live up to our responsibilities as a nation.

Viewed in its unity, then, this volume dramatizes the interrelationship of thought and action: the irrepressible power of ideas in a revolutionary world.

Over the years Chester Bowles has grown from a local to a national to a world figure. Through all of these years he has worked ardently and selflessly to set national goals and shape the national conscience, ceaselessly reminding his countrymen that this is the time for greatness. And he has himself been one of those to whom the great words of Pericles apply, that "knowing the secret of happiness to be freedom and the secret of freedom a brave heart, he did not idly stand aside from the enemy's onset."

HENRY STEELE COMMAGER

Amherst, Massachusetts
June 15, 1962

━━ BOOK I ━━

THE UNITED STATES AND THE WORLD REVOLUTION

A Personal Note on Book I

I am grateful to Professor Commager for bringing together these selections from my writings and speeches since the war.

Book I is concerned with our world objectives as I see them, and what I believe is required to achieve those objectives. As a series, these papers underscore our gradual progress toward a national bipartisan consensus on many key questions of foreign policy.

This consensus includes agreement on the need to oppose overt and covert aggression and to provide an adequate defense with effective international security arrangements, side by side with a deep national concern about the continuing arms race. It also includes an acceptance of the importance of the United Nations, a commitment to expanding world trade, and a belated recognition of the importance of Asia, Africa, and Latin America, where a majority of mankind lives.

Yet as I reread these pages I am also reminded of our lingering disagreements over priorities and objectives in regard to the developing nations, and our sluggishness in applying our national consensus to new situations.

The Alliance for Progress, for instance, is a very late substitute for twenty years of indifference to our Latin American neighbors.

Our freedom of action in Asia continues to be impeded by an accumulation of myths at home and commitments to the status quo abroad.

Each year prodigious efforts are still required to persuade a Congressional majority that our best hope of eroding the alleged Soviet monolith and expanding the areas of freedom lies in the economic, social, and political development of the free nations.

There is no doubt that we Americans have come far and fast out of a century of neutralism and isolationism. But have we come far and fast enough? Are we making the best use of our extraordinary national assets?

And most basic of all: Can a nation as rich and fortunate as ours become an active participant *in a revolutionary struggle for a world of peace and increasing justice for all men?*

Our answers to these questions in the 1960's will almost certainly shape our world for the remainder of this century.

CHESTER BOWLES

Section I

OUR WORLD OBJECTIVES

The least that the less timid among us can do is to go out into this generation and stand for the essential truths of our time: that man's future on earth need not be canceled; that we need not resign ourselves to catastrophe; that our political ingenuity still may rescue us from ruin; that our moral standards still are here; that some things, like war and injustice, may seem everlasting, but that these things are everlastingly wrong, must be everlastingly fought and must someday be conquered.

July 26, 1954

OUR CHANCE TO TURN THE TIDE

Mr. Bowles voices one of the earliest proposals for long-term economic and technical assistance to the underdeveloped nations and for the erection of a new integrated Europe in an address at Freedom House, Willkie Memorial Building, New York, January 17, 1947.

IF THE American people will support the investment of 2 percent of our total income each year for the next twenty years in the development of less fortunate countries, we may change the tide of history.

This sum of money, in addition to private investments abroad, would help to harness the power of many of the great rivers of the earth, eliminate floods, build great power plants and provide irrigation for the benefit of tens of millions of people. It would go a long way toward the building of modern transportation systems throughout the East, in South America and in Europe.

With this investment, the American people could help to modernize peaceful industries in many parts of the world, which, in turn, would substantially raise living standards in Europe, Asia, India, South America and Africa, and enable countless people to become customers of each other and of American enterprise.

Two percent of our national income—four billion dollars—represents only one-third of our present expenditure for defense. It is only one-half the sum which we spent each *month* in waging the war against the Nazis and the Fascists. And yet we can be sure that it will be ridiculed by many as a wasteful extravagance, as another example of Uncle Sam transformed into "Uncle Sucker."

The viewpoint of these critics is wrong, and I pray that it will be rejected. Such an expenditure would be one of the shrewdest investments ever made by the American people. It would bring immeasurable economic benefits to hundreds of millions of human beings all over the world. It would be the living proof of the ability of our American system not only to provide a high standard of living for ourselves, but to help others get a start toward a more prosperous life with a greater measure of dignity. It would be our cheapest peace insurance.

These investments should not be conditional or for narrow political advantages. We should support loans to Poland, Czechoslovakia, Yugoslavia and the war-devastated nations of Eastern Europe as well as to the other European, Asian, African and South American countries.

We must make sure, however, that the money is spent with the greatest possible effectiveness. Natural resources, for instance, do not follow national boundary lines. Therefore the more efficient use of natural resources, which is basic to higher living standards, calls for increased regional planning throughout the world.

Here in America we are blessed with a large enough geographic area to allow for development of the broad markets necessary for a high industrial output. The U.S.S.R. has a similar potential and for the same reason. If there is to be peace based on orderly economic expansion and political growth, the same opportunities must be increasingly held out for the remainder of the world.

Europe offers a good example of the possibilities of such economic integration. To encourage integration, our expenditures to speed European growth and eventually *political* growth should be made through some kind of European Economic Authority. This Authority should establish an over-all economic plan for the European Continent, allocate resources, and see that the plan is carried out.

It should include a European power system, a European communication system, a European transportation system, a coordination of European agriculture and steel production.

America should offer generous help to this European Economic Authority, provided that tariffs between European nations and between our own nation and Europe are eliminated or sharply reduced so that goods can once again move freely. The funds should be used in a way which would assure a steady increase in living standards for all of the three hundred odd million people of the European area, including our former enemies. The Authority should be so organized, however, that the potential military power of Germany will be curbed forever.

Similar plans for over-all economic authorities as a basis for American financial aid should be developed for certain sections of South America and Africa, for Southeast and South Asia, and for the Near East.

A first step in our effort to build a lasting world peace must include the imaginative and vigorous export of American technology and industrial equipment on a basis of regional planning in order to raise gradually the standard of living in other countries.

It would be folly to expect a millennium of world understanding in the next ten years, or in the next generation. But an even greater folly would be to delay in making a bold start along the only road that can lead us toward the establishment of world peace and the achievement of human freedom.

══ 2

WE NEED A PROGRAM FOR
AS WELL AS AGAINST

*Mr. Bowles pleads for greater emphasis on moral, economic,
and social aspects of American foreign policy in a
revolutionary new world.* New York Times Magazine,
April 18, 1948.

THERE are only 145 million of us and we live in a revolutionary world of two billion people. Under such circumstances, our success in creating the basis for a lasting peace will depend in large measure on the strength of our ideas and our relationship to other free people.

Even though our military forces were double their present size, we could not expect to impose our leadership by force or the threat of force. We can influence tomorrow's world only if the people believe in us, and they will never believe in us unless they are confident that we are their sincere champion and friend.

In order to win their respect we must first understand them—and, most important of all, understand their yearning for some semblance of economic security.

If we choose to think of them in terms of governments instead of people, and to base our decisions primarily on strategic considerations rather than on ideas and concepts which move people, we may stumble into a catastrophe.

The average American believes not only in political democracy, but in economic democracy as well. He has been called upon to fight throughout our long history against the domination of vested economic interests.

Moreover, his fight has been remarkably successful. Through broad land ownership, minimum-wage legislation, labor unions, cooperatives, social security, the income tax, child labor laws, public schools, fair-employment practices and a hundred other devices, we have gone a long way toward the ideal laid down in President Roosevelt's Economic Bill of Rights.

Yet when we speak of "democracy" in international terms, our concept seems limited to *political democracy*. We have failed to emphasize economic democracy—the peasant's right to landownership, the city worker's right to his fair share of food and shelter, the right of people everywhere to a decent minimum of education and health.

The Communists have taken advantage of this omission by posing as the one great power which concerns itself with the interests of the impoverished millions. Communist leaders exclaim cynically but with telling effect: "Communism stands for economic democracy, which means higher standards of living through state planning. America stands for political democracy, which you cannot eat and which will not protect you when it rains."

The economic democracy advanced by the Communists through state planning, state ownership and land reforms, however dishonest their *objectives* may be, has a direct and practical appeal to the hundreds of millions who have never known anything but poverty and oppression.

The tyrannical aspects of Communism, which are so shocking to those of us who have grown up in the political democracies of the West, seem less important to a majority of the people in Asia, Africa, Eastern Europe and South America for the simple reason that political oppression in one form or another has always been more or less an accepted part of their lives.

Communism has won many victories in the last two years. It will win more in the years to come unless our policies are made more sensitive to the forces which are now shaping history.

Generally speaking, there are two forces in Europe, Asia, Africa and Latin America which are opposed to the growth of world Communism. First, the feudal landowners, semi-Fascist industrialists and old aristocracy, which fight Communism not because they object to dictatorships as such, but because Communist dictatorships threaten their own power and positions. Second, the liberal democratic forces, which fight Communism because they cannot and will not accept police state tyranny.

The only hope of establishing mass opposition to Communism abroad lies in supporting consistently the democratic groups which share our concept of human freedom. This we have often failed to do —sometimes because these groups were weak, sometimes because we were opposed to their economic ideas as "tending towards socialism" and sometimes because of the pressure of military strategy.

We have on occasion thrown our support behind reactionaries simply because they dislike Communism as much as we, and are in a position to use force in opposing it. With an able assist from Communist propaganda, this has served to identify us in the minds of hundreds of millions of people with the forces which they view as the primary obstacle between themselves and a future of security.

What are the alternatives? How can we strengthen our strategic position with the two billion people who do not live in North America? How can we best avoid war? And, if war comes in spite of our efforts, how can we be sure to develop the maximum support behind us? There are many things that we can do.

Let us start by taking our stand unequivocally beside the hungry and oppressed people all over the world in their fight for increased economic security.

Let us convince them that we stand wholeheartedly for long-overdue economic and social reforms, and that with our help they can achieve higher living standards and political freedom, too.

Through the International Bank we can promote river valley developments on the TVA model on the Tigris, Euphrates and Jordan. We can press the rulers of this area toward long-needed reforms designed to raise the standard of living, of literacy and of health.

The European Recovery Program offers us an unusual opportunity in Europe. It is a bold concept for which Secretary Marshall deserves great credit.

But a major question lies in how our money will be used. Will our efforts lead to the traditional concept of competitive nationalism which has made Europe a cockpit of war since the days of the Romans? Or will we find practical ways to lay the basis for an integrated United States of Europe, friendly to the United States and ready to work with us to create a peaceful world?

We can also take up the case of the oppressed millions in South America and offer our tangible help, under specific conditions, in improving their living standards. If we did so, we would capture the imagination of people not only in South America but throughout the world.

The same approach could be applied to India, not merely to compete with Communism when it starts to gain a foothold, but before Communism gets its start. A reasonable amount of material aid over these critical early years could, with the aid of American technicians, help in raising the living standards of the people whom Gandhi and Nehru have awakened from their long slumber.

Offers of material aid, however, will not be enough. We will need imaginative leadership to go with it. If we are successfully to combat Communism and lay the basis for lasting peace, we cannot afford to compromise with inefficiency and graft, with reaction or Fascism.

Let us demonstrate that we, as Americans, stand not only against tyranny in any form, but for the sweeping economic and social reforms which are so long overdue, and the lack of which now provide such an easy opportunity for the Communists.

Historically, great nations have lost their position of leadership because as they grew prosperous they have tried to stand still, and so lost touch with a world which is forever on the march. As they lost touch, their fears for their own security increased, and with the increase in their fears came even greater conservatism, slowly emerging as out-and-out reaction.

The spotlight of history is now upon us Americans. If we are to remain a great people, we must stand for a bold, world-wide program of economic, social and political democracy, skillfully conceived and aggressively programmed.

Only by so doing will our country continue to flourish as a symbol of hope in a world of two billion people who are determined not to go back.

━━ 3

A PLEA FOR ANOTHER GREAT DEBATE

*The celebrated announcement by U.S. Secretary of State
John Foster Dulles of a new policy of massive retaliation
prompted this strong rebuttal and challenge in an article
in the* New York Times Magazine, *February 28, 1954.*

To LIST the Great Debates over our foreign policy since
World War II is to call the roll of the historic steps America has taken
to accept the world responsibilities thrust upon her. The Truman Doctrine, the Marshall Plan, the North Atlantic Treaty, the dispatch of
troops to Europe, the refusal to expand the war in Korea by an attack
on China—all these were basic decisions and all were made after full
vigorous public discussion.

I believe the time has come for another Great Debate. We need
urgently to debate the doctrine—the so-called Dulles Doctrine—of
"instant retaliation."

In his address before the Council on Foreign Relations on January
12, Secretary Dulles outlined the "new look" of our world strategy,
and in doing so he revealed what appears to be a far-reaching shift
in our foreign policy. What, precisely, did Mr. Dulles mean?

In parts of his speech, parts upon which he lays very heavy stress,
he seems to propose the virtual abandonment of the local resistance,
limited-war concept. He emphasizes the "deterrence of massive reliance on deterrent power and less dependence on local defensive
power."

14

Formerly, he says, "we needed to be ready to fight in the Arctic and in the tropics, in Asia, the Near East and in Europe; by sea, by land and by air, with old weapons and with new weapons." This need is now said to be changed by a new "basic decision . . . to depend primarily upon a great capacity to retaliate, instantly, by means and at places of our own choosing."

The term "instant retaliation" has always been associated with strategic atomic bombing. Retaliation at "places of our own choosing" implies places beyond the area of aggression, for that area is chosen by the enemy.

All told, the Administration seems to be saying that in dealing with future armed Soviet or Chinese aggression into non-Communist territory anywhere in the world, it proposes to rely chiefly upon atomic attack by the Strategic Air Force against the major cities in Communist countries. This interpretation is supported by background statements of high government sources that "this is the most important speech that Mr. Dulles has ever made or is ever likely to make."

If this is the new policy, what are its chances of success, first, in discouraging aggression, and second, in repelling aggression if it should break out? Will it really, as Mr. Dulles maintains, give us "more security at less cost"?

First, it should be said that in Western Europe such a policy is neither new nor untested. Russia undoubtedly has long known that we would consider an attack on Europe as an attack on ourselves; and that in response to such an attack we would use the atomic bomb against her, even though the ensuing general war would probably involve widespread atomic destruction in our own country.

But would America be willing to accept these same terrible risks to meet local aggressions in Asia—say, in Afghanistan, Burma, Iran or Indochina? Our deep-felt reaction to the war in Korea and to the bare prospect of an even more limited involvement in Indochina seems to say clearly that we would not.

In any case, how vulnerable is vast, decentralized China to our atomic attack? China, unlike the Soviet Union, has no major industrial concentrations. The entire steel production of Manchuria is no more than one-half that of the new United States Steel plant on the Delaware.

The Chinese economy is not dependent upon highly articulated transportation and communications networks. Chinese armies are mobile, schooled in guerrilla warfare and in survival on the land, and they operate without the elaborate supply and support formations of Western armies.

We cannot hope that the atomic devastation of Chinese cities would mean anything but a lengthy, sprawling, indecisive conflict in which China's main asset, manpower, might occupy most of continental Asia.

And is there not a broader issue, indeed a fundamental moral issue, implicit in this new policy, which in all conscience we should resolve with our eyes open? We are a religious people, who believe that man is sacred to God. We pride ourselves on our democratic faith in the ultimate worth of the individual. It is these beliefs that distinguish our way of life from that of the Communists.

Yet, if we threaten to bomb China's cities, we would seem to be proposing to wipe out tens of millions of Chinese men, women and children, huddled in metropolises which, unlike those of the Soviet Union, are almost devoid of legitimate military or industrial targets. Are we prepared to exact this frightful toll of helpless people in order to punish the rulers who control them?

Communist propaganda has already convinced hundreds of millions of Asians that we dropped the atomic bomb on Japan and not Germany because we considered Asians inferior people. Would not the atomic destruction of defenseless Chinese cities, while Russian cities remained untouched, turn all Asia into our bitter and unrelenting enemies?

What of Europe? Does Mr. Dulles' new policy fulfill the requirements of our most delicate diplomatic problem, which is keeping the coalition of European nations intact and vigorous? Will the new policy announced by Mr. Dulles make our European friends more or less eager to be associated with us?

We Americans may be willing to accept the all-or-nothing risk of a third world war which the new policy of "atomic retaliation" entails. But our war-weary European allies, only a few hundred miles from Soviet bases, would suffer even more grievously than we from atomic counterattack. Suspicion that our new policy incurs unnecessary risks of a third world war may thoroughly dampen their enthusiasm for the essential task of European defense.

Another fundamental question is: What effect will the new policy have on whatever hope still exists for international atomic control?

One of the most important steps we have taken to create confidence in our goals has been to press wholeheartedly and with imagination for workable international control of atomic weapons under the United Nations.

If we move toward almost complete dependence on atom bombs to keep the peace, we may kill the dream of atomic disarmament for which most human beings have yearned since the Atomic Age began. And for this we would bear the full responsibility before the world.

Still another question which I believe should be soberly considered concerns the basic structure of our government. Under the Constitution, Congress, and Congress alone, has the power to declare war.

If Chinese troops invade, say, Indochina, will the President ask the consent of Congress before he launches a retaliatory atomic attack on China itself? If so, how can retaliation be "instant," and will he not run the risk that, while Congress deliberates, the Russians will deliver their own savage anticipatory atomic attacks on American cities?

Or, faced with such a possibility, would he launch the Strategic Air Force bombers on his own Presidential authority, and start or invite World War III without giving Congress an opportunity to exercise its constitutional authority?

Another question: In conceiving of the situation before us almost exclusively in terms of military power, and one type of military power at that, does not the new policy seriously underestimate the range and scope of the Communist threat?

One of the most striking things about the cold war is the fact that nowhere have the Communists resorted to overt action by *Russian* armies. Indeed, only in Korea has even the attempt been made to change the boundary line of the Iron Curtain by means of external *military* aggression.

Instead, we have been confronted with a wide variety of effective Soviet techniques. In Iran, in 1946, the Russians lent their support to a rebellion in the northern provinces which was clearly stimulated by the Iranian Communist party on orders from the Kremlin.

In Greece, Burma, Malaya, Indochina, Indonesia, the Philippines and in China itself, the fighting has been carried on by well-trained and well-organized *local* troops or guerrillas, often supplied with Soviet arms and advised by Soviet experts.

These Communist onslaughts have been successfully resisted and defeated in every country where the government has earned the allegiance of a clear majority of its people. But where colonial power has persisted, as in Indochina, or where the opposition to the Communists has been led by men in whom the people have ceased to believe, massive Western military and economic aid, and even the intervention of Western troops, have not yet proved decisive.

In other cases, notably in Czechoslovakia, the Soviet Union has depended upon the well-organized subversive efforts of local Communist parties. Thus the Kremlin, seeking world domination, has always used a highly flexible strategy.

How does the new policy deal with these most frequent Communist threats, which do not take the form of external aggression?

Further, Moscow seems to be moving into additional fields. There is every evidence, for instance, that Russia plans to use her rapidly increasing production to launch an aggressive trade effort designed, not only to aid the Soviet economy, but to create new divisions in the Western world and to establish close ties with the new governments in Asia.

There are even signs of a forthcoming Russian Point Four program. In the face of Russia's diversified challenge by political, economic, and paramilitary means, can we afford to put all our eggs in an atomic basket?

Have we ceased, for instance, to hope and work for the development of dynamic, independent nations in Asia, willing to fight, not for us, but for their own right to remain free?

What about our own lagging Point Four programs, which Mr. Dulles barely mentioned?

Any substantial reduction in our burden of defense effort and expenditure is dependent upon the development of *indigenous* strength in the areas of the globe which may be threatened by Communist aggression or subversion. This indigenous strength can only arise with the growth of truly independent governments and healthy, expanding economies.

Although we may hope that such governments will support our views, day-to-day agreement with us is far less important than their success in creating a dynamic faith of their own for which, if necessary, they are prepared to fight against all comers.

Atomic striking power has a vital and continuing function. Yet it will be foolish to assume that it offers a guarantee against Communist aggression, much less subversion and internal revolutions, in the tempting vacuums of Asia.

For example, when we announce to the world that under no circumstances will we become directly involved in Indochina, we are hanging out the welcome mat for the Communists to a far greater extent than it was ever hung out in Korea.

Flexible, mobile, military units which the world knows we are prepared to use in a crisis will do far more to discourage aggression in such situations than threats of wholesale atomic retaliation which every informed person on both sides of the Iron Curtain knows we are unlikely to carry out unless our European allies are directly attacked.

Our diplomacy must be both resolute and profoundly alive to the revolutionary forces in the world which are shaping the future. It must be alert to seize and exploit internal contradictions in the far-flung Communist world.

It must avoid the danger of becoming hypnotized into negation by the actions of Communist nations. It must support, to the absolute limit of practicability, the aspirations of all people to be free.

Most important of all, it must maintain an attitude which our forefathers in the Declaration of Independence described as a "decent respect for the opinions of mankind."

Out of a Great Debate on these critical questions we can seek the balanced solutions that will enable us to meet the challenge. Such a debate, in which the Congress and the people participate, is the only enduring and proper way to develop foreign policy in a democracy.

4

HAVE WE NO CHOICE BUT DESPAIR?

In 1954, when the world first realized the fearful meaning of the H-bomb, Mr. Bowles suggested some hopeful alternatives that he asserted are open to us under vigorous national leadership. From an article in the New Leader, *July 26, 1954.*

EDMUND BURKE once advised his colleagues in Parliament that "when bad men combine, the good must associate; else they will fall one by one, an unpitied sacrifice in a contemptible struggle."

That the struggle which threatens us may be atomic and total renders it no less contemptible. How shall good men associate to avert it? What alternatives are left for us to choose?

In the last eighteen months we have been presented with impossible alternatives, many of them so sloganized as to be empty of content. We have been asked to choose between "preventive war" and "appeasement," between "containment" and "liberation," between "give-away programs" and a tariff-ridden "trade, not aid" proposal, between a domestic economy "within our means" and "virtual bankruptcy."

It is defeatist and intolerable to say that we have reached a point of no return where all decent choice is foreclosed. Men of good conscience cannot admit, even to one another, that they have reached that point until the day the bombs begin to fall.

If we shrug our shoulders and default responsibility to others, none of us can evade individual, moral responsibility for a historic betrayal. There are more hopeful alternatives to an H-bomb future, alternatives more in keeping with our traditions and our principles.

These alternatives are not new. All we have to work with is variations on old and universal themes. The new, awesome H-bombs have simply dramatized and sharpened into immediate focus some long-standing human dilemmas. And the essential *morality* involved in these dilemmas is inescapable:

When our budget-cutters throttle Point Four, they profess to make an economic judgment, but it is a *moral* one as well.

When the emergency refugee program is cluttered up with administrators and regulations out of sympathy with the spirit of the legislation, it is not just an admihistrative matter, but a *moral* one, too.

When we discriminate against minority groups, we are not only exercising a prerogative that we can no longer afford, but we are making a *moral* estimate of the inferiority of a fellow human being.

When local vigilantes become hysterical over the U.N., they demonstrate not just a quirkish provincialism, but a lack of *moral* balance.

We must disengage ourselves from the pursuit of phantoms that can never contribute to freedom or safety, and instead devote our time and talents to making the long-postponed inroads on the human problems that matter.

The H-bomb has arrived at a time when much of the world is seething with revolt against the status quo. This revolt takes many forms: nationalism and anticolonialism in Asia and Africa, intense frustration with the cold war conflict in Europe, the struggle of the Negro against second-class citizenship in the United States, the fight for agrarian reform and industrialization in all underdeveloped areas.

The Communists did not create these issues; they merely exploit them.

Our assertion that we will meet "overt aggression" by military action is absolutely right and essential in itself. But it is inadequate to deal with the far more likely contingencies of internal popular turmoil, manipulated and eventually led by Communists, but with its roots deep in misery, oppression and poverty. Our recent failure in Southeast Asia underscores this essential point.

As long as the Kremlin commits itself to the goal of world revolution, there is no basis for a permanent settlement with the Soviet bloc. But this does not mean that we should cease to propose plans for workable atomic control, enforceable disarmament and a stronger U.N.

We should strive to cut loose from the psychological grip that the Kremlin seems to have fastened upon us. We should get on with the business of solving the fundamental problems which are at the heart of the world's sickness, regardless of what Russia says or does.

There are so many constructive actions that the Russians cannot control. For instance, Russia cannot veto a United Nations World Development Authority. Russia cannot veto the growth of successful U.N. agencies like the World Health Organization, the Food and Agricultural Organization, UNESCO, the Children's Fund and the General Assembly itself.

Russia cannot veto an atomic-energy pool agreed to by those nations which wish to cooperate without her.

Russia cannot veto enlightened leadership in Washington or active goodwill in the hearts of the American people.

America, once the hope of history, has lately been providing only slender fare for the minds and affections of the world's two billion people. Why are we not saying the things Americans were born to say? Why did we, who dropped the first big bombs in Asia, return to test our new ones there? Why do we leave it to others to apologize publicly on behalf of mankind to the Japanese fishermen who were the innocent bystanders?

Why did we leave it to Mr. Nehru, at the recent Ceylon Conference, to paraphrase the words from our greatest Inaugural: "With malice toward none, with charity for all." Why are such words not on the lips of Lincoln's countrymen at home and across the world?

Even the cynical men of Moscow have pitched their appeal to the poor and the disinherited. They have stolen our slogans and parodied our principles. It is a shabby stunt on their part, but it may in the long run be productive of much good. We cannot continue to ignore this apocalyptic appeal, this false vision of a classless society, this hollow cry of brotherhood, this empty claim to offer a society based on justice.

We shall have no relief from this challenge, and we deserve none. We must expose the hypocrisy of the Communists the only convincing way we can: by ending our own.

The least that the less timid of us can do is to go out into this generation and stand for the essential truths of our time: that man's future on earth need not be canceled; that we need not resign ourselves to catastrophe; that our political ingenuity still may rescue us from ruin; that our moral standards still are here; that some things, like war and injustice, may seem everlasting, but that these things are everlastingly wrong, must be everlastingly fought and must someday be conquered.

5

THE POWER OF PEOPLE AND IDEAS

In an address to the Naval War College, Mr. Bowles
challenges conventional reliance on military power alone,
and stresses the powerful ability of ideas and people to
bring about revolution and change. Newport, Rhode Island,
June 7, 1956.

AT DINNER one night in Washington I asked a dozen friends for their definition of "power." The group included military people, Congressmen and members of the State Department.

"When we speak of power," I asked, "what do we really mean?"

One by one they listed the ingredients that they felt constituted power. The composite list included naval, air and ground forces, steel-making capacity, industrial productivity, geography, overseas bases and the like.

This definition overlooks the essential dynamic of our time. In the short period of eight years, some 1.2 billion people—half the population of the world—have changed their form of government with but little regard for "power" as we so narrowly defined it.

Indeed, in each case the traditional concept of power had been overwhelmingly on the side of the status quo. Over and over again such power had proved to be inadequate, and the changes which took place had underscored its inadequacy.

China is one such example. Here Mao Tse-tung, starting with only

24

two hundred rifles, one thousand men and a concept of Communist totalitarianism which was persuasive within the pattern of the old Chinese society, developed a mass movement that rode to a national triumph in twenty years. Although the traditional military and industrial power in China had by and large supported the Kuomintang, Mao and the Communists became China's masters.

In Indochina we have again seen the power of an idea, this time linked with nationalism. Because of the failure of the French to respond affirmatively to the challenge of Indochinese independence, Communism and nationalism were merged into a powerful and explosive mixture. In Southeast Asia, as in China, the tanks, the planes and other traditional components of military power supported the status quo. The French had competent troops—one of the best professional armies in the world—and we poured in three billion dollars' worth of equipment to help them. Yet the French lost; and we lost with them.

In India we see the triumph of a constructive democratic idea. Gandhi's concept of freedom through nonviolent action fitted the temperament and aspirations of the Indian people. This simple technique manipulated by Gandhi with his great political skill and capacity for administration and organization eventually forced the British to leave India, Pakistan, Ceylon and Burma.

The British had possessed an abundance of military power in its traditional sense; they were still the third military nation in the world. Yet they were unable to cope with the power of Gandhi's idea.

Again, in Indonesia it was the Dutch who had the Sherman tanks, the P-38's and the modern machine guns. Yet it was the idea of freedom which ultimately carried the day.

The lesson should be clear: Realism compels us to expand our definition of "power" to include the power of *people* and the power of *ideas*. In our new, revolutionary world, these are forces of decisive strength through which hundreds of millions of people, eager for greater opportunity and freedom, can be organized into movements capable of bringing impossible pressures to bear on status quo governments.

Unhappily, we have often been led by expediency to place our prestige behind those who are determined to protect the *past* in situations in which millions had their hearts set on *change*. As a result, we have often turned up on the losing end.

Soviet policy has also had its share of failures, largely due to Stalin's ignorance of what Asians and Africans really want. Just as we have often failed to understand the basic forces which are at work, so also the Soviet Union has failed to grasp them thoroughly.

During the years following the war, with all their effort of subversion and propaganda, the Soviets were unable to add a single square mile of European territory beyond the ability of their Red Armies to advance. There was an equal Soviet failure—and a rather extraordinary one—in Asia.

In 1923 President Sun Yat-sen of China, who had tried in vain to get American support in financing his struggling new government, finally turned in desperation to Russia for assistance. He was confident that somehow he could borrow ideas, techniques and capital from Lenin and the Soviets without becoming absorbed by them.

China was saved from Sun Yat-sen's folly largely by the mistakes of Stalin. The Borodin Mission came to China at the invitation of the Chinese Government to demonstrate how a modern underdeveloped nation could be organized and brought into the twentieth century. What an opportunity this offered the newly established Soviets!

Yet the mission failed dismally. Its members operated on the Marxist premise that revolutions are created by city workers and students. They totally ignored Lenin's advice that in an agricultural country the peasants hold the *ultimate* key.

Mao Tse-tung saw the folly of the Soviet-directed effort and, turning his back on the cities, moved out into the villages to organize the peasants within the simple context of the age-old injustices which they had experienced.

His formula was appealing and powerful. "Destroy the landlords and the moneylenders," Mao asserted, "and you will be free!" Within twenty years Mao and his dedicated associates had succeeded in spreading their gospel throughout China.

In the meantime, the lessons of his failure in China were almost totally lost upon Stalin. Throughout Asia he continued to base his revolution and efforts on students and the largely nonexistent proletariat, ignoring the peasants who constituted 80 percent of the people and who were the political key.

The results of this inept approach were clearly evident in the Communist efforts in India even as late as 1949-50. Toward the end of 1948 a stormy peasant revolt broke out in Hyderabad. This revolt was developed by a group of "deviationist" Communists who defied the Stalinist party line by concentrating in the rural areas. In so doing they succeeded in taking over many thousands of villages. Only with great difficulty and considerable casualties was the Indian Army finally able to quell the revolt.

These "deviationists" who followed the teachings of Mao, contrary to the orders from Moscow and to the wishes of their own Communist party in India, came perilously close to success. If they had been strongly supported by Indian Communists generally, they might have succeeded in creating a permanent base of operations in India. Fortunately for us, the Kremlin with its lack of awareness of the peasants' decisive *political* power refused to support them.

Russian tactics following the death of Stalin have undergone a profound change. Without altering their ultimate objective of world domination, the Soviets now seem to be striving to establish bonds with Europe, Asia and Africa on the basis of *economic* self-interest.

Their political aims, although *basically* unchanged, are now kept discreetly in the background. Their public emphasis is on basic reforms which everyone agrees are long overdue; their purpose is gradually to draw Asia into the Soviet orbit.

The new tactics could become a serious threat to our interests. Today we are importing something like 50 percent of our industrial raw materials from Asia, Africa and Latin America. The Paley Report suggests that this figure may rise to 70 percent by 1965-70.

If we were to be shut out of these great continents by this new Soviet "Operation Strangle," we would find our military power gradually undermined and our living standards jeopardized.

This is precisely the result which the Russians have always had in mind. Now their tactics are increasingly skillful.

One factor is of special importance to our own policy-makers: It is natural and human for us to favor those nations which are ready to stand up "on our side" and to condemn those which refuse to do so.

Yet we cannot buy loyalty to the United States of America. We cannot expect Asians, Africans and Latin Americans to die to keep America's living standards roaring ahead. Like all of mankind, they will sacrifice only for their own country and for what they believe to be their own interests.

Therefore we must identify our own self-interests with theirs. We must do this not through slogans but through action. We must be prepared to expand and to defend the common objectives that *they* think are important.

Fortunately, these objectives are easy for us Americans to understand and to accept: freedom from colonial rule; human dignity for all, regardless of race, creed or color; and expanding economic opportunities.

══ 6

HOW REALISTIC HAVE WE BEEN?

*Strongly challenging the "ideological emptiness" of our policies
abroad, Mr. Bowles pleads for a major change of
emphasis, a fresh approach worthy of America's greatness.*
From the New York Times Magazine, *May 20, 1956.*

FUTURE critics of current American foreign policy may focus on a factor that now receives little comment—its lack of widely
shared purpose, its ideological emptiness.

Many Republicans, as well as Democrats, are demanding a reappraisal of our foreign policy, and an agonizing one at that.

Yet if this is limited to a review of budgets and tactics, it is too
narrow an approach. Foreign policy is not an end in itself. It is the
means by which a nation pursues its national objectives beyond its
frontiers.

This poses a fundamental question: What is America's national
purpose? What does she want from the world? What is she prepared
to contribute?

What we need is not simply a reappraisal of our military program,
our alliances and our foreign aid program, but, even more important,
a reappraisal of our relations with our fellow men, our proper role in
world affairs, our national purposes and aspirations.

It is an indication of ideological bankruptcy in world affairs that
anyone who suggests that principles have a legitimate place in Amer-

ican foreign policy is at once charged with being out of touch with reality.

Principles, they agree, are important enough in personal dealings. But foreign policy is a more critical business. Here, they say, our primary concern must be a tough-minded understanding of power.

I wonder if the Maginot Line concept of power, which so many accept as the ultimate in international "realism," does not lie at the very heart of our present world-wide dilemma? Let us examine for a moment a few of the dangerous dead ends into which this narrow approach has already taken us.

How realistic were we in the 1940's to assume that the narrow-based government of Nationalist China, based on feudal landlordism and a leadership which had lost touch with the Chinese people, could keep a lid on the revolutionary surge released by Mao Tse-tung?

How realistic were we to assume that the Communists could be stopped in Indochina, even by one of the ablest of professional armies, as long as the anti-Communist effort remained based on a dying French colonialism tied to an outmoded land system and strangled by local corruption?

How realistic were we to lead the United Nations forces across the Thirty-eighth Parallel in Korea on the assumption that Peking's warning was a bluff and that the Chinese would not dare to enter the war—only to be forced to accept a truce at that same line three years later?

How realistic have we been to assume that a military program which upset the balance of power in South Asia by arming our good friends, the Pakistanis, thereby frightening Afghanistan into accepting Russian aid and India into a major increase in its own military, will increase the security of that critically important area?

How realistic have we been to discount the powerful, inevitable growth of nationalism in Africa in order to avoid differences with our Western colonial allies?

How realistic have we been to assume that a NATO without effective political or economic roots could not be weakened by new tactics; that Germany can be united on our terms?

The parochial views that are reflected in such thinking suggest that many of our policy-makers have lost sight of the power of ideas and people in a period of global revolution.

As long as ideas influence the minds of men, and as long as men and their aspirations are a major component of power, ideas, both good and evil, will continue to upset nations, defy armies and write history. A recognition of this essential dimension of power is, I believe, the New Realism. Wilson and F.D.R. understood this; the leaders of our generation have often ignored it.

What we must seek is a balance between ideas and defense; on the one hand, the bringing together under the banner of a militant new freedom of those people of the earth—and today they are by far the majority—who seek the goals that we seek: self-determination, human dignity and expanding opportunities; and, on the other hand, the power of a massive, competent defense to provide a screen behind which those goals can be vigorously pursued.

If we consider our interests in the framework of the revolutionary, fast-changing world in which we live, we may be surprised at the extent to which they coincide with those of others.

A year ago at Bandung the representatives of twenty-eight Asian and African nations outlined their four primary objectives: freedom from colonial domination; dignity of the individual regardless of his race, creed or color; expanding economic opportunities; and peace.

These concepts are not Marxist. They are Western and American—no more and no less than a reflection in these two vast continents of the continuing American Revolution for which Jefferson, Lincoln, Wilson and Roosevelt spoke so eloquently.

If we have a purpose on this earth—and I profoundly believe that we have—it is to assure the preservation and the ultimate expansion throughout the world of the spirit of liberal democracy with its primary regard for the dignity and integrity of man.

This calls for a major change of emphasis in our relations to other peoples and a fresh approach to the problem of American security, development and growth.

Everywhere, throughout my travels across the United States—east, west, north and south—I have found Americans seeking earnestly to throw off their frustration, to achieve a new sense of direction.

Where the public vision of America's world role is too narrow, it is because leaders of both political parties have failed to offer the broader vision which great Americans have provided in earlier critical periods of our history.

═══ 7

OUR OBJECTIVE IN EUROPE— AND RUSSIA'S

Both sides might benefit, says Mr. Bowles, from a phased reduction of military forces in the heart of Europe. This article in the New York Times Magazine *of May 12, 1957, discusses Mr. Khrushchev's reaction to this proposal.*

WHAT precisely do we Americans want in Europe? Our primary security objective is to make certain that Europe's industrial and military power will never be organized against us.

Britain fought five major wars to prevent the domination of Europe by any power or combination of powers. When British military capacity faltered following World War II, some farsighted American leaders understood the critical importance of filling the breach.

Thus the pressure of the Soviet Union on the Mediterranean in 1947 led us to the bold decision of the Truman Doctrine. The Soviet refusal to withdraw from Central and Eastern Europe induced us to station substantial military forces in Germany, and to help organize and equip the North Atlantic Treaty Organization defense line.

Because we also understood the close relationship between the prosperity of Europe and its political stability, we invested tens of billions of dollars, first to repair the war damage, and then to create solid foundations for Europe's spectacular postwar economic expansion.

Most Americans, however, see Europe as more than an exercise in geopolitics. Our cultural, historical, religious and ideological relations with Europe are close; indeed, 90 percent of us are of European stock.

Although the nations of Eastern Europe have been largely under Soviet domination since 1944, our concern for the people of this unhappy area, with their millions of relatives and friends in America, has remained intense and genuine.

By and large, we believe that American as well as European objectives can best be served by an increasing degree of integration and federation that ultimately may include even the nations of Eastern Europe. As Europe draws together, her people will gain new confidence and purpose. In such a Europe, Britain, France and other colonial nations may find it easier to adjust to the loss of the global power which they held for centuries.

But how does the situation look from the Kremlin? On February 20, in a two-hour discussion in his Moscow office, Nikita Khrushchev outlined the Soviet view to me in the following terms:

1. The present "unnatural" situation in Central Europe is not in the interest of the Soviet Union, America or the Europeans. For one thing, NATO-Soviet forces could be drawn by some unexpected spark into a conflict that no one wanted.

2. Although neither the Soviet Union nor the United States can determine the economic and political future of Germany, unification should come in stages in order to protect the Sovietized "economic institutions" which have been developed in East Germany.

3. The Kremlin will agree to withdraw all Soviet troops to the Russian border provided American and British troops agree to retire to their own. Peace in Europe, with guarantees against excessive armaments, could then be assured, Mr. Khrushchev said, by an agreement between NATO and the Warsaw Pact nations. The Soviet Union would prefer to see both organizations disband and their places taken by a new organization which would include the United States and the Soviet Union. But he would not insist.

4. Although Khrushchev said that Premier Bulganin's offer of a gradual withdrawal to President Eisenhower was genuine, he asserted that the American Government would not accept it. Why? Because of the pressure of the "billionaire munitions-makers," who, Mr. Khrushchev maintained, "oppose any relaxation of the cold war."

In my reply I said that as a private citizen I could assure him that Americans of both political parties are anxious to see Europe develop in its own way. The presence of our troops in Germany and the development of the NATO alliance had been brought about by the Soviet refusal to withdraw the Red Army to its own borders following the war.

Under present tense conditions it seemed unrealistic for the Soviet leaders to expect us to withdraw across three thousand miles of ocean while their own armies withdraw only a few hundred miles along good roads to the Russian border.

Mr. Khrushchev could hardly expect us to do so unless the Soviet Union agreed to keep all concentrations of troops and equipment some distance *east* of its western frontier and granted the right of full military inspection by United Nations observers throughout this area.

Nor could Mr. Khrushchev expect us to abandon our air-base system in other parts of the world until there was either a drastic change in military technology or an agreement on universal disarmament.

For several reasons, I said, it was difficult for most Americans to believe that Mr. Khrushchev and his colleagues, when faced with the final, fateful decision, would, in fact, agree to withdraw Soviet troops from their present advanced positions in Europe under guarantees which would be acceptable to America and her NATO associates.

For one thing, events in East Germany, Hungary and Poland seemed to indicate that withdrawal of Soviet troops from Eastern Europe would be followed by a rapid lessening of Soviet political and economic influence in that area.

The living standards of the East Germans, for instance, are substantially lower than those of the West Germans. Why would they stick to an economic system which has proved less productive than the freer system of West Germany? Once the Red Army had been withdrawn, how could Mr. Khrushchev expect to keep the Germans from developing their united country in their own way?

Moreover, the withdrawal of the Soviet Army would likely lead to an integrated Europe in which the Eastern sections would be drawn into a close relation with Western Europe.

Mr. Khrushchev replied that the Kremlin leaders had carefully considered these questions. It was their opinion that an integrated Europe would not be in the long-term interest of the United States, Britain or France. Such a Europe, he said, would be dominated by Germany, which "in time of peace would secure all the objectives which it failed to win in war."

I asked him if the Soviet Union would go to war to prevent the integration of Eastern and Western Europe if it should develop as I had suggested. "Certainly not," he replied, "unless our European neighbors should become bellicose."

During the last few weeks I have discussed this conversation with people who have studied the Soviet Union for many years, several of whom personally know the present Soviet leaders. They include not only foreign diplomats stationed in Moscow, but members of the Polish and Yugoslav governments, American officials in Moscow, Belgrade, Berlin and elsewhere, and students of the Soviet Union here in America.

Although most of these men do not believe that Bulganin and Khrushchev are serious, this judgment was by no means unanimous.

One impressive foreign military leader, who has had an opportunity to know the members of the Kremlin, offered an interesting counterview. "I have no idea what Mr. Khrushchev had on his mind," he said, "but I shall hazard a guess as to what is going through the mind of Marshal Zhukov. I would expect him to be thinking along the following lines:

" 'In East Germany I have twenty-two Soviet divisions, thrust like a thumb into the center of Europe. Their communications run across Poland and Hungary. We now know that the people of all three nations are ready to turn on us.

" 'We of the Red Army have been made particularly aware that our policies in Eastern Europe have been a failure. For thirteen years our *political* leaders worked to draw this area into our Soviet orbit and to win the confidence of the people. In this they have failed utterly. Because of their failure I was forced to order Soviet soldiers to kill thousands of Hungarian civilians in the streets of Budapest.

" 'But that is not the end of our military difficulties. During the last thirteen years we have organized more than sixty divisions in the Eastern European countries and equipped them with modern Soviet guns, tanks and planes. What we saw in Budapest and what we can sense in Poland and East Germany indicate that if war should come, these formidable forces may turn against us. In the circumstances the Soviet Union has much to gain by any agreement that strictly limits the military power of Eastern and Central Europe.

" 'Then there is the economic question. Each year since the war we have drained billions of rubles in capital, equipment and raw materials from Eastern Europe to strengthen the Soviet Union. If we are to avoid trouble there, we must now reverse this flow of capital. Would we not be wiser to put this money into Asia and Africa, where we have a clean sheet of paper on which to work?

" 'Surely our propaganda people must be skillful enough to twist an offer to withdraw from Germany to our political advantage. Can they not demonstrate that we are the ones who are trying to relax tensions? If the Americans refuse, it will be they who will appear to insist on a divided Europe.' "

As my European military acquaintance finished his outline of what might be in Marshal Zhukov's mind, he cautioned, "It will be Khrushchev and others, of course, not Zhukov, who make the final decision."

I doubt that the Soviet Union will seriously negotiate a meaningful, long-term *global* settlement as long as hope exists within the Kremlin that Asia and Africa may be first associated with Moscow through economic and political ties and ultimately brought into the Soviet orbit. Nor would a floating neutralized Germany be in our interests.

However, neither the Soviet Union nor we ourselves have anything to gain from the continuation of a situation in Central Europe that by some accident may suddenly erupt into a nuclear war which both sides are anxious to avoid.

A NEW POLICY TOWARD EUROPE

*Europe is at the beginning of a new era, says Mr. Bowles.
If America is to cope with the implications, it must reassess
its objectives and its methods. From the* New York Times
Magazine, *December 20, 1959.*

PRESIDENT Eisenhower, Prime Minister Macmillan, President de Gaulle and Chancellor Adenauer are holding their presummit talks in Paris against a background of unease about American policy in Europe.

The President's triumphal tour has helped allay concern over our immediate intentions. But doubts remain about our insight, our capacity and our will to move confidently and effectively into what is generally assumed to be a new and different period in European affairs.

An objective review of both our short-term and long-term aims is long overdue. The roots of our European policy must continue to be based on the closest political, economic and military association with the nations of Western Europe. But if we are to deal effectively with the new conditions which are rapidly unfolding, these policies must be given new tone, direction and vitality.

Mr. Khrushchev has made a heavy personal political investment in proposals to substitute negotiations and economic competition for the harsher techniques of the cold war. Whatever his motivations, his promises have raised certain expectations both at home and abroad—

expectations which neither he nor anyone else can quickly or easily erase.

China's growing intransigency must surely constitute a disturbing factor in the Kremlin's calculations. Peking's apparent determination to increase tensions runs counter to Moscow's new approach. Maintenance of the Sino-Soviet Axis will remain critically important to both parties for the foreseeable future, but the specter of an adventurous and aggressively minded Chinese "junior partner," with more than three times the population of the U.S.S.R., must concern Soviet planners deeply.

If the spreading revolution in weapons technology and strategic concepts continues uncontrolled, all the world's major powers will be confronted with enormous increases in costs, dangers and tensions in the next few years. Yet, as France and other nations become nuclear powers, the means for achieving a dependable control system will become increasingly complicated.

Economic and political relationships within Europe, and between Europe and America, are also changing. The rate of economic growth in much of Western Europe is three times our average annual rate of 2.5 percent since 1953. Comparatively speaking, Western Europe is having an industrial boom while America is having an industrial slowdown.

In the face of such developments, many of our present attitudes and tactics have become obsolete. We have reached the end of the postwar period. We are at the beginning of a new era of readjustment, experimentation, pragmatism and flux.

The objectives of American policy in Europe, as I see them, are threefold:

1. We must re-establish a confidence in our firmness at such pressure points as Berlin.

2. We must encourage the establishment and growth of a free European community friendly to us and capable of standing on its own feet.

3. We must recognize the deep desire of men of all nations for a peaceful long-range settlement, and devise and offer practical proposals which may someday form the basis for such a settlement.

The first essential is to check the drift of the NATO alliance into weakness and confusion. As long as some thirty Soviet divisions remain west of the Soviet frontier, it is folly to consider further weakening of our already inadequate European defenses.

The recent inept official suggestion that we may in the near future embark on further unilateral cuts in our European ground and air forces should be repudiated by the Commander-in-Chief himself. This is an important first step in restoring, as far as may now be practicable, a position of firmness in regard to Berlin.

No one likes the situation there. It is dangerous to us, disturbing to the Russians and frustrating to the incredibly brave Berliners, and indeed to all Germans. Yet as long as the over-all situation in Central Europe remains what it is, any effort under pressure to satisfy the Russians on the details of the Berlin situation will serve only to frighten our friends and to encourage further Soviet demands.

It gains us nothing, for instance, to haggle over a possible reduction of the ten thousand Allied soldiers in Berlin. Their number is militarily irrelevant both to us and to the Russians. No one assumes that they could successfully defend the city against a Soviet attack. Their purpose there is to maintain a solid symbol of our occupation rights.

Soviet pressure for a reduction, therefore, is designed solely to gain concessions which would be interpreted by the Berliners and by Germans generally as a sign of diminishing American fortitude and strength.

If the Russians react to a firmer Western position on such questions by actually turning over their prerogatives in Berlin and its approaches to their agents, the East Germans, let us consider turning over to the West Germans, as our agents, all of our remaining prerogatives in West Berlin except for the retention of our troops and the preservation of our present legal occupation rights in the city.

Firmness on the essential questions does not suggest blind inflexibility in minor matters. Nor should firmness in regard to our rights in Berlin be allowed to evolve into recklessness in dealing with East Germany or the rest of Eastern Europe. The promise to "liberate" the East European nations made during the 1952 Presidential campaign as a lure for the Polish, Czech and Hungarian vote was irresponsible, fraudulent and demonstrably self-defeating.

A realistic awareness of Soviet interests on the one hand and the limits of American power on the other, plus a sensitive exploitation of the opportunities of American policy, will be far more productive of concrete results. Diplomacy, exchanges, consultation, economic assistance and our agricultural surpluses can help in the creation of what should be a basic objective of our East European policy—the diversification of politics and economics in that area.

From such diversification can grow a ferment that may make possible an increasing measure of independence for the people of this unhappy area. Our goal is not the chaos and catastrophe of Hungary, but the kind of national resurgence that grew out of the bloodless revolution in Poland, which, in spite of recent government crackdowns, has provided far more freedom than was possible under Stalin.

In the second place, American influence should be exerted on all possible occasions for the growth of the European idea. Regardless of the enormous obstacles to its fulfillment, the concept of a united Europe, held out steadfastly to all people who consider themselves Europeans, is profoundly in America's interest.

This further underscores the crucial importance of the Coal and Steel Community, Euratom and the Common Market now covering France, West Germany, Italy, Belgium, the Netherlands and Luxembourg. These new institutions are now gradually combining their functions. The pace of political and economic integration is without doubt moving much more rapidly than most Americans think.

If these six nations plus the United Kingdom with their very substantial industrial potential come together, they may begin to take on the flesh and blood of a United States of Europe. This in turn may provide the constructive, dynamic political force which will ultimately save Europe from being perpetually divided.

Precisely because American military policy is and must remain identified strongly with NATO it is essential that we encourage this unifying movement to play an active political and economic role in softening, not hardening, the present military dividing line from the Baltic to the Black Sea. Let us hope that it may develop in a way that will enable it to offer a continuing invitation to the rest of Europe, including the satellite countries, to associate themselves with the integration of Europe, however tentative or timid the initial steps. Associate membership in the Common Market for Greece and Turkey, for instance, could conceivably lead to future association of a similar kind for Yugoslavia.

In other words, the new organization should not appear as a closed door but as an open one—and not only to the Yugoslavs, but to the Poles, Hungarians, Czechs, Rumanians and Bulgarians. It can also help create the framework in which the future of Berlin and East Germany may ultimately be settled.

It may be argued that our short-term interests, as well as those of the Soviet Union, favor a divided Germany; surely a united one is impossible under present conditions. But over the long haul a divided Germany is an aggravation of the problem of a divided Europe, and a divided Berlin is an aggravation of the problem of a divided Germany. These divisions are threats to everyone concerned.

Only a united Europe can safely contain a united Germany, and only in that kind of Germany and in that kind of Europe can Berlin resume her logical role as a major capital city. Concrete evidence that a united Europe is gradually being built may therefore be expected to exert a constructive gravitational pull on the sentiments and hopes of East Germany, Poland and other East European countries.

This appeal will be sharply increased if a greater effort is made pledging American policy to firm support of the largest possible nonrestrictive European market. If a free market should develop in Europe, let us view it as an opportunity and not as a threat. For example, the Common Market gives us a chance to secure the easing of import restrictions, quotas and tariffs against American goods in a single agreement rather than through separate negotiations with six countries. Since our bargaining position in regard to trade is strong, we should use it vigorously toward this end.

By all means, let us also use every opportunity to encourage the wider participation of prosperous Western European nations in joint efforts to aid the underdeveloped world. Such aid should not only include the African countries most closely associated with the European governments concerned, but should also, particularly in the case of Germany, be extended elsewhere in Asia, Africa and Latin America where need and utility coincide.

Economic integration inside Europe can help, too, in solving the acute problems of poverty and economic injustice that still persist. Effective progress toward ending these economic injustices, particularly in Southern Europe, is long overdue.

In all West and South European countries, "economic recovery" has created an impressive façade of luxurious apartments and smart shops, along with a well-publicized increase in the indexes of production. But in several of them the even more important indexes of distribution, sharing and justice are far less impressive. Because the economic gap between rich and poor has persisted, political divisions have remained deep.

Fourteen years after the end of the war, 37 percent of the Italian people still voted for Communist or fellow-traveling candidates. The

Communist vote in France is 21 percent. Despite a civil war and the outlawing of the Communist party in Greece, the Communist-controlled EDA (Union of the Democratic Left) won nearly 25 percent of the votes at the last election.

This does not mean that about one-fourth of the people of Italy, France and Greece believe in Communism. The heavy continuing left-wing vote is largely a protest against governments that may effectively be charged with favoring the rich and the powerful at the expense of the people. Yet the continuing size of the protests dramatizes the need for reforms still long overdue.

Third and finally, most Europeans and non-Europeans alike are now ready for a bold and genuine proposal which, if accepted by the Kremlin, would open up prospects for a more peaceful future. It must be a reasonable and believable proposal. Without sacrificing our strategic commitments in Europe, it must be one which the Soviet Union conceivably could accept as a basis for negotiation.

Is there a proposal which is consistent with this objective, which is specifically applicable to greater Europe, which preserves NATO commitments, which avoids the recognized pitfalls of old "disengagement" theories and which nevertheless would constitute a constructive effort toward a new negotiation? No one can say with assurance that such a proposal exists, or what its precise content might be. But I believe that an acceptable point of departure for it may have been suggested last spring by President de Gaulle and Chancellor Adenauer.

On March 25, de Gaulle said: "If disengagement does not cover a zone which is as near to the Urals as it is to the Atlantic, how . . . can we prevent an aggressor from coming by a leap or by a flight across the German no-man's land? Certainly we are supporters of control and limitations of all weapons of war. But these measures . . . must cover an area deep enough for France to be covered and not exposed."

Two weeks later Chancellor Adenauer added at a press conference in Bonn: "As the result of discussion with responsible military bodies, I am in a position, putting it quite generally, to subscribe to what General de Gaulle has said about the size, extent and nature of a so-called zone of relaxed tensions. . . . Such a zone would only serve its purpose if disarmament were carried out from the Atlantic to the Urals."

A zone of limited military activity of these broad dimensions in the area most directly affecting the security of greater Europe may indeed provide a plausible basis for further exploration. The carefully phased, step-by-step reduction of nuclear-strike bases, rocket and missile sites and massive concentrations of conventional forces, with full inspection and control, would help us to draw the increasingly difficult distinction between aggressive and defensive capabilities. It could be presented as either part of a global arms-control settlement or in a more limited regional context.

Such a reduction of forces in greater Europe would permit both the Soviets and ourselves to by-pass the critical issue of growing Chinese military might, which, for the time being at least, limits the possibilities of a world-wide arms-control agreement. This proposal also has the added advantage of not requiring the withdrawal of all foreign troops from the European Continent, or the "demilitarization" of any one country or group of countries, both of which concepts are likely under present conditions to create more problems than they solve.

Regardless of the nature of the Soviet response, such a proposal, persistently put forward, would serve to replace fears with hope, and to reassure the world that American diplomacy is alert, creative and again ready to seize any realistic possibility for progress toward peace.

━ 9

IT'S TIME TO RECOVER THE INITIATIVE

*A blind obsession with what the Kremlin may do next is,
Mr. Bowles asserts, unworthy of America's dynamic
traditions. In an address to the Minnesota Foreign Policy
Association in October, 1960, he proposes some vigorous
new guidelines for American foreign policy.*

WHAT will Mr. Khrushchev do next?

Month after month his threats, blandishments, maneuvers and
speeches have dominated our newspapers and television screens, the
minds of our political leaders and the shaping of our foreign policy.

Like rabbits transfixed by the blinding headlights of an oncoming
car, we have been focusing on the every move of the Soviet Premier.

Historians will surely regard this as odd. Why, they will ask, should
twentieth-century America, with its vital people, its dynamic industrial system, its boundless resources and all its magnificent traditions
in behalf of human freedom, become so blindly obsessed with what
the Kremlin says and does?

The situation calls for new faces and new ideas. It calls for a new
leadership which will switch our national focus from the Kremlin,
about which we can do relatively little today, to those broad opportunities which are beckoning us to do a great deal.

Let me list a few of the areas for action on which a new Administration can speedily move next January, regardless of what Mr. Khrushchev does or says.

1. *We can put our defenses in better order.* Our military power must be brought into balance to provide nuclear striking power that cannot be crippled by surprise attack, plus far more flexible and mobile ground forces to enable us to handle localized conflicts should they confront us again as they have in the past.

Our present defense policies have left us prepared to fight the only kind of war we say we will never fight: an all-out nuclear war initiated by us.

2. *We can simultaneously and drastically upgrade all our efforts in the field of disarmament and arms control.* In a new Administration, defense and disarmament must be seen for what they are—not inconsistent, competing policies, but the twin essentials of world stability in the months ahead.

By its statements and actions, the next Administration can demonstrate that we know the new facts of life and death, that we recognize the vulnerable nature of a peace based on a balance of nuclear terror, and that we are committed to an unending search for new approaches which will ease, if not end, the present disarmament impasse.

These approaches should include fresh proposals for arms control under realistic safeguards based on sound research and negotiated with patience and skill.

3. *We can create a more effective partnership with the 400 million industrialized skilled people of the Atlantic Community,* with whom we share a common cultural and political heritage.

Our mutual fear of Khrushchev is perhaps the greatest single factor holding the NATO alliance together. NATO waxes and wanes depending on his frowns and smiles.

This mutual fear is inadequate to sustain our long-term relations with our European allies. We must return to the roots of those relations, and extend the political, economic and cultural ties that link us together.

The strengthening of the machinery of cooperation in the Atlantic Community should be the first order of business for the new Administration.

4. *We can reorganize and reappraise our economic assistance programs.*

These programs need new standards assuring increased assistance to those nations which can use our aid most effectively and which are willing to make the necessary sacrifices to help assure their own rapid progress.

By committing our assistance on a long-term basis in those cases where the problem justifies such a commitment, we can also encourage more orderly and more economic planning.

5. *We can switch American emphasis in the U.N. from participation in cold war name-calling to the promotion of orderly political and economic development in Asia and Africa.*

The U.N. has a key role to play in these continents, where its functions should be expanded in all areas of need, from civil service to economic assistance, and from arms control to education.

6. *We can stop treating Latin America on a crash basis with belated proposals adopted under pressure.* Instead we can reaffirm Mr. Roosevelt's "Good Neighbor" policy in practical terms to meet present-day needs.

This includes the strengthening of the Organization of American States and the implementation of the new Act of Bogotá.

In the absence of progress on arms control between the Soviet Union and the U.S., we can at least encourage regional disarmament efforts. Latin America is an excellent place to begin.

7. *We can develop a more realistic perspective on China.* As long as the Peking Government threatens the peace of Asia and lays claim to the sovereignty of Formosa, recognition is out of the question.

Meanwhile, questions of U.N. representation, Chinese trade with Japan and Southeast Asia, Chinese-Soviet relations and the cracking of the bamboo curtain will become increasingly urgent aspects of the Chinese problem which any new Administration will have to face.

Although we have heard a great deal of talk about our tough policy toward China, the threat is really greater than the Eisenhower Administration seems to think. The fact is that the Administration has consistently underestimated the dangers which are basic to the whole situation.

We can meet Chinese expansionism effectively only if we understand that it stems not only from Chinese Communism, but also from the Chinese imperialistic tradition and her lack of adequate land, oil and other resources.

A realistic policy in East Asia must concentrate on building situations of real strength, economic and political as well as military, that will counterbalance the impact of 650 million mainland Chinese on their neighbors.

What we do or fail to do in helping to build the foundations for political freedom and orderly economic growth, from Japan and Formosa around Southeast Asia to India and Pakistan, will be vital to the future of free Asia.

8. *Finally, there are a tremendous number of things we can do about ourselves to make the U.S. better equipped for leadership.*

We can speed up our economic growth so that we have the people, the production and the machines which we need to cope with the challenge of our explosive but infinitely promising world.

We can build the modern schools and universities and train the able teachers that are necessary to assure every American boy and girl all the education each can effectively absorb.

We can clear away our slums and rebuild our cities.

We can provide better and more accessible hospitals and medical care.

We can put our farm abundance to work as a fundamental asset for American foreign policy around the world.

We can prove to all men everywhere that we still believe the words of the Declaration of Independence, that all men are created equal, by removing the barriers to equal dignity throughout America.

These are but some of the major opportunities facing us, and they by no means exhaust the list. In each of these crucial areas it is not Mr. Khrushchev that holds us back. It is the inertia, confusion and lack of faith in the present leadership of our government.

FIVE DECISIONS THAT WILL SHAPE
OUR CENTURY

*Mr. Bowles believes that we met two of these decisions
successfully, failed in regard to two others and that the fifth
hangs in the balance. From an address before the annual
convention of the American Booksellers' Association,
Washington, June 12, 1961.*

TONIGHT I would like to look far ahead to a group of authors—the historians of a generation or so hence—who will write in judgment on our nation, its relations with the world and its contributions to increased world stability.

What will these historians say about America's influence over the course of events in the mid-twentieth century?

What will they say about our success or failure in turning our extraordinary new industrial capacity to serve the cause of peace and plenty?

In considering the first seven decades of the twentieth century, I believe that they will focus their attention on at least five areas of decision. In two instances they may say that we failed, in two others that we succeeded; the fifth still hangs in the balance.

What are these five decisions?

First was our tragic failure in 1919 to join the League of Nations and to throw our power and prestige behind a program to preserve the newly won peace in Europe.

Second was our equally costly failure, following the collapse of the Manchu Empire in 1911, to understand the revolutionary upheaval in China and its relevance to our future security.

Third was our success in meeting the Nazi threat to Western Europe.

Fourth was our brilliant and decisive response to the awesome challenge posed by the postwar economic and political chaos in Europe.

Fifth, and finally, is the decision which we face in the 1960's in regard to our relations with two-thirds of the people of this earth who live in Asia, Africa, the Middle East and Latin America, whose rising hopes and demands for a better life have created the most powerful, the most dangerous and yet most promising revolution in the long and eventful history of the human race.

This final decision involves a deep-seated, totally unprecedented and far-reaching commitment, not only by the American Government, but by the American people as well.

Let us therefore briefly examine our reaction to each of the first four areas of decision in the hope that it may provide us with a fresh approach in dealing with the fifth.

1. *Failure to Join the League of Nations*

There is no need for more than a brief reference to the consequences of our failure to join the League of Nations in 1919.

Over and over again Wilson warned us that if we rejected his vision and seceded from the emerging world community, we would not only "break the heart of the world," but would pay for our failure in blood.

But the habits of isolationism were still strong, and its advocates skillful and determined. We had acted generously enough, they said, in sending our boys and our dollars overseas to "solve Europe's problems."

And so Woodrow Wilson was repudiated, and his League of Nations rejected. Thus our father's generation, which could have provided the spirit and the sinews necessary for the beginnings of world order, turned its back on the future. I believe that the historical judgment of 2000 A.D. upon America's withdrawal from world responsibility in 1919 will be severe.

2. *The Challenge of the Chinese Revolution*

The second great area of decision grew out of the challenge of the Chinese Revolution. At the birth of the Chinese Republic, we were admirably positioned to understand the physical and psychological needs of the emerging new China and to exert a positive and perhaps decisive influence over economic and political developments there.

Yet in 1920 and 1921, when Sun Yat-sen urgently pressed us for substantial loans with which to further the unification and economic development of China, we abruptly turned him down. At that time only a handful of farsighted Americans were even conscious that the question had been posed.

And so, following a similar turndown in the capitals of Western Europe, a now desperate Sun Yat-sen turned to the new Communist Government in Moscow for the help which the Atlantic nations had denied him.

At the Washington Disarmament Conference in 1922, the Harding Administration compounded our failure. By agreeing to dispense with a major part of our new Navy in return for Japan's agreement to accept some limitations on her own forces, we abdicated our power position in the Western Pacific and opened the door for the series of Japanese aggressions which led to Pearl Harbor nineteen years later.

But more opportunities and more blunders were yet to come. In 1927, when Sun's successor, Chiang Kai-shek, turned against the Communists and outlined his plans to establish a modernized non-Communist state, we were granted another opportunity to retrieve past mistakes. But once again America, fat, contented, far away, secure, failed to understand the challenge.

In 1931 the Japanese Army moved into Manchuria. Firm American action there might still have checked Japanese aggression and given China a chance to emerge as an independent and politically stable nation. But the 1930's found us caught up in our own problems, unwilling to provoke the naval power of Japan or to give the wobbly Chinese Government the assistance it needed so desperately.

No one knows precisely when we finally lost our capacity to influence events in China.

Some observers assert that as late as 1941 a comprehensive American military, political and economic effort might have provided an effective democratic alternative to Communism. By the end of the war, however, it had become clear that nothing less than massive American military intervention could change the course of events.

In view of public weariness with war and crisis and the efforts of political leaders in both parties to cater to this natural state of mind, the necessary action was not even debated.

So it was that we failed to meet the second great foreign policy challenge of our century. The world will live with the consequences of this failure for many generations to come.

3. Opposition to Nazi Germany

The third challenge was one which we belatedly but effectively recognized and met.

Franklin Delano Roosevelt, with his powerful sense of history, understood that a Europe under Nazi domination would mean a world in which America's own freedom would be fundamentally challenged. In 1937 he began gradually to move the American people toward a similar understanding.

Our first instinct was to reject Roosevelt's appeal and to withdraw into isolationism. The Neutrality Act, curbing shipments to the Western European nations, expressed our national mood.

Yet the old myths of self-sufficiency were weakening. We were beginning belatedly to recognize the interdependence of nations that Woodrow Wilson had pleaded with us to accept. And so in Britain's darkest and finest hour we came to her support.

4. The Challenge of Postwar Reconstruction

The fourth challenge began to take shape soon after the end of hostilities in Europe.

Western Europe's cities were in ruins from years of bombing and street fighting. Food, fuel and building materials were inadequate. The entire European economy was on the verge of collapse, with mounting inflation everywhere.

In the meantime, a few hundred miles away in East Germany and Poland stood nearly two hundred Soviet Army divisions ready and able to roll, almost unopposed, to the English Channel.

The initial Soviet pressure was aimed at Greece and Turkey. The British, who for two centuries had provided the shrewd diplomacy and military power that had effectively blocked Russia from the Mediterranean, were no longer able to meet the challenge.

Simultaneously, all through Western Europe Communist parties which had been effectively associated with the underground resistance to Nazism were vigorously on the move to sow confusion, to establish united fronts and ultimately to seize power.

At this critical moment we were fortunate to have as our Secretary of State General George Marshall, a towering figure of integrity and intelligence. In Harry Truman we had a President whose raw courage and unswerving sense of purpose will assure him a privileged position in the history of our times.

The men and the crisis came together, and the result was a brilliant creative national effort that checked the Soviet military, political and economic threat, rebuilt the foundations of a new free Europe, and almost certainly saved us from a third world war.

The Truman Doctrine for the defense of Greece and Turkey was followed by the Marshall Plan for the economic and political recovery of Western Europe. Then came the North Atlantic Treaty Organization for the military defense of Western Europe, and the dramatic Berlin airlift with which we demonstrated that we Americans and our allies had the will as well as the resources.

In 1949, as the fresh challenge of the newly free, desperately poor, yet largely undeveloped nations began to emerge, we again broke new ground through the Point Four proposal for a constructive partnership with Asia, Africa and Latin America.

These were years of brilliant, creative, nonpartisan response to an unprecedented challenge. They were years in which our leaders *led,* and the American people, aroused and informed, responded with the dedication and intelligence which mark a great nation.

5. *The Challenge of American Leadership in the 1960's*

We come now to the fifth and greatest challenge in this series of momentous situations which have so sharply tested us Americans in the first sixty years of this century.

In the nineteenth century and the first decades of the twentieth, world peace could be said to rest almost exclusively on the balance of power in Europe. Since the end of the Second World War, this had been fundamentally changed.

Hundreds of millions of Asians and Africans, who once responded to orders from London, Paris and The Hague, have won their freedom. The emergence of these new and underdeveloped nations inevitably has created a wholly new challenge for the American Government and its people.

This situation, with its new and far broader dimensions, has been further compounded by the fact that this revolutionary development has occurred at precisely the time when modern technology is rapidly widening the already highly explosive gap between the rich white minority, on the one hand, most of whom live around the North Atlantic basin, and the poor colored majority on the other, who live largely in the Southern Hemispheres.

Meantime, moving toward the forefront in world affairs, is the new Chinese giant, intent on overnight industrialization, with 650 million dynamic people, a doctrinaire, aggressive leadership, inadequate natural resources, facing a tempting power vacuum in Southeast Asia, which is rich in the petroleum and rich producing lands that China needs so urgently.

Finally, there is the Soviet Union, with a steel capacity of sixty million tons, an annual rate of industrial growth nearly three times our own, graduating twice as many engineers and scientists, and with enormous power in nuclear weapons and conventional military forces.

In recent years Soviet leaders have developed a new understanding of the decisive importance of the underdeveloped areas, and a new flexibility, new subtlety and new economic and political skill in dealing with them.

Together, these developments pose the greatest challenge that any society has ever faced, a test of our values, our nerves and our intelligence. What will be our national reaction to this ultimate test of our capacity to serve and to prosper as a free society?

Let us examine more precisely what is required of us.

The first essential is that we understand the nature of the forces which are upsetting the old order, disrupting old societies, creating fervent new hopes and expectations, often threatening the peace while offering the promise of a better future to hundreds of millions of people.

At the heart of the revolution lies the universal promise of expanded human dignity, greater opportunity for the individual and an increased measure of justice. Although its ways are often violent, irrational and destructive, this revolutionary promise is based on the human values which may be found in almost every religion on earth.

Although the Soviet Union did not create this revolutionary wave, it is seeking to divert it to its own purpose. In this effort the Soviet Union has some very major advantages.

The Kremlin understands these revolutionary forces. Its image is not blurred by racial conflicts or a record of discrimination against the darker-skinned people of the world. Through its totalitarian government it can focus its resources—educational, industrial, economic or political—where they can best serve the Soviet cause, which is usually at the weakest point in the internal structure of the new nation.

Yet there are many formidable obstacles in the way of Soviet success. For one thing, the announced national and ideological objectives of the Soviet Union are sharply opposed to the new nationalism which has become the driving force of the new nations of Asia and Africa and the awakening lands of Latin America. Because the Soviet Union is opposed to nationalism, it is also opposed to an effective United Nations, where these new nations have found a global forum in which to express their views.

The Soviet Union is also deeply opposed to formal religion, which it considers "the opiate of the people." It is committed, not to the expanded freedoms which the whole world seeks, but to the harnessing of the individual to the service of the state.

Now what about the strengths and weaknesses of the United States?

Our *disadvantages* as we approach the challenge of the decisive 1960's are substantial. The most damaging of these is the fact that the American people and their Congress have not yet fully awakened to the requirements. They are uncertain about the nature of the problem and are skeptical of its meaning for their own future.

In addition, we are plagued with a long record of racial discrimination. Finally, while our economy is gradually recovering from a recession, we are nowhere near producing to our full capacity.

Although these disadvantages are sobering, it would be a profound mistake to underestimate our very great strengths. Our first great asset is that we were born a revolutionary people, under a towering revolutionary leadership. Even more important, this revolution has been a continuing one.

The most important advantage of all, however, is one of which we appear least aware: *the fact that what we want for the people of the new emerging continents is precisely what they want for themselves.*

We have no desire for satellites or nations subservient to our will. For the people of Tanganyika, Bolivia, Burma, Korea and of other nations, young and old, we want expanded economic opportunities, increased dignity and justice, more doctors to take care of their sick, more food to feed their hungry, more and better schools to wipe out their illiteracy, improved communications so that we can better understand each other, the right to travel, to trade, to move freely, to speak, to think and to worship in their own way, within cultures of their own choosing.

This identity of objectives is the primary, overriding advantage of the United States in its efforts to create a peaceful, prosperous, non-Communist world partnership. The fact that the Soviet Union's objectives for the people of the new nations are so deeply antagonistic to their own is the fundamental point of Soviet weakness.

Yet the central question remains: Can we muster the understanding to meet the challenge and to rally our forces to deal with it effectively?

If we are true to our heritage, there can be but one answer.

Let us see to it that the historians of the year 2000 will be able to record that America's response to the fifth and most critical of the five great decisions of our century was confident, bold, compassionate —and everlastingly right.

━━ 11

WHERE THE UNITED NATIONS
HAS SUCCEEDED

*Mr. Bowles assesses the world's greatest experiment in
international cooperation before a United Nations Day
luncheon in Washington, October 24, 1961.*

WE ARE contending with two mighty rival tides, running at crosscurrent. At times these two tides seem so contradictory that we are tempted to conclude that one is the reality and the other an illusion.

On the one hand, we have the massive tide of cold war conflict. This is the world of barbed wire and stone walls, of sneak raids in the jungle and threats of nuclear destruction, the world of violence, distrust and fear, of standoff and fallout. This rampaging tide of cold war conflict has dominated the headlines since Stalin first threatened Greece and Turkey in 1946.

And yet, parallel to the arms race, coexistent with tension and largely obscured from public understanding, another tide has been running toward freedom, toward hope, toward increased understanding and justice among nations and men.

What are the components of this less dramatic but perhaps decisive tide of human effort?

First is the movement toward national independence through which 900 million Asians and Africans have thrown off the rule of the old European trading empires to create forty new countries within fifteen years. This wave of liberation may earn more pages in the history of our time than the cold war itself.

The second aspect of this hopeful tide is the world-wide determination to attack the hunger, disease and despair which for centuries have been the lot of the vast majority of the people of the underdeveloped world.

The new nations have made an impressive start in dealing with these problems. Although progress in many areas is slow, in others we see an extraordinary capacity to plan, to initiate reforms, and to organize domestic resources.

Until recently the United States was one of a handful of noncolonial nations that were willing and able to provide essential capital and technical support. Now some fifteen industrialized nations are offering their capital and technical skills to help speed the progress of economic and social development in the less developed areas. Much of this assistance is now being coordinated through regional and international institutions.

So here we have more positive evidence that the countertide of hope is running strong in world affairs.

A third hopeful phenomenon has been the rapid emergence of new international communities of sovereign states which are learning to work in free association for common purposes of security and growth. Since the end of World War II there has been a great reaching out across national frontiers, a groping for new forms of international cooperation, and the sudden appearance of new institutions in what remains an unplanned and still embryonic world community.

It is these three factors that constitute the tide of hope.

Now how does the United Nations relate to these developments? And how do we relate to the U.N.?

In our frustration with the complex and largely unfamiliar world around us, there is a temptation even among the most thoughtful and informed observers to see the possibilities only in terms of the black and white contrasts. The task of dealing with varying shades of gray is unfamiliar, uncomfortable and unsatisfactory to many Americans.

Our experience in building this great nation has conditioned us to believe that there are only two sides to every question, one right and one wrong; that if there are problems, there must be solutions; that if there is open conflict, there must be total victory for one and total defeat for the other.

The new world with which we must deal, however, is one of infinite complexity in which simple solutions are rarely available. We represent only 6 percent of mankind, and even with all our great industries and military power there are strict limitations on what we can do.

It is inevitable that Americans who fail to understand the complexities with which the United Nations must deal should charge that this great world organization has failed to do what it was set up to do.

Yet, in spite of the determined opposition of one of its most powerful members, the U.N. and its family of specialized agencies have acted with increasing vigor and imagination on a wide variety of fronts.

The World Health Organization, for example, is now conducting a world-wide campaign to eliminate malaria, a disease which has caused more deaths and more loss of work than any other in history. It also has launched a campaign to help bring clean water to every village on the globe.

Last year the United Nations Children's Fund, with ninety-eight governments participating, brought better care to 55 million expectant and nursing mothers. It also examined 75 million children for yaws, at an average cost of fifteen cents a head.

The World Meteorological Organization is planning a world-wide weather-reporting system. The International Telecommunication Union now allocates radio frequencies for the whole world.

Moreover, in every field the binational and multinational agreements for regional economic and social cooperation to which I referred earlier are matched by the development of vigorously creative U.N. regional agencies such as ECAFE, the Economic Commission for Asia and the Far East, and ECLA, the Economic Commission for Latin America.

The capacity of the United Nations General Assembly for positive political and economic action was brilliantly demonstrated in the Congo during the past year.

The Congo also illustrates the U.N.'s capacity to create a more solid base for peace and security. The remarkable performance of the United Nations in throwing together, under the most difficult and urgent circumstances, an emergency force of nearly twenty thousand men drawn from twenty-eight countries is a recent dramatic example. The ability of this organization to mobilize, transport, supply and command a major peace-keeping force on short notice exceeded almost everyone's expectations. Nor should we forget the record of the

U.N. as a peace-keeper in Iran, Greece, Palestine, Suez and Korea.

Finally, in addition to promoting economic and social progress and to keeping the peace, the United Nations has served with considerable effectiveness as an international forum for the airing of disputes. Although its detractors refer to this function as a debating society, the debates which take place there, in spite of the bitterness and demagoguery with which they are often conducted, are of the utmost importance.

The issues that come before the United Nations are the oldest and most intractable issues of history, which cannot be effectively aired in any other arena.

How, then, can we assess the United Nations in the real world of 1961?

Clearly, we cannot say that it has abolished the threat of war or even that it has narrowed the gap of disagreement among the world's great powers. Yet the record is in many ways extraordinary.

Although sorely hampered by the vast ideological struggle which commands the unflagging energies of free men everywhere, the United Nations has somehow grown and developed by associating itself ever more effectively with the powerful currents of hope.

Where great issues of justice have been raised, it has served as a meetinghouse for the opinion of all humanity.

Where violence has threatened, it has time and again proved its growing capacity to divert the pressures and to preserve the peace.

Where peoples have been striving for an end to the tyranny of poverty, it has opened new paths for the indispensable cooperation in the battle against human misery.

We live in a raucous, restless, ill-mannered world in which a Community of Hope exists side by side with a Community of Fear. The cold war conflict is paralleled by a growing partnership between the United States and the peoples of Asia, Africa and Latin America. It is this evolving world which helps shape the United Nations and which, increasingly, may be shaped by it.

One final word. I cannot close without paying tribute to the man who more than any other of our generation has helped to make the United Nations what we all know it must become.

In his final report to the organization whose voice and conscience he became, Dag Hammarskjöld issued this quiet warning:

"The effort through the Organization to find a way by which the world community might, step by step, grow into organized international cooperation within the Charter, must either progress or recede. Those whose reactions to the work of the Organization hamper its development, or reduce its possibilities of effective action, may have to shoulder the responsibility for a return to a state of affairs which Governments had already found too dangerous after the First World War."

In Dag Hammarskjöld was combined an inspiring idealism with the hard common sense of the practical politician. The real world of 1961 was precisely the world with which he was concerned, and it was in that world that he enabled the United Nations to operate with growing effectiveness.

We who carry on can do no better than to follow in the course which he charted. We must continue to maintain the vision to which the United Nations has always aspired. Only by so doing can we make the United Nations the instrument of the world-wide community of hope which its founders intended it to be.

THE NEO-ISOLATIONISTS

This analysis of the well-publicized extreme right-wing view of foreign affairs and its dangers to our national interests was given in an address to the National Adult Education Conference in Washington, November 5, 1961.

THE NEW world emerging is not only intricate but vast, and we Americans constitute only a small minority of mankind. Wise, courageous policies will enable us strongly to influence the shape of world affairs, but we are beginning to see that we cannot control them. For many of us this is a new experience.

Is it any wonder that frustration and exasperation with new problems and new forces should lead some of our most respected fellow citizens to seek short cuts?

There are at least three types of neo-isolationist thinking in the United States today which reflect such frustration.

First, there are those who have come to believe that sooner or later war is probably inevitable. This is defeatism of the most dangerous kind.

We cannot, of course, achieve peace by running away from the prospect of war. Until controlled disarmament and international justice under law are fully agreed to, our military power remains essential, not only to our own national security, but to the vast majority of mankind, who have no desire to live in a Communist world.

The present strengthening of our defensive capacity does not suggest the inevitability of war; on the contrary, it provides the essential barrier behind which creative forces may work to lay the foundation for a rational world society.

A second reflection of present-day isolationist thinking is the concentration of many Americans on the activities of our small minority of domestic Communists to the exclusion of the far greater challenge abroad.

Every intelligent man knows that a world-wide Communist conspiracy exists, and that the Soviet empire has agents in almost every nation on earth, including the United States.

But in our concern over internal subversion, let us be careful not to hit the wrong target. Some frustrated Americans seem to be saying that Communism arises from socialism, which in turn stems from liberalism, which in turn emerges from the democratic ideas written into our Declaration of Independence by Thomas Jefferson. This notion will not hold water.

The only realistic answer to Communist challenge is more democracy and progressivism, not less, not only here in America but everywhere in the world.

The third group of isolationists, and perhaps the most unhappy, are those who in effect seem to be saying, "Stop the world, I want to get off." If they had their way, we would retire from world affairs and leave the future to others on the assumption that somehow we can isolate ourselves from the ebb and flow of human events.

Can any thoughtful man question the ultimate result of such a policy? Indeed, is this not almost precisely the line of action that we followed with disastrous results following World War I? What troubles me is the nagging question: Has the lesson been fully and finally learned?

Again we hear the voices of earnest but misguided men who assume that we can ignore the lessons of history, disregard the vital importance of the United Nations, recklessly raise our tariffs, cut off foreign aid, abandon our allies, attack any nation that we don't like and somehow escape the consequences.

I respect their sincerity and understand their honest desire for simple answers. But would their undoubted patriotism and good intentions lessen by one iota the catastrophe that would surely occur if we accepted their mad advice?

The unprecedented world challenge that confronts us now stems not from foreign aid, not from international trade, not from the ups-and-downs of U.N. debate, not from the views of our neighbors with whom we may disagree, but from the unprecedented revolutionary forces of today's world.

It will take great energy, patience and wisdom to deal effectively with these powerful forces. It will take all the rich variety of tools which our pluralistic society can provide: the art of diplomacy, the warmth of person-to-person relationships, the helping hand of economic and technical aid and the protective shield of military strength.

Yet, with one essential proviso, I remain confident of our capacity successfully to meet the challenge. This proviso can be simply stated: Do we clearly understand the nature of the struggle? At this crucial moment in history, what precisely do we Americans seek?

Some will answer that our national purpose is self-evident: to preserve the American way of life. But in today's tightly interrelated world is this answer still adequate?

Imagine yourself for a moment talking to Mohan Chaudri, a young Indian schoolteacher on the banks of the great Brahmaputra River. "Why," he might ask, "should we Indians associate ourselves with you Americans in the struggle against Communism?"

And suppose you should answer, "Because we need your help in protecting the American way of life." Could you expect anything less than total bewilderment?

Why should Mohan Chaudri, a simple Indian schoolteacher, agree to risk his life to assure the continued comfort of the richest people in the world twelve thousand miles away?

Others may suggest that America's national purpose should be expressed in broader terms. "Is it not our true objective," they may ask, "to use economic aid and skilled diplomacy to bring other nations into line behind American leadership?"

But does even the most cynical among us seriously believe that our government can purchase the loyalties of whole nations?

Such arguments have a hollow ring in the ears of most of mankind because they are so totally unworthy of us. What, then, are America's true purposes, and how can we present them to the world in understandable terms?

Surely the present challenge is not simply to the privileged minority of mankind who have the most to lose in a material sense. It is a challenge to all men who cherish freedom and the right to work out their destiny in their own way within the framework of their own history and culture.

Again let us imagine ourselves in the village on the Brahmaputra as Mohan Chaudri again puts the crucial question, "Why should we Indians associate ourselves with you Americans in the struggle against Communism?"

And suppose you should answer, "Although you and we are thousands of miles apart in a physical sense, we share certain universal beliefs for which generations of our forebears have fought, which we are prepared to defend today, and for which your own great Gandhi died.

"Therefore we say to you, and to all others who share these convictions: Let us work together to create a world in which men may free themselves from the sterile grip of totalitarianism which denies these basic human values."

When we learn to speak in these universal terms, the faces of hundreds of millions of people of all races, creeds and cultures will light up in new confidence and understanding.

Our historic role as a nation has always been clear. It is time to reaffirm it at home and abroad.

═ 13

A REVOLUTION INTENDED
FOR ALL MANKIND

*Can a well-fed, prosperous nation such as our own help
spearhead a world-wide revolution of peaceful change among
the developing nations? Mr. Bowles believes that we can
—provided we are true to our own revolutionary traditions.
From an article in the* New York Times Magazine,
December 10, 1961.

CAN A nation as well fed and comfortable as our own participate as a leader and partner in a world-wide revolution of peaceful
change? Or is it fated by its own fears and inhibitions to become identified with a doomed status quo, or at best to watch uneasily from the
sidelines?

These are questions that stand at the center of the challenge to
American foreign policy. Wherever I have traveled in Asia, Africa and
Latin America, the core of our dilemma remains the same: Can we
understand, can we adapt, and can we act effectively?

Over the past four months, the reorganization of our overseas diplomatic missions and my attendance at the annual Colombo Plan meeting in Malaya have taken me into every continent except Europe. And
everywhere these questions have repeated themselves: in the problems
raised by our ambassadors to new African nations; in the obstacles

65

facing our economic aid administrators in Latin America; and in the doubts and hopes of our critics and well-wishers in the governments of South and Southeast Asia.

We are unquestionably in the midst of a world revolution. Has any nation of great wealth and material advantages ever taken off its coat, rolled up its sleeves and become an active, contributing partner in such a revolution? My reading of history discloses none.

Can America, then, become history's first exception? Almost certainly our answer to this question will shape, not only our own future, but the course of civilization for generations to come.

In Africa, Asia and Latin America impatient millions are straining against the old established order—against the old economic order of landlord and tenant, against the old social order of master and servant, against the old political order of the rulers and the ruled.

In each of these developing continents, the most dangerous gap is still the gap between the very rich and the very poor. In the background we Americans stand as the most spectacular international example of the rich and, to make our task more difficult, as a predominantly white nation in a world that is two-thirds colored.

How can such a nation identify itself with the world-wide revolution, let alone help to guide it? How can a man with two cars in his garage talk to a man dreaming of his first bicycle? What can a housewife worrying about calories say to a woman whose children are hungry?

Although the obstacles to our success are massive, we approach the challenge with certain advantages. The first of these is our own American revolutionary tradition. As a nation we were born with a will, first to secure our national freedom, and then to take whatever action was required to assure increasing justice and economic and social opportunities for all our people.

Nor has our revolutionary zeal been confined to our own continent. From the very beginning, our founders focused their vision on a larger horizon. It was Jefferson who said, "The American Revolution is intended for all mankind." And the mass of mankind, he added, "was not born with saddles on their backs, for a favored few, booted and spurred, ready to ride them by the grace of God."

Jefferson's vision of a democratic revolution whose benefits were meant to be shared by all men has stayed with us throughout our history. President after President has supplied the stirring words and acts that have kindled men's spirits.

"The right of revolution," said Lincoln, "is a most sacred right; a right which we believe is to liberate the world." Wilson's Fourteen Points in 1917, with their advocacy of the rights of self-determination for subject people everywhere, were deeply rooted in the American tradition.

So, too, were Franklin D. Roosevelt's Four Freedoms—freedom of speech and expression, freedom to worship God in our own way, freedom from want and freedom from fear—each specifically earmarked for people "everywhere in the world."

The first of our moral and ideological resources, therefore, is the idealism of our own revolutionary tradition. The second is the economic, political and social content of that tradition. As a nation we have not only given lip service to revolution; we have legislated revolution. In the context of today's world, many economic and social laws and programs that we Americans take for granted are radical in their conception and revolutionary in their results.

For example, many Asian, African and Latin-American leaders still look on the graduated income tax, which we Americans accepted fifty years ago, as a profoundly radical doctrine. Yet most Americans, regardless of party, have long since accepted this mechanism, which not only raises revenue, but also sharply reduces the gap between rich and poor by redistributing wealth.

Similarly, such concepts as social security, public housing, regulation of utilities and transportation, collective bargaining between labor and management, and substantial corporation taxes, which are now an established part of our economy, are still associated in the minds of much of the world with "radicalism."

The revolutions which are now in progress in Asia, Africa and Latin America are striving to raise living standards, to distribute national wealth, to provide minimal security for men and women and children. These are goals which we have sought for ourselves, and which we continue to seek.

A third basic consideration which relates us to the world-wide revolution of today derives from our deep-rooted belief that every rural family should have an opportunity to own its own land. And nothing is more fundamental to the tide of revolution on three continents today than the desire of the landless and the tenant farmers for just such landownership.

From the days of our colonial youth as farmer-proprietors and militiamen, we have expressed our opposition to rural feudalism in all forms through far-reaching legislation. One hundred years ago we wrote our beliefs into the Homestead Act which gave 160 acres of land to every family willing and able to till them. In later years we strengthened this concept of independent landownership with agencies for rural credit, cooperatives and agricultural improvement.

These three great American resources—our anticolonial revolutionary tradition, our commitment to economic and social reform and our dedication to the private ownership of land—are tremendous potential assets in helping us meet the test that today's revolutionary world imposes upon us.

Yet many Asians, Africans and Latin Americans today feel that we Americans have lost touch with our traditions. It is essential, therefore, that we carefully consider and clearly define our national purposes in the framework of the modern revolutionary world. Precisely what do we want in our relations with the world? What are the necessary steps to fulfill our objectives? Why do we seek to win the understanding and support of other peoples?

These are questions we must constantly ask as citizens and voters. They are questions that our policy-makers and embassy personnel have been reviewing in the past several months. For they lie at the heart of all our overseas operations.

For instance, is our national purpose merely to counteract Communism? Communism poses a vast challenge to free institutions everywhere, and the battle against Communism is part of our struggle against all forms of tyranny.

Yet anti-Communism alone can hardly be accepted as the sole national purpose of the nation of Jefferson and Lincoln. Indeed, when we relate all our actions to the presence or absence of a Communist threat in any nation, we tend to turn Communism in that nation into a natural resource like uranium or petroleum that may be exchanged for dollars at the United States Treasury.

Or is our purpose, as we are so often told, to "capture the minds of men"? On analysis, this objective falls equally short of both practical reality and our democratic faith. Wasn't it the *liberation* of men's minds to which Jefferson pledged our efforts, and does not this aim run throughout our entire history?

Finally, there are those who suggest that our purpose is to demonstrate the advantage of private ownership over public ownership. Yet here, too, the suggested objective is woefully narrow. Capitalism has worked wonders for our own country, and it can perform major services in other parts of the world. But the universal acceptance of capitalism is not America's ultimate national goal; capitalism is a means to an end, not the end itself.

Our true national purpose, as I see it, is something far simpler, far more universal and far more compelling. It is no less than a dedication to partnership with these non-Communist peoples to develop a world community where freedom of choice is possible; where people can live their own lives in conditions of widening economic opportunity and deepening social justice; and where nations can make their own choices within the framework of their own cultures and traditions.

It is one thing to understand our assets and to clarify our aims; but it is quite another to apply our new awareness through specific programs and policies.

It might be useful to review the answers that have developed from our search for ways to translate our national purpose into wise and constructive programs for this revolutionary world.

First, it is abundantly clear that we must maintain our military power as the prerequisite to all action, as long as potential aggressors continue to exist. At the same time, however, our defense posture must remain one of clear restraint, never of provocation.

Second, it is equally clear that we must never forget the appalling danger of the spiraling nuclear-arms race. In the pursuit of effective, tightly safeguarded disarmament plans our patience must be inexhaustible.

Third, we must put aside arrogance and frustration, and forever resist the temptation to judge that those who are not with us must therefore be against us.

Let us not forget that "neutrality" from Europe's "everlasting quarrels" was a cornerstone of American foreign policy from George Washington to Woodrow Wilson; that the new nations of the world, which have only recently managed to throw off the grip of European colonial powers, are now as preoccupied with their own pressing problems as we were at a similar stage of our own development; and that, in all probability, they will continue to underestimate the Communist challenge which properly concerns us.

A fourth and critically important element in the application of our national purpose is our program of overseas economic and technical assistance.

A fifth and final element, in our overseas effort, is our information programs. These programs should describe us as we are: fortunate, yes, but not smug; a nation still struggling with unsolved problems of education, of housing, of race relations; a nation still on the move toward a more just and democratic society. We should·speak of what we are still seeking to achieve, and of what we seek to accomplish abroad in partnership with others.

With all its excesses and confusion, the present surge for human freedom in Asia, Africa and Latin America is basically a continuation of the fight for those universal objectives which our forefathers in the Declaration of Independence proclaimed to be self-evident.

If our generation of Americans can effectively understand and meet this challenge, there is little reason for anyone to fear that the developing new nations will become subverted by the sterility, bitterness and false values of the Communist counterrevolution.

TOWARD A NEW DIPLOMACY

Foreign aid, the Peace Corps, Food for Peace, and other overseas development programs have dramatized the expanding dimensions of mid-twentieth-century diplomacy. In an article in Foreign Affairs in early 1962, Mr. Bowles reports on how the new Administration has organized its overseas missions to meet this challenge.

BEFORE the last war, the tasks of American foreign policy were comparatively well defined. Secretary Cordell Hull, with a Washington staff of less than one thousand, presided over our entire global diplomatic establishment from a building shared with the War and Navy departments.

The function of the seventy-eight ambassadors and ministers stationed abroad consisted largely of reporting and analyzing the flow of events and representing the President in negotiations and ceremonial events.

Twenty critical years have changed this traditional pattern dramatically. As our responsibilities in world affairs grew, the task of our diplomacy became more complex and its instruments multiplied correspondingly.

For the ambassador, the transformation has meant a change of emphasis from discreet observation to active operations. In terms of budget and administration, the transformation has resulted in a 38,-

71

000-man Department of State, including the Foreign Service and the Agency for International Development (which accounts for 17,000 of the total).

In addition, there are a Peace Corps, a Food for Peace program, a United States Information Agency, a Central Intelligence Agency, a variety of military programs, and expanded overseas operations of the Labor, Commerce, Agriculture and Treasury departments.

Moreover, we now have diplomatic missions in more than one hundred countries, in addition to 166 consulates and consulates general. In many of these posts the mission chief presides over what amounts to a cabinet. For instance, on the eve of World War II our Paris Embassy employed seventy-eight people, including the staffs of four other agencies. Now it employs seven hundred, including the staffs of twenty-three other agencies.

This extraordinary multiplication of activities and agencies reflects the complexity and interdependence of our modern world. Much of it would have occurred even if there were no Soviet challenge. Yet the increasing competition between our two societies, between the Soviet and the liberal-democratic approach to human development, has greatly hastened the process, and we know that this competition will be with us for the foreseeable future.

The challenge of our new age was initially—and understandably—interpreted by both the executive and legislative branches of our government as primarily a challenge to policy-making. But the development of an effective foreign policy is only the first step; we must also devise effective means to carry it out. And this challenge to our instruments of policy, to the organization, administration and operation of our efforts at home and abroad, has only recently begun to be appreciated and acted upon.

It is against this background of challenge and growth that the Administration has been seeking to coordinate its overseas activities to increase their effectiveness. This effort has taken three forms: (1) a critical review of the special qualities now required of our ambassadors; (2) a Presidential clarification of the ambassador's greatly expanded responsibilities in the country of his assignment; (3) a program to coordinate our far-flung activities wherever we maintain diplomatic or consular missions.

The transformed demands of diplomacy have clearly altered the qualities required in our ambassadors. Although personal charm, an attractive wife, political perceptiveness and analytical ability are still highly useful, they are no longer enough.

The modern ambassador must also be an administrator capable of supervising a wide range of operations; a creative leader capable of taking initiative, inspiring subordinates, delegating authority and cutting through details; a diplomat of tact and persuasiveness who knows how to combine toughness and restraint.

In these circumstances, the Administration concluded that the time-honored practice of awarding a number of ambassadorships to wealthy campaign contributors was something we could no longer afford. Thus the percentage of Foreign Service career ambassadors appointed in 1961 was the highest in history. In addition, a special effort was made to provide rapid promotion for outstanding younger men in the service who were likely to be flexible and perceptive in dealing with the special problems of young and newly independent nations. The twenty or so new, noncareer ambassadors were, almost without exception, men with extensive foreign policy experience. Most of them were drawn from university faculties and foundations. With a handful of exceptions, all ambassadors now speak the language of official discussion in the country of their assignment.

An effort was also made to see that each ambassador received an assignment which he felt personally qualified to handle. The hair-shirt tradition of sending Foreign Service officers to precisely those places to which they did not want to go in order to "strengthen their character" was abandoned. The normal term of an ambassador and his principal associates at a post was extended to four years. The ambassador and his wife were considered as a team. And he was given increased authority over the choice of his assistants and associates.

The selection of better-qualified personnel was the first essential step. The next was to clarify the ambassador's authority.

Thus, on May 29, 1961, President Kennedy sent a letter to each American ambassador in which he reaffirmed the ambassador's role as the President's personal representative, with clear authority over all other U.S. Government activities and personnel in the country of his assignment. "I shall count on you," the President wrote, "to oversee and coordinate all the activities of the United States Government. . . . You are in charge of the entire United States Diplomatic Mission, and I shall expect you to supervise all of its operation." The President's letter sought to eliminate once and for all the problem of conflicting lines of responsibility. The ambassador was clearly established as the final authority, as the President's top representative.

The next step in the effort to modernize the practice of American diplomacy and to increase its effectiveness was a series of six regional conferences to which were invited, not only ambassadors, but their wives, their administrative officers and their principal aid, information and military advisers.

Although the ambassadors had been armed with new statements of authority, many were still skeptical as to whether the new directives really meant what they said. Moreover, administrative procedures had remained largely untouched, and communication between Washington and the field had left many operational questions unanswered. Nor had representatives of the Pentagon, the new AID administration, USIA, the Peace Corps, Food for Peace, the Central Intelligence Agency, the Bureau of the Budget and such departments as Commerce and Labor had an opportunity to thrash out specific details of operations, responsibility and cooperation with the ambassadors and their staffs. These conferences provided the opportunity. In many cases, on-the-spot decisions were made on questions which had been previously swept under the rug.

One of the innovations of the regional conferences was the attendance of the ambassadors' wives. As every Foreign Service officer knows, the wife who is sensitive to local problems, aware of our national purposes and anxious to help carry them out is an invaluable addition to any embassy. Likewise, one who lacks such qualities can be a serious liability. It is the ambassador's wife, for better or worse, who sits regularly beside the highest officials of the government at dinner parties and official functions.

At each conference, in order to broaden their knowledge and understanding, the wives accompanied their husbands to all but the highly classified meetings.

These conferences produced nearly two hundred proposals for administrative improvements within the State Department alone, more than half of which have already been acted upon. The proposals ranged from the desirability of smaller official automobiles to more intensive language training for clerical and officer personnel. A large number of constructive measures were suggested for eliminating operational red tape, for speeding up communications between Washington and the overseas missions and for better coordination with international agencies.

It is fair to say that we have made only a start in the essential re-tooling and integration of the instruments by which American foreign policy can be made effective in this age of total diplomacy. More public education will be needed to persuade the American people, and some officials as well, that nearly everything we do, whether it involves labor, civil rights, food surpluses, trade, science or tourism, now bears in some degree on our foreign policy. And the problem, once we have recognized the interrelation of these many aspects of our foreign affairs, is to learn how to administer them with greater skill and effectiveness.

In this respect, we are fortunate in that the President's Cabinet today is made up of men who have a world view, who understand foreign affairs and the role of their departments in carrying out an integrated foreign policy. This is immensely important, for the progress we have made in coordinating our activities in our missions abroad under the ambassador's leadership must be backstopped by correspondingly better control and coordination of foreign policy in Washington.

The logical focus for such coordination lies in the regional assistant secretaries of state. By increasing the authority of these officials we can make them the actual coordinators of all our wide-ranging operations in their areas of responsibility. This is one of the many essential innovations which may meet resistance.

But the task ahead necessarily calls for new approaches, more imaginative techniques and tougher-minded administration if the instruments of our foreign policy are to keep pace with its requirements. Although a good start has been made, much remains to be done.

PATTERNS OF ECONOMIC ASSISTANCE

The over-all objective of our aid program is clear, urgent and profoundly worthwhile: to develop indigenous political and economic strength among the nations of the free world so that they can survive, not to serve America's interest but their own.

As they succeed in meeting the needs of their people, their confidence in democratic methods will grow, and with it their determination to defend their achievements against all adversaries, either from within or without.

With such nations, America can form a free and dynamic partnership which over the years will ease the threat of Communist aggression and gradually establish the foundations for a lasting peace.

December, 1954

═ 15

AMERICA'S FOOD IN A HUNGRY WORLD

*America's astounding feats of farm production during the
war prompt Mr. Bowles to suggest American leadership in a
world-wide agricultural revolution to banish hunger. An
address at the eleventh annual convention of the Supermarket
Institute, Chicago, May 25, 1947.*

FAR INTO the future, America has a tremendous role to fill
in the production and distribution of food, not only for her own people,
but for the hungry millions throughout the world.

In 1939, three-quarters of all the people in the world were engaged
in the production, processing and distribution of food. And yet, two-
thirds of mankind, in what we used to call normal, prewar conditions,
were not getting enough to eat.

No one of us would choose to live as a rich, privileged individual
in a community of hungry, insecure people. And yet that is exactly
the situation which we Americans are facing today. In effect, we have
created a luxurious mansion, labeled "the U.S.A.," in the midst of a
world slum.

There can be no peace or security for ourselves and our children
until other members of the world community are able to live a better
life. And food is the basis of that better life.

Although the process of raising world living standards through higher food production is easy to outline in theory, it will be a staggering task to put into effect. What we must help to accomplish on a world basis in the next generation is suggested by what we have accomplished in food production here in the United States in the last 150 years.

In America in 1795, 90 percent of the people raised their own food and sufficient extra food to feed the 10 percent of the people who were not then living on farms.

In the United States today, thanks to modern equipment and improved agricultural methods, some 20 percent of the people are raising food, not only for themselves, but for the remaining 80 percent of us who live in cities and towns, with a sizable amount left over for export.

It is this development in large part which has enabled us to free the millions of skilled workers who were required to create our great mass production industries, and to raise our living standards to the highest levels in the world.

What we must do now, laboriously and painfully, is to help others to duplicate this development throughout the world. We must find means to help increase world food supplies substantially; some experts say we must double them in the next generation. In the meantime our own "surpluses" must help fill in the gap.

We will need nothing less than a revolution in world agriculture. We will need broad planning for river valley developments on the model of the Tennessee Valley Authority for the great rivers of Asia, South America and Africa.

We will need greatly to increase the production of modern farm machinery. We will need vast irrigation projects and tremendous new fertilizer plants.

Above all, in many countries we will need to encourage land reform programs so that the land can be owned by those who work it, rather than by absentee landlords.

This will require broad and imaginative planning. It will require the breaking down of old rural taboos, prejudices and traditions. It will call for a strengthened United Nations Organization and a greater willingness on the part of all nations—including our own—to work through the United Nations rather than on a direct, unilateral basis. It will take a lot of doing.

In the Farm and Agricultural Organization of the United Nations, in the General Assembly and in the Economic and Security Council, we Americans should take the lead.

In programs to reorganize agriculture throughout the globe, courageously conceived and vigorously pushed forward, we will find unlimited stimulation and opportunity for the use of our best skills and resources. This kind of approach is right from the standpoint of human decency. It is right, too, from the standpoint of our own economy and security.

As long as the peace of the world remains disturbed, let us make sure that our powder is not only dry but ample. But let us never forget that the future cannot be won with rockets, tanks and long-range bombers.

If civilization is to mean anything, it must be bolstered as well as protected by democratic people with dynamic ideas and the skill and boldness to put those ideas into effect. The future of all mankind may depend on our willingness to accept the challenge which our hungry, chaotic world presents to us.

━━ 16

TO BRING HOPE TO CHILDREN
WITHOUT HOPE

*After visiting war-devastated Europe, as Chairman of the
United Nations Appeal for Children, Mr. Bowles pleads for
help and food for Europe's "new generation." From an article
in the* New York Times Magazine, *February 1, 1948.*

I HAVE just returned from an intensive five weeks' trip to
Europe, where I was sent by the Secretary General of the United
Nations, Trygve Lie, to study the effects of the war on children and
to suggest programs to deal with their needs.

Like most Americans I had some understanding of the vast difficulties of postwar reconstruction in Europe, of what Europeans are
doing to help themselves and of the help they are getting from beyond
their borders.

But I was totally unprepared for many of the things I found: the
devastation in Warsaw; the bitterness of the Czech people over the
murdered men of Lidice; the tragic spread of tuberculosis among
the children of France and Hungary; the tight-lipped patience of the
English.

Above everything else, I was impressed with the courage and intensity with which all these people are attacking their own problems, and

the hard work being put forth by men, women and children, many of them weakened by malnutrition.

Equally inspiring has been their reception of the United Nations Appeal for Children—even in countries which have themselves suffered terribly. For the people of Europe, the appeal means more than food alone. It means the hope for enduring peace and a chance for all peoples to cooperate directly in an international undertaking. In this, I think, they are in advance of their governments.

Words and figures are not adequate to convey some of the impressions which have been burned into my mind on this brief trip. All I can do is to pass on the facts about some of the things I can never forget.

In an industrial town near Paris, in a windowless one-room shack, an eleven-year-old girl was caring for three smaller children—and for her father, whose legs had been amputated, and who would have to wait for several more weeks for artificial legs.

Her mother was at work at a ten-dollar-a-week job, trying to earn enough to keep the family alive—and together. The little shack was neat. The children were clean. Most surprising of all, the eleven-year-old was singing.

In Warsaw, in a ten-by-fourteen-foot corner of the cellar of a blasted house, lived what was left of the Marshy family—a boy of seven, his sister aged ten and their grandmother. The father, mother and a baby boy and a girl who would be fifteen now were killed in the Warsaw uprising of 1944.

The grandmother found the children wandering in the streets and moved them into her cellar home. To support them, she earns a few cents an hour removing rubble by hand. In addition, she receives two dollars monthly from the Welfare Department. The children take turns going to school because there are not enough clothes for both of them.

They are among the fortunate few who get a little bread given by the government, spread with lard and washed down with milk contributed by the United Nations Children's Fund.

There are millions of children living like this in the countries which I have visited. But I shall remember not only the misery, hunger and squalor. I shall remember the neatly tied ribbons in the little girls' hair in the Warsaw and Budapest orphanages; the pathetic decorations in the peasant huts in Italy and Czechoslovakia; the cheerful nursery group in the devastated Polish schools; the grateful appreciation of

Hungarians and French doctors for new hospital equipment just received from the Swiss; and the calm, quiet, cheerful determination of teachers and social workers, nurses and physicians in every country as with meager resources they attack the problems of a new generation born in war.

The children of Europe and Asia are living in a world of misery created by our generation. It is our responsibility that they shall have an opportunity to build a new world infinitely better than the one their parents' generation helped to destroy.

POINT FOUR BEGINS AN
ASIAN REVOLUTION

*In 1951-52 India launched the first and largest of America's
new Point Four programs of technical and economic aid under
an agreement negotiated by Ambassador Bowles. Here Mr.
Bowles reports on the program's potentials in the* New York
Times Magazine, *November 16, 1952.*

ANYONE in Asia who watches Point Four in action soon
comes to a challenging realization. Point Four is no mere program,
however bold and new. Potentially, it is a revolutionary concept.

If we understand it and nourish it, Point Four may go down in
history as the most important idea of our generation, the counter-
revolutionary movement with which world Communism could not
cope.

Arnold Toynbee recently suggested that our age will be remembered
"not for its horrifying crimes or its astonishing inventions, but because
it is the first age since the dawn of history in which mankind dared
to believe it practicable to make the benefits of civilization available
to the whole human race."

Most thoughtful people who have lived and worked in Asia will
agree with him. To the hundreds of millions of long-oppressed people
here, the new surging conviction that a better life is somehow attain-

85

able has deep revolutionary significance. It is the driving force and ferment that is changing the face of Asia, and which may change it even more profoundly in the coming years.

In cooperation with effective, progressive Asian governments, Point Four can offer these millions the hope of a better life, and the tools and encouragement to achieve it. It can guide their energies away from explosive frustration and into tangible opportunities for advancement —bigger crops, more schools, literacy, tube wells, better plows, healthier children and relief from smallpox and malaria.

Point Four, in other words, intelligently administered and adequately financed, can help accomplish a dynamic, bloodless, non-Communist revolution from poverty, hunger, disease and ignorance. It is little wonder that this program is vigorously berated by Communist agitators, who know better than many of us the almost unlimited positive possibilities of this down-to-earth, bullock-and-plow approach to mankind's problems.

Point Four is a tremendous challenge. It is also a great responsibility.

We should understand how this dynamic concept must blend with the indigenous forces with which it works, and the awakening drive for human betterment which is rapidly arousing the billion people who live in the so-called underdeveloped areas.

There are several points that will bear repetition.

First, Point Four is not a ready-made program that can be exported neatly wrapped, complete with a guarantee to cure the economic and social ills of underdeveloped countries. The objectives of Point Four can be simply stated: the conquest of poverty, disease and ignorance through the democratic use of modern tools and technical assistance.

These broad objectives must be worked out in specific terms for each country; and the specific program must be individually tailored to the country, to its economy, to its customs and culture and to its government.

Second, Point Four is not a charity basket program, but an approach to human betterment based on the most modern principle of social work—self-help. This approach, although sometimes slow and frustrating, is the only enduring way.

Unless the people themselves participate, unless they see how by their own efforts, plus a little outside help in money and materials, they can build a better future, the advances gained will never take root, but will eventually lapse in apathy.

Third, in each country Point Four must encourage the broadest possible attack on human problems. A limited number of Point Four developments carried to a high standard of perfection will accomplish far less than a larger number which touches more people, stirs them to activity in their own behalf and gives constructive help to the universal drive for advancement.

What is needed is not so much model hospitals, model schools and model farms, as a mass attack on the problems of public health, literacy, agriculture and stimulation of local industry, built solidly on the participation of the people themselves—and as many of them as possible.

Fourth, we should not embark on a Point Four program in the naïve belief that it will enable us to buy favors in the recipient countries or even to win their gratitude. Indeed, the principal reason why some underdeveloped countries hesitate to accept American assistance is the fear that we may attempt to use Point Four to curb their newly won freedom or to influence their national policies.

There is only one basis on which America and the underdeveloped countries can grow closer together, and that is mutual desire to build a more secure and freer world. If democracy succeeds in India, Pakistan, Japan, Indonesia, Ethiopia, Liberia, Egypt, Brazil, Venezuela and other Asian, African and South American countries, every American will have increased reason to hope for a better existence for himself and for his children.

If we cannot be satisfied with this simple objective, our efforts are doomed to failure. We will have lost not only the chance for a partnership with the hundreds of millions of Asians and Africans who wanted to be our friends, but also the hope of the bloodless, democratic revolution that alone can lay the basis for a world of peace and increasing human dignity.

=== 18

WORLD PARTNERS IN
ECONOMIC DEVELOPMENT

*Military assistance is not enough to stop the cunning Communist
effort to subvert the revolution of rising expectations for
their own ends, argues Mr. Bowles. In the December, 1954, issue
of the* Atlantic Monthly, *he outlines what we can do to help
the developing nations protect their own freedom.*

SINCE Stalin's death the Soviet Union has moved steadily
to capture the diplomatic offensive and to divide the free world. Day
by day it is striving to convince millions of people in Europe, Asia
and South America that the Communist nations are the true advocates of peace, and that America, toward whom the world looked with
such fervent hopes in 1945, is a power-hungry aggressor.

That this incredibly distorted picture is now widely accepted is a
measure of the problem which we face. If we are to change this picture, we must develop a fresh concept of our relations with other free
nations, a broader understanding of the nature of power in a revolutionary world, and a bold new approach to match that understanding.

What we do or fail to do in Europe is of crucial importance. But
what we do in Asia, Africa and South America is of at least equal
importance. In these underdeveloped areas our concentration on military answers and our indifference to economic and political factors
have been particularly damaging.

If the world Communist movement closed up shop tomorrow, the underdeveloped areas would still be of profound importance to every American. Although we produce 40 percent of all the industrial goods in the world, we have only 6 percent of the world's population. As our own natural resources dwindle in relation to the demands of our economy, we have become more and more dependent on trade with Asia, Africa and South America—which now amounts to 50 percent of our world-wide total.

Today these underdeveloped nations are going through a revolutionary period which would affect our lives regardless of the cold war. In Asia, Africa and South America the people, confident that science can quickly erase their poverty and misery, are determinedly seeking a better life.

The Communists did not create this turmoil and ferment. If Marx, Lenin, Stalin and Mao had never existed we would still be contending with it. What the Communists strive to do is to ride the revolutionary wave like surf riders, and to work with all their skill and ideological fervor to speed the destruction of the old order and fill the resulting vacuums.

The government of every underdeveloped nation is now on trial. In the next few years these governments must demonstrate to their people that democracy can provide, not only political freedom for each individual, but also steady and even spectacular economic growth.

Demands for higher living standards, for more food, for freedom from disease, for schools and roads, for the damming of rivers to provide irrigation and hydroelectric power, for the expansion of railroads and communications, are growing steadily more insistent. Any government which consistently fails to meet these demands, however honest and democratic, will eventually go under.

The obstacles in the way of rapid progress are great, and one of the most stubborn is lack of capital resources.

Whether the country is rich or poor; whether the economy is capitalist, Communist or socialist, capital accumulated through savings is the essential dynamic motive force which determines the speed with which industry can be expanded and living standards raised.

Today every underdeveloped nation is struggling with the question: Where can the savings be found to push forward development at a pace that will satisfy their impatient people?

If a democratic government piles the taxes too high, it will face defeat at the polls. Yet if it fails to match the progress of the Communist nations, it will be swept aside in revolutionary upheaval.

We cannot cope with this challenge by simply adding more atomic bombs to our already massive supply. Indochina should have taught us that Western military power in revolutionary Asia has its limits. Nor can America "save" Asia from Communism by lectures and threats.

If Asia decides finally to reject the Communist doctrine, it will be because Asians have become convinced by their own experience that steady economic progress and individual freedom can both be attained under democratic governments, and that the bloody totalitarian road is a political and economic dead end.

The situation calls, among other things, for a fresh new approach to foreign economic assistance that is practical, acceptable and within our capacity.

If we are concerned solely with stopping Communism, our effort will start under a grave handicap. We will tend to concentrate our efforts solely in those areas where Communism already exists as an active threat, and this will hang a political label on everything that we do.

If, for instance, a new American assistance program is concentrated in Communist-threatened South Asia, while Africa and South America remain largely neglected, Asians will promptly assume that we are interested, not in their welfare, but purely in thwarting the Communists. We will be charged with attempting to buy their loyalties and to draw them into the "Western camp." Many free Asian leaders, although desperately anxious for assistance, will accept our aid only with reluctance or not at all.

Why, indeed, should it take the cold war to goad us into doing what we should do for its own sake? To reach out a helping hand to others less fortunate than we was basic to our religious beliefs and our traditions long before the Moscow-Peking Axis came into existence.

The over-all objective of our aid programs is clear, urgent and profoundly worthwhile: to develop indigenous political and economic strength among the nations of the free world so that they can survive as free people, not to serve America's interest but their own.

As they succeed in meeting the needs of their people, their confidence in democratic methods will grow, and with it their determination to defend their achievements against all adversaries, either from within or without.

With such nations, America can form a free and dynamic partnership which over the years will ease the threat of Communist aggression and gradually establish the foundations for a lasting peace.

For this reason the purpose of any effective program must be broader than the easing of poverty. Misinformed people tell us that "a man with a full stomach will never become a Communist." History does not bear them out. Revolutions are led, not by hungry peasants, but by middle-class, frustrated and normally well-fed intellectuals.

* * *

OUR aid programs to non-Communist nations must be free of *political* strings. But it is essential that workable requirements be established for long-range economic planning, land reform, tax reform and a ban on the use of foreign exchange for the purchase of luxuries for the wealthy.

Today in several underdeveloped countries the effect of American aid is not to speed such reforms but to postpone them. If we dodge this issue, a large proportion of our aid money will be wasted, and we will be charged with subsidizing feudal economics which serve the few and not the many.

Finally, we must forego our search for a simple, glib, all-inclusive formula. The problems of economic development are infinitely complex, and the solutions which we bring to bear must reflect their complexity.

For instance, lower tariffs and increased trade will greatly reduce the amount of aid that is needed. The underdeveloped nations are willing and anxious to pay for their own progress as far as that is possible. But there are only two ways that they can get dollars: they can earn them by selling us things which we need, or they can get them through American grants or loans.

The easier we make it for these nations to sell part of their production to the United States, the less assistance they will require from us. Moreover, the higher their living standards rise, the more goods they will be able to buy from American manufacturers.

We should also take steps to bring a greater element of stability into the prices of raw materials which we buy in the underdeveloped areas. The incomes of three-fourths of all the families in Malaya are tied to the price of rubber in America. In many of the tea, coffee, cocoa, tin and oil producing nations, the link is almost equally close.

Surely we are ingenious enough to develop some system of minimum and maximum prices that will avoid the violent swings of the market which cause such suffering and bitterness and which benefit only the speculators. A price band with maximum and minimum limits might be set up for normal fluctuations, which could ordinarily be controlled through adding to or subtracting from stockpiles.

If production remains beyond the capacity of the market to absorb it, an orderly planned movement into other fields of production could be set in motion. No responsible person would suggest that such a program could easily be put together or agreement quickly reached. But the time to make the attempt is now, while there is latitude to give it considered attention.

Freer trade and assured markets for raw materials at stable prices will strengthen the economies of the underdeveloped nations and enable them better to help themselves. But a substantial program of direct assistance is also urgently needed. Such a program must be as bold and imaginative as the Marshall Plan, which helped put the economies of Western Europe on their feet between 1947 and 1951.

Only to a limited extent can these capital needs be met by private investment from America and other Western nations. Since the war, private investment in the United States has averaged $46 billion annually. In this same period our total overseas investments were only $10 billion. Most of this was in Europe and Canada, and it came largely from profits earned in those countries by American corporations. If we eliminate American oil expansion in South America, American private investment in the underdeveloped nations since the war totals scarcely one billion dollars. In India, during this period, it has been less than $100 million.

There are valid and understandable reasons for this meager flow. Conditions in most underdeveloped nations are uncertain. Often there has been unreasoning prejudice against foreign investors based on colonial experience. In some cases tax laws make it difficult to take out a reasonable share of the profits once they are made. There are often nagging bureaucratic difficulties in operations.

But even under ideal conditions it is folly to expect that the essential foundations for economic growth in the underdeveloped nations can be built through private capital. The investment that is required is too great and the profit opportunities too limited and uncertain.

Such basic primary needs as increased electric power, adequate port facilities, more efficient railroads and improved communications must largely be created with government funds. Only after these foundations have been built and colonial fears have receded can we expect broad opportunities for private investment to be opened up. Hence, in most underdeveloped nations direct government loans and grants on a substantial scale are essential to adequate progress.

The poverty which exists throughout much of Asia, Africa and South America provides the soil in which Communism is most likely to grow. When we restrict our willingness to assist the underdeveloped nations on the grounds that we cannot *afford* both economic development and defense at the same time, we simply offer the Russians one more reason to maintain the present arms race.

Why cannot we break loose from our obsession with the Russians? Why cannot we take those measures which are clearly in line with our own American heritage and which will begin to meet some of the most impelling demands of our fellow men?

The time has come for members of both political parties to set a new measure of action for the future. Let America put her hesitation behind her and boldly offer the free, underdeveloped and uncommitted people of Asia, Africa and South America a partnership to quicken their economic progress.

═ 19

A NEW APPROACH TO FOREIGN AID

*The dilemma of the underdeveloped nations—how to step up
economic growth and yet raise living standards at the same time
—calls for a more realistic focus for our foreign aid as shown
in Mr. Bowles' testimony at a hearing before the House
Foreign Affairs Committee in November, 1956.*

MANY reasons have been advanced to explain the lessening
of our influence in the underdeveloped and largely uncommitted areas
of the world during the last few years. One of the most important of
these is our failure to come to grips with the mounting crisis in
global economics which is developing under the pressure of the new
Soviet tactics.

Most of the new leaders of non-Communist Asia and Africa are
Western-educated and largely committed to democratic objectives and,
in varying degrees, to democratic methods. But they are also subject
to unprecedented internal pressures generated by low living standards,
made even more explosive by a new public understanding of the po-
tentialities of modern technology.

This poses for them a critical dilemma.

Because industrialization has become synonymous with national
purposes and power, and because of widespread public knowledge of
the new technology, the political pressures for extremely rapid growth

94

in Asia and Africa are now much greater than during the early period of our own industrial development.

At the same time, public attention in democratically inclined nations has been focused, not on building the essential heavy industrial base, but on the immediate improvement of living standards. The people have been conditioned by the rival promises of their political leaders, by United Nations and Point Four surveys, and by Communist propaganda to judge the effectiveness of their government largely by its ability to deliver here and now more food, more clothing, less disease, more literacy and improved welfare services.

Thus a nation which chooses to develop its resources by democratic methods must keep its taxes within acceptable limits; it must divert enough productive capacity to consumer goods and service to satisfy the public demand for tangible improvement in living standards; at the same time it must match within reasonable bounds the highly publicized industrial achievements of comparable Communist nations.

The government of a Communist country, however, using police-state methods, can squeeze far heavier taxes from its people, invest practically all its forced savings in heavy industry and military defense, and postpone indefinitely any substantial improvement in living standards.

Totalitarian China and democratic India offer striking examples of the practical effects of the two alternative systems in action. China is now concentrating 22 percent of her annual gross national product in expansion, most of it in heavy industry, transportation and power development. India, although governed by men of great ability and political courage, has so far been able to push the annual rate of savings available for similar developments to only 8 or 9 percent.

This brief analysis brings into sharp focus the decisive role of an intelligent American economic assistance program for those new Asian and African nations which seek to avoid totalitarianism, that is, to keep the internal sacrifices and strains which are an inevitable by-product of rapid economic growth within limits acceptable to a free people; to enable democratic governments to avoid police-state methods and still approach, if not match, the Communist rate of economic growth.

Most underdeveloped, democratically inclined nations require not only technical assistance but substantial amounts of capital to finance industry, transportation and power development, side by side with a visible increase in consumer goods and services, all within a tolerable domestic tax burden.

The traditional means of effecting a flow of capital from the developed to the less developed nations has been through private financing. Yet, to a large extent, this means is not now available on a sufficiently massive scale to effect the final outcome.

Direct American private investment in nations seething with political unrest will also remain limited as long as the high profit levels, which would alone justify such investment, are politically unacceptable to those nations. With the exception of the petroleum and mining industries, less than $200 million of private American capital has been invested in Asia and Africa since 1948.

Private investment abroad should be encouraged with considerably more ingenuity than we have shown so far. As the industrial base of modern transportation, adequate power and heavy industry begins to develop, political stability in Asia and Africa may grow, and then private investors will have an increasingly important role to play.

In the meantime, the chief vehicle of substantial capital investment in the new non-Communist nations of Asia and Africa will remain, by default, the American Government. Only direct government action can enable American capital and technology to fill the gap between available local resources and the minimum development objectives which are commensurate with stable democratic government in present-day Asia and Africa.

A new global approach to economics will almost certainly be developed under the pressure of events in the next few years. This new approach may differ as much from our present view as Roosevelt's domestic economic program differed from that of Calvin Coolidge.

Because almost no serious effort has been made to explain its crucial importance to our future security, most Americans have continued to look on nonmilitary economic aid as a short-term, do-goodish scheme of doubtful value.

As a result, this program has received less than one percent of the funds we have invested in military defense. Moreover, the funds which Congress has made available for nonmilitary assistance have often been spent on the wrong projects, in the wrong places and for the wrong reasons.

In Asian countries we also find that substantial increases in output achieved through American assistance have not always been matched by a corresponding increase in political stability. The reason is our assistance programs have too often underwritten the old patterns of life with all their built-in inequities, although at a higher productive level.

In addition to creating more wealth, our aid program must place heavy emphasis on the development among the workers and peasants of a healthy, cooperative attitude toward their national governments and their communities.

This requires steady progress toward three essential objectives without which political stability in Asia, Africa and Latin America will almost certainly fail to develop:

1. A recognizable increase in economic output.

2. A sense of widespread personal participation in the creation of this increase.

3. A public conviction that the fruits of the increase are being fairly shared, with injustices steadily lessening.

Because we have focused our efforts in Asia and Africa largely on objective No. 1—sheer production increases—and because in many areas a growing percentage of the new wealth created with our assistance has been diverted into the hands of the ruling hierarchy, we now find ourselves identified in many parts of the world with the despised status quo.

American-trained students from certain Middle Eastern and South Asian countries often tell a tragic but familiar story. They return from their studies in the United States excited about the prospects of working to promote democratic growth and development among their own people. But upon reaching their homelands, they find semifeudal regimes bolstered and even kept in power by American assistance.

They find governments which tax the rich only a fraction of the degree to which we Americans tax ours. They find ridiculously low corporate taxes. They find scarce foreign exchange spent, not for necessities, but largely to pay for imported luxuries.

In other words, they often see our economic assistance used, not to speed reform, but to postpone the need for it, and thus to protect the power and prestige of the antidemocratic, right-wing groups which are clinging hopelessly to the past.

Economic assistance grants designed "to stop Communism" by such narrow means must ultimately fail. By underwriting an unpopular, feudal status quo which could not conceivably survive through its own resources, American aid programs may even turn large numbers of people against us and ultimately lead them to accept Communism as the sole way to change an intolerable situation.

*   *   *

I SHALL list briefly certain considerations, which it seems to me would form the core of a positive plan of action in the field of international economic assistance.

1. We should clearly define the purpose of economic aid. We must know what it can accomplish; equally important, we must know what it cannot accomplish.

Being human, we may hope that other people will like us and support our views. But a desire for friends, allies and approval should never be our prime motivation for assistance.

Further, although the implications of the Soviet challenge are clear, arguments which tie our economic assistance to the "duration of the Communist menace" dangerously oversimplify the problems which now confront us. So do proposals which would relate our assistance proportionately to the extent of the Communist danger in each country under consideration.

Our objective is not to win a short-term global popularity contest, but to help other nations achieve a degree of internal stability that will enable them to remain independent masters in their own houses, determined to defend their freedom against all foreign intruders.

2. Foreign economic aid is a long-range project. Its results cannot be immediate, and we will experience only frustration and bitterness if we fall prey to premature expectations.

We are entering a potentially promising period of rapid international development based on new achievements in technology and communications. Yet societies in which economic growth and a deep belief in human rights develop together in the balance essential to political stability will not be created cheaply or easily.

This time factor, of course, poses a practical legislative problem. Congress simply cannot lay down a precise five-year program and commit itself totally in advance. Yet our long-term support for the Marshall Plan, the United Nations, the Export-Import Bank, farm support price programs, the Commodity Credit Administration and the Social Security program, among others, give us a series of practical precedents.

In a given year Congress could refuse appropriations; but once the general confines of a long-term program had been agreed upon, such a refusal would be unlikely unless a drastic change occurred in international relations.

3. The volume of our aid should be adequate to the demands of the new world situation. To trim our commitments below the actual sums required to meet the most immediate and crucial needs will be the utmost folly.

We can no longer ignore the fact that a sizable and dangerously explosive gap exists, and will continue to exist, between what most of the new democratically inclined nations can save and spend on internal development and what the Communist nations can save and spend.

Some of our aid will undoubtedly take the form of technical assistance, commodity grants and commodity loans whose nature will vary considerably among nations. Our agricultural surpluses in a world that cries for food and clothing can and should be turned into a major economic asset. Perhaps a World Commodity Bank will eventually provide the mechanism to facilitate their full use.

4. Nations receiving loans should be encouraged to spend a portion of these loans on management training. The contracting firm would take responsibility for planning and building the factory, training its personnel and operating it until its own indigenous managers are capable of taking over.

The central role of American business in such an overseas development program deserves urgent study. One of the principal techniques of economic assistance should be the export to Asia, Africa and South America of first-rate American and West European technological and managerial knowledge. This inevitably places a responsibility on American business.

It will not be easy to persuade American firms to accept this responsibility on the terms which will ordinarily be offered. Yet American industry has many leaders who are ready to look constructively beyond today's dividends to tomorrow's survival.

5. We should consistently seek to associate ourselves with the fundamental economic reforms which are a prerequisite to the creation of a free society where democratic political processes can flourish.

If we succeed in so doing, we will see our prestige and influence in the underdeveloped continents steadily grow.

A precise, pat rule of operation is impossible. But through tactful pressure I believe we can encourage, in almost every situation, steady progress by recipient nations toward the equitable redistribution of land, the alleviation of economic injustice, a more democratic tax system and the like. I must emphasize again that without this essential human progress pure production gains will almost certainly create more political troubles than they solve.

6. Finally, there remains the question of economic assistance channeled through the United Nations. It has been persuasively argued that we should distribute much of our economic assistance through the U.N.

The United Nations might well provide an effective channel for such development funds through the establishment of an international loan agency as a subsidiary of the World Bank. Another potential distributing agency exists in the facilities of the Colombo Plan Organization.

A coherent and comprehensive economic development program for Asia, Africa and South America will involve a departure into new realms of thinking and new areas of activity. It will demand dynamic leadership at the executive level of our government, a comprehensive program of public education that only the President can undertake with bipartisan support in Congress.

NEED FOR STANDARDS IN DISTRIBUTING FOREIGN AID

*As the new Congressman from Eastern Connecticut, Mr.
Bowles, in one of his first speeches on the floor of the House of
Representatives (April 20, 1959), calls for a re-examination of
our military assistance programs and proposes new and now
accepted standards for administering economic aid.*

MR. SPEAKER, few subjects on the minds of the American
people and the agenda of Congress are as important as foreign aid.
And probably on no subject is there so much disagreement, misunderstanding and frustration.

One of the principal reasons why we now face grave difficulties in
securing adequate funds for foreign aid is the failure of the Administration to explain honestly and frankly why it is so urgently needed.

I know of no greater tribute to our national intelligence than the
public opinion polls, which consistently show that 70 percent of all
Americans strongly support the foreign aid program in spite of their
government's failure to spell out its true, long-range objectives.

The official purposes which are now most often advanced for foreign aid are inadequate for several reasons.

They fail to do justice to America's real goals in world affairs.

They fail to appeal to the common concern for the dignity of man
which we share with people all over the non-Communist world.

And they fail to take into account the intelligence and decency of the American people themselves.

The preamble to the Mutual Security Act now implies that it is "the policy of the United States to continue" the aid program only "as long as [the Communist] danger . . . persists."

In the market place of the cold war, a noisy Communist minority has become by our own Congressional definition worth its weight in American dollars.

Another specious supporting reason for the foreign aid program, which is often officially offered in discreet, off-the-record talks, is its alleged usefulness in buying majority support for our policies in the United Nations General Assembly.

But, Mr. Speaker, is this second reason any more valid than the first? Suppose a wealthy man came to live in a typical American community to finance a series of community improvements in return for public acceptance of his political views. Would not most upstanding, civic-minded people urge him to take his benefactions and go live elsewhere?

Can we expect the proud new nations of Asia and Africa and the older nations of Europe and Latin America to react differently?

A third mistaken argument for foreign assistance is that Communism appeals only to hungry people. "Just fill everyone's stomach with rice," we sometimes hear, "and that will be the end of Communism in the underdeveloped world."

This view reflects a massive lack of understanding of the Communist appeal and, indeed, of human nature. Frustrations which grow from injustice and the absence of a sense of belonging are far stronger motivations toward Communism than pure hunger.

The objectives of American assistance have not always been advanced in such negative terms. For example, in the Foreign Assistance Act of 1948, which laid the basis for the Marshall Plan, the 80th Congress called for steps designed to strengthen "the principles of individual liberty, free institutions, and genuine independence, based upon a strong production effort, the expansion of foreign trade, the creation and maintenance of internal financial stability and the development of economic cooperation."

Against this background, Mr. Speaker, the 1954 statement of purpose retained in this year's bill appears unworthy of us. Its implied motivations are negative, expedient and unrealistic.

In this critical period in history, I believe we should stop under-estimating the American people. It is time to put aside the sales gim-micks and to do what needs to be done for the right reasons.

What does America really want? We have no desire to control the nations or the resources of Asia, Africa and Latin America. We seek no satellites. We have no wish to impose our ways on others.

Indeed, our own nation was born in revolution and since our earliest days we have associated ourselves with the efforts of people every-where to gain and maintain their freedom, and to create their own future in their own way.

Our global objective remains what it was in Jefferson's time: a world of peace in which all men may have the opportunity to develop freely and independently within the framework of their own cultures, religions and national capabilities.

The time has come to give the American people and the world a positive indication that the objectives of our Mutual Security Program are worthy of our historic political convictions and of our democratic beliefs.

Mr. Speaker, my first proposal is that we clearly spell out these objectives.

I shall now turn to my second proposed change. I am impatient, and I believe others here are too, with the present wasteful, and often ineffective, methods of allocating some of our military assistance. In many cases we have inadvertently created situations which have played into the hands of the Communists and increased their influence.

I realize, of course, that in certain areas which are clearly threat-ened by Communist aggression military considerations often must take precedence, at least for the short haul. Western Europe, Greece, Turkey, Yugoslavia, Korea, Formosa and Vietnam are all cases in point. Here substantial American military assistance remains abso-lutely essential.

But in two whole continents—South America and Africa—and in much of the vast arc of Asia that stretches from Lebanon to Manila, the principal threat to world peace comes, not from Soviet tanks and jets, but from economic strangulation, injustice and human frustration.

In these areas, haphazard shipments of American military equip-ment seldom coincide with our long-term security interests, much less with those of the people in the countries concerned.

Such military assistance given on an expedient basis is almost invariably self-defeating. It adds to internal economic strains. It diverts internal efforts from constructive development. It paves the way for palace revolutions. In some cases it ties our prestige and our influence to the dubious tenure of dictatorships which are destined sooner or later to be swept aside.

Military assistance injected into these surging continents may be particularly harmful if it is given without proper regard for regional political considerations. By disrupting the delicate balance of power between a recipient nation and its non-Communist neighbors, indiscriminate arms shipments jeopardize the military and political stability of the entire area.

For all these reasons I believe it is essential that we reconsider on a country-by-country basis the effectiveness of our military assistance program.

I do not propose that we recklessly repudiate old arrangements. But I believe we should insist that they be shaped to new objectives and that new agreements which fail to meet these standards should be ruled out.

* * *

LET me consider, Mr. Speaker, the need for a more realistic approach to the distribution of economic assistance.

Why is it that a dam can be built and operated with great success in one country, while in another country a similar dam is a miserable failure? Why is it that modern equipment can make a vital contribution to increasing the agricultural and industrial productivity of some countries, while similar machinery sent to other countries lies rusting on the docks?

In most cases it reflects basic differences between the countries and the governments in question—differences which we have often lamentably failed to take into account.

I suggest the following five standards to measure the capacity of each country to use our long-term economic development assistance. I believe they are both practical and urgently necessary.

1. The most important standard for granting American economic loans and other assistance should be that of self-sacrifice.

To become eligible for substantial long-term assistance, a nation should demonstrate that it is making a substantial effort to finance its own national development from its own resources.

Such evidence should include a reasonably effective program of national taxation based on individual ability to pay, controls over the importation of luxuries and nonessentials which otherwise rapidly eat up foreign exchange, and a determined and continuing effort to assure the maximum number of peasant families ownership of their own land.

2. To qualify for major American investment assistance, an under-developed nation should have put together a practical, comprehensive set of economic objectives and itemized the allocation of all available resources to achieve those objectives.

This assures that important tasks will be given priority, that the development program will be relevantly related to private and public income, and that the need for international help will be more accurately assessed.

If there is already a significant private business sector, it should be considered side by side in such a plan with government-sponsored agricultural, power and transportation projects in formulating the national development scheme.

3. A qualifying country should have a reasonably substantial, competent and graft-free civil service. Without able technicians, tax collectors and administrators, large amounts of investment capital cannot be used to economic advantage.

4. In order to qualify for long-term investment assistance, a country should also have a relatively stable government with popular roots.

Our democratic tradition makes most Americans unsympathetic to authoritarian governments of whatever persuasion. But this does not mean, Mr. Speaker, that our aid should be restricted to parliamentary democracies modeled on the West.

Indeed, we must face the fact that most of the new nations of Asia and Africa, over the long haul, may consider our own institutions unsuitable. Only one thing can we be sure of: The governments *least* likely to succeed are those whose power is based on the shifting loyalties of feudal landlords and moneylenders.

By foregoing the support of both the middle-class center and the non-Communist left, such governments open the door wide for the Communists to pose as reformers and to press for united fronts. When we support such governments and they fall, our prestige and influence may tumble down with them.

Ataturk, who ruled Turkey for nearly a generation, was a dictator of the non-Communist left. We could not always endorse his methods. But since his government was rooted in popular support, he was able to put through vitally needed reforms, encourage the participation of his people and lay the foundation for increasing democracy. Such a government deserves our help.

5. Finally, in granting economic assistance, a country's political importance must be taken into account. This will be measured by its population, the size of its territory, its resources, its influence and its location.

Countries which are not unable to meet these minimum development standards should tactfully be told that they cannot expect investment assistance from us until they have created their own internal basis for successful growth.

Most emphatically this does not mean that we should turn our backs on them. On the contrary, there is much that we can and should continue to do to help.

We should offer to assist them in the creation of a comprehensive economic development plan which enables them to use their own resources to the best possible advantage.

We should help provide tax experts, engineering survey teams and other technicians to create a workable administrative base.

We should encourage them to place import controls on luxury imports purchased for their wealthy upper class so that their scarce foreign exchange can be used for the essentials needed by the people.

We should urge them to inaugurate land reforms and suggest expert advisers to help them. In Japan and Formosa American Government experts took the lead in promoting a program of private landownership that has helped the peasants in these two countries set records both for agricultural productivity and for the expansion of rural democracy.

More specifically and immediately, we can help these nations to finance individual projects that are worthwhile in their own right, that are not dependent on the economy of the country as a whole and that are clearly in the people's interest.

An example might be a modern hospital in the national capital, with training facilities for doctors and nurses and an outpatient clinic system for the villages; or an expanded and improved university or agricultural experiment college.

I recognize the fact that some form of economic aid—officially called "defense support" or "special assistance"—is needed for straight political purposes, for compensatory economic reasons, to backstop military aid or as an expedient rental fee for the use of a military base. In recent years such aid has been unduly expanded.

Mutual security implies a partnership. To be effective it must be a two-way street. American representatives abroad should make a more determined effort to place our mutual security efforts in the military field on a true partnership basis.

* * *

MY CRITICISMS of the planning and administration of many of our foreign aid programs involve both military and economic assistance. Iraq provides a case in point. A brief review of developments there illustrates the need for a more realistic and less military-oriented approach.

On several occasions in 1953 and 1954 Egypt requested arms from the United States. This assistance was wisely refused, largely on the grounds that it would disrupt the balance of power with Israel, and thereby increase the danger of a clash between these neighboring nations.

However, in the spring of 1954 the Administration agreed to send military aid to Iraq, which not only threatened the destruction of Israel, but which also was in direct conflict with Egypt for the leadership of the Arab bloc.

The Egyptians protested on the ground that this assistance represented a deliberate American effort to split the Arab world, and that it ignored Egypt's interest. These protests were disregarded.

In February, 1955, the Baghdad Pact was set up to add the military weight of Iraq, Iran and Pakistan to that of Turkey. Its stated purpose was to deter Soviet military aggression toward the Persian Gulf.

In Cairo other Arab leaders did not fail to recognize that the Baghdad Pact called for much more substantial American arms shipments to Iraq. After his protests over these shipments had again been rejected, Nasser announced in November that Egypt had negotiated a military agreement with the Soviet Union.

These were not the only factors in this cause-and-effect relationship, to be sure. But these events were part of a chain of events that ended with the British-French-Israel attack on Egypt.

During this period, substantial American economic and technical assistance was also flowing to Iraq. Those responsible for administering this program reported to Congress that this help, together with the oil revenues available from the Iraqi Government, seemed to assure Iraq's economic success.

However, little effort was made to see that the people of Iraq benefited directly from our joint efforts. Thus the new irrigation programs, while vastly increasing the income of the landlords, brought only minor gains to the cultivators.

Iraq's gross national product rose rapidly. But because luxury imports were not curbed, because progressive tax programs were not introduced and because land reforms were postponed, the increasing income served only to expand further the already explosive gap between rich and poor. In the summer of 1958 this situation, as many of us had predicted, blew up and Colonel Kassem's government took power, while Communist influence gained.

Here we have an example of what happens to our interests when we overlook the political, economic and local realities in quest of a nebulous military security.

The Iraq example and others raise an obvious further question. What about the effect of the standards which I have proposed on the leaders of unprepared nations whose goodwill is essential to us? Will the system which I have proposed be construed and resented as political interference by nations which fail to qualify?

If we were to use our aid to pressure such nations into following our lead in the cold war, resentment would be inevitable. But is it unreasonable for the American people, who themselves pay such heavy taxes, to ask that their assistance be efficiently and honestly used?

My own practical experience in Asia and Africa leads me to believe that the principles which I have proposed will be readily accepted, provided they are presented by tactful American negotiators, supported by a firm Congressional mandate.

Indeed, I am confident that most governments can be persuaded that these criteria are essential in their own long-range interests. Many of them welcome such standards as a lever with which to persuade reactionary elements within their own countries to cease blocking constructive reforms.

Therefore I propose that the Mutual Security bill should clearly outline the basis on which we intend our technical assistance and development loans to be distributed.

If the new direction and emphasis which I have proposed is accepted by the Congress, we will demonstrate to the world that our Mutual Security Program is more than a temporary cold war gambit, and that we have embarked on a determined, long-range program designed to give men everywhere the opportunity to live under governments of their own choosing in a world of increasing prosperity and peace.

══ 21

A PROPOSAL FOR FOOD BANKS ABROAD

How America's farm surpluses can be used to feed a hungry world was the subject of a hearing of the Senate Foreign Relations Committee, in which Mr. Bowles on July 8, 1959, proposed the establishment of scores of "food banks" in the developing nations.

HISTORIANS of the future looking back on our generation will note many startling things, but none will be more paradoxical than the picture of the United States of America sitting on a pile of so-called "surplus" agricultural commodities valued at almost ten billion dollars at a time of world hunger, political crisis and a desperate need for a positive peace effort.

At this point in the mid-twentieth century, we are prone to call our blessings "burdens," while in most of the world men are short of food, and nearly every country has to import or go hungry.

The biggest single economic problem of the Soviet Union has been food and fiber. Today the problem that I believe may break the Communist Chinese regime is food—trying to feed their people on 1.7 acres of land for an individual family. Yet here we are, with our enormous capacity, wondering what in the world to do with all our food.

In a sense, we are now facing much the same situation on a *world* scale that we faced here in America in 1933 when sixteen million unemployed workers in search of work, many of them suffering from malnutrition, were daily walking past stores loaded with spoiling food which they were prevented from eating by what economists described as the "iron laws of economics."

Ultimately, we elected a government that recognized the immorality and fantasy of this situation. Without really knowing how to handle it, we started to experiment, first with this move and then with that move, imaginatively seeking solutions. Gradually we learned how to rewrite the "iron laws of economics" and match abundance with need.

Now we face a similar problem on a world scale, with two-thirds of mankind undernourished while we Americans sit uneasily on stores of food for which there is "no market." Yet I have a feeling that in the next few years we may be looking back on this period of confusion with the same astonishment that we now look back on 1933 when Americans went hungry in the midst of plenty.

In any event, it is high time that we begin to convert our so-called burdens into assets. The virtue of the bill now before your committee is that it would go a long way toward enabling us to do just that.

I am particularly intrigued with the creative, constructive possibilities of Title 5 of the bill.* This concept of national "food banks" can become highly significant.

The idea of food reserves set up in various countries has been discussed for many years in our own government, in the United Nations and elsewhere. But we have yet to tackle it on an adequate scale.

Today we know that we are confronted with not only a moral but an economic deadline. Our stored commodities, unless used, are a wasting asset. The problem of preventing spoilage is a continuing and growing one. With the prospects for another good crop year, we will be confronted soon with a new burden of storage.

Dramatic situations require dramatic solutions. The time has come for action.

I suggest that we take one-half of our entire grain surpluses and store them *abroad* in designated depots as a vivid and reliable guarantee to hundreds of millions of people against famine and disease, and as an earnest demonstration of our determination to see that no one starves while we have so much food to spare.

* The Humphrey International Food for Peace Bill of 1959.

Thirty or forty such depots could be placed in India alone, another ten in Pakistan. Others could be placed in the Middle East, North Africa, Indonesia and parts of Latin America.

Such a constructive effort on our part could also save us money. From all of the statistics which I have seen, any amount of surplus commodities could be shipped abroad for considerably less than the cost of storage in this country for a three-year period. The savings from such a procedure would accelerate geometrically after the second year.

Let us therefore store one-half of our grain in these overseas "food banks." Let us make sure the banks are well constructed, so that they will protect the grain against spoilage as well as we protect it in this country. Then let us make arrangements with these governments to draw on the grain for local consumption according to a set of standards that could be mutually agreed upon.

One obvious standard would be the actual failure of the harvest. A second should be soaring food prices, due to shortages causing a critically inflationary situation in the price of food. A third might be related to certain degrees of malnutrition.

A whole chain of these American-sponsored food banks established all over the world, with their building paid for by counterpart funds, would in effect become pipelines between the vast food abundance in the United States and the hungry people who would receive this food. If it requires taking more American ships out of storage to supply them, we should welcome that opportunity.

By utilizing the concept of Title 5 of this bill, and expanding it as I have suggested, we would be providing solid assurance to hundreds of millions of people that they and their children would be forever freed from the specter of starvation, famine and disease which has plagued men from the beginning of history.

There are few things we can do which would serve more usefully than this to put a fresh, affirmative face on American foreign policy.

22

RURAL DEVELOPMENT: KEY TO DEMOCRATIC GROWTH

Bringing the benefits of the twentieth century to the impoverished and neglected majority of mankind living in the rural areas must become a primary objective of economic development assistance, says Mr. Bowles. From an address to the White House Conference on Conservation, Washington, May 24, 1962.

THIS YEAR marks the hundredth anniversary of two of the most decisive documents of American history, documents which assured that American land would be used for the common good—the Homestead Act of May 20, 1862, and the Morrill Land Grant College Act of July 2, 1862.

Although the importance of this legislation to our national development is dramatic in terms of physical progress, its greatest importance may lie in the way it shaped our national character and gave depth to our belief in the dignity of the individual.

The right of a man to own his soil and the obligation of government to educate its citizenry to be useful and productive human beings were part of a long-established American tradition.

The family-owned farm, the county agent, the village schoolhouse, the self-help community organization, the use of resources to achieve

113

the greatest good for the greatest number, and the university in the service of the people spring from deeply rooted and widely shared democratic values that go back in many respects to Colonial days.

Nor have American farmers ever shown any hesitancy in fighting for what they believed to be right. Our rural tradition has always been marked by a radical strain of protest against injustice by government or exploitation by bankers or railroads.

Do the principles which found expression in our national legislation a hundred years ago and the willingness of American farmers to speak out against injustice have relevance today to the impatient, developing nations of Asia, Africa and Latin America?

I am convinced that they do. Indeed, I believe they may be the decisive key to a successful United States policy in Asia, Africa and Latin America. Against this background let us examine the challenge which we face.

For most Americans the unrest of Asia, Africa and Latin America is symbolized by pictures of unruly, shouting students and protesting industrial workers. Yet the future of these developing continents is more likely to be decided in the remote muddy villages where nearly 80 percent of the people live.

The peasant majority in Asia, Africa and Latin America is important for two reasons: first, because of its potential *political* power, and second, because of its *economic* role as producers and consumers.

As long as three-fourths of the population in a developing country are denied a measure of political participation and personal dignity, they will be fertile ground for subversion and unrest. As long as they lack the capacity to buy anything beyond the bare essentials, industrial output in the urban centers will remain hopelessly stifled.

For centuries the rural areas in many of the emerging countries have been dominated both economically and politically by landlords and moneylenders. The land rent may still take three-fifths of the crop. Interest on loans often exceeds 30 percent annually.

Yet everywhere these conditions are now being vigorously challenged. Word is spreading that poverty and illiteracy are not part of God's plan for the unfortunate, but evils to be met and conquered.

Many factors however combine further to slow progress and to prevent new governments from coming to grips with the challenge itself. One of these is an unbalanced emphasis on rapid industrialization and too little regard to people and institutions.

Industrialization is, of course, essential to the growth of modern societies, and a major objective of our economic assistance program must be to promote such development. But a reading of our own history will demonstrate that industrial growth by itself is not enough. A politically stable society requires a solid rural foundation which brings the peasant majority into the mainstream of their national development.

A key objective of our aid program, therefore, is an effective working balance between urban and rural development. Otherwise we will fail in our objective, regardless of how many billions may be spent on industrialization, power plants, docks and highways.

Although it is dangerous to generalize about the specific problems faced by nations in different stages of growth, certain lessons in regard to balanced rural development emerge from our own experience, together with that of the Japanese and others. These lessons can be grouped under seven headings:

1. At best the modernization of an old society is a disrupting process. Therefore an unbalanced emphasis on rapid industrial growth is likely to *increase* rather than decrease political unrest in the cities and rural areas as well.

Indeed, there is no evidence that increased national income *in itself* brings increased political stability. This is dramatically demonstrated in Latin America, where average per capita gross national production ranges from a high of over $1,000 in Venezuela to a low of $55 in Bolivia, with no pattern of political stability between these extremes. Cuba under Batista had the second highest average per capita income in Latin America.

The evidence is clear: Orderly political growth requires, not only economic progress, but also social progress and political reform.

2. A comprehensive program of land reform, therefore, is a political and economic must. Peasants who do not own their own land have little incentive to practice wise husbandry and to put in the longer hours and hard work necessary to expand their production. A tenant farmer is likely to be listless and apathetic, to mine his soil without thought for tomorrow and to waste the potential of his lands. His distrust and resentment usually lie close to the surface.

Therefore the great feudal estates, where they still exist, must be broken up and the land distributed to the people who till it, with fair compensation to the former owners.

3. Although widespread landownership is essential to a stable rural society, it is only one element in the process. A comprehensive system of community development should have an equally high priority. This should include an agricultural extension service to help introduce improved seeds, tools, fertilizer, insecticides and the more effective use of irrigation water.

Unless land reform is supported by a community extension program of this kind, it will almost certainly lead to lower production; with such a program, output per acre, as in Japan, will almost surely be increased.

A community development effort should also encourage local initiative in building schools and roads with freely contributed local labor, improved health standards and the encouragement of village self-government.

In this regard the means by which development is achieved may be even more important than the extent of the actual development. For instance, a simple mud school or a connecting road built by the villagers themselves in the tradition of our own rural development gives everyone concerned an exciting new sense of participation in the building of the community.

Such projects, therefore, will contribute far more to the orderly political growth of the village than a better-constructed school or road provided by the government with no local involvement.

4. A rural credit system with lower interest rates is another important element in rural community development. Such a system enables the peasants to by-pass the moneylenders and secure funds on reasonable terms for the purchase of fertilizer and simple farm implements.

5. Marketing cooperatives should also be organized on a democratic basic. Such cooperatives will help to reduce the middlemen's profit margins and thereby assure the peasant-producer a larger share of the consumer price. Nineteen thousand such cooperatives have been organized in Japan.

6. Developing countries should be encouraged to use some of their military budgets to create engineering battalions modeled on our United States Corps of Army Engineers.

These units can play an important development role in building bridges, roads, schools and clinics and at the same time establish close relationships with the rural people whose freedom they are seeking to defend.

7. Finally, in assisting developing nations to create healthy rural societies, we Americans must realize that not all of our own successful
agricultural experience is relevant.

For instance, the costly and complex farm machinery on most
American farms is designed primarily to reduce the cost of labor, not
to increase the output per acre.

In relatively underpopulated countries such as Afghanistan and certain new nations of Africa, agricultural machinery has a substantial
role to play. But in India, Pakistan, Ceylon and most other developing nations where there is a *surplus* of rural labor, agricultural tasks
can be performed most economically with simple tools and the power
of bullocks and buffalo.

The highest yields of rice, wheat and vegetable in the world are from
three- or four-acre farms in Japan and Egypt where each plant is individually cultivated as in a private garden.

* * *

ALTHOUGH we have made a good beginning, there is
much more to be done. The demand for change in rural areas of Asia,
Africa and Latin America is insistent and cannot be denied.

This situation poses a decisive question for every thoughtful American: Can we become creative participants in the unprecedented revolutionary changes of our era, changes that most privileged people will
oppose tooth and nail, but which for the bulk of mankind offer the
hopeful prospect of a little more food, a little more opportunity, a
doctor for their sick child and a sense of personal dignity?

The mood of awakening peasants throughout the world is expressed
in a poem written many years ago by Edwin Markham as he reflected
on Millet's famous painting "The Man with the Hoe":

> Bowed by the weight of centuries he leans
> Upon his hoe and gazes on the ground,
> The emptiness of ages in his face,
> And on his back the burden of the world.
> Who made him dead to rapture and despair,
> A thing that grieves not and that never hopes . . . ?
> O masters, lords and rulers in all lands,
> How will the Future reckon with this man?

How answer his brute question in that hour
When whirlwinds of rebellion shake all shores?
How will it be with kingdoms and with kings—
With those who shaped him to the thing he is—
When this dumb terror shall rise to judge the world
After the silence of the centuries?

What do we well-fed Americans have to say to this man? Do we have the capacity to understand him and effectively to respond to his challenge? The next decade of our century may be largely shaped by our answer to these questions.

Section III

THE DEVELOPING CONTINENTS

The real choice in Latin America, as in Asia and Africa, is citizenship or serfdom, hope or despair, orderly political growth or bloody upheaval. Our failure to understand this choice, or to support the vital new elements which are striving to assert leadership, would be catastrophic.

November 22, 1959

THE DEVELOPING CONTINENTS

=== 23

ANSWERS TO A FELLOW TRAVELER

In a unique interview for the leftist Indian weekly Blitz, *in July, 1952, Ambassador Bowles answers questions reflecting the then current anti-American party line—and some of the deepest Asian fears of American "interference."*

BLITZ REPORTER: *What is the purpose behind U.S. economic aid to India which you have initiated? Is it intended to further the cause of U.S. foreign policy or just philanthropy?*

MR. BOWLES: Before answering your question, let me say this: If every Communist in India handed in his card tomorrow, India's problems would remain. The Communists did not create these problems, although they are now doing all they can to take advantage of them.

Americans sent aid to India from churches, foundations and other private sources long before Communism here or anywhere else was ever thought of. Tens of millions of dollars have come over here as gifts from individual Americans to build hospitals, schools, and to pay for food and medicines for the Indian people.

Nearly a million dollars in food and medical gifts came over this year. Seventeen ambulances were sent as American gifts from private sources to Indian hospitals. There has been no fanfare or publicity about them or any desire to be anything but helpful.

As far as U.S. Government aid is concerned, it is our earnest hope

121

that India in the next few years can demonstrate something that has never been clearly demonstrated before—that a democratic government in an underdeveloped country can guarantee, not only individual freedom, the right of free vote, free speech and freedom of religion to all of the people, but also higher living standards, increased agricultural production and the foundations for expansion in steel, power, chemicals and other industries.

If democracy fails to meet that test in Asia, then democracy will eventually fail in Asia. The major testing place is right here in India. Therefore if we Americans can do anything to help the Indian people succeed in their great efforts, we will do it. That is our purpose.

BLITZ REPORTER: *Do you really believe that the paltry sums of money that have been made available under the Technical Cooperation Administration and Point Four would substantially aid India's economic development? Would it be wrong to say that this meager economic aid is at best a propaganda expenditure?*

MR. BOWLES: The sum granted by us last January to be spent between January and June 30 of this last year is not "paltry"—it totals $54 million. This money is now providing 100,000 tons of fertilizer; helping to dig 2,200 tube wells, which will irrigate some 800,000 acres, the biggest tube well program in history; and providing DDT to make a long start on driving malaria from India.

Our U.S. aid program will also provide some forty or fifty thousand tons of steel for small-implement manufacturers. It will make a big start in helping to modernize India's fisheries. It will help to provide bulldozers, earth-moving equipment for your first great river valley developments, and assist in many more projects.

Some of the fertilizer has arrived, the DDT is here, the jeeps for Indian village workers are starting to arrive this fall. On all these projects our funds, of course, are matched by Indian expenditures in your own rupees. We pay in dollars for what is purchased abroad. You provide local material, labor and so on.

No, I would hardly call it a "paltry" effort, and the news that India is setting out to solve the problems of the people in a vigorous, dynamic way through democratic methods is not propaganda; it is a hard fact that the Communists cannot wipe out of existence.

BLITZ REPORTER: *How is it that the whole emphasis of the U.S. aid program is on India's development as an agricultural country? Why is no stress being laid on India's industrial development?*

MR. BOWLES: That is a fair question. Many of my friends in America bring up the same point. Here is the situation.

Through partition in 1947 India lost some of her best food- and cotton-producing lands. As a result, she now has to buy between three and five million tons of grain each year and over one and a half million bales of cotton to keep her textile mills going and the people fed adequately.

The India Planning Commission, which wrote the Five-Year Plan, supported by other students of the Indian economy, feels that India's first problem, therefore, is to be self-supporting in wheat grains, other foods and cotton.

Last year three million tons of grain came from America alone. In order to pay for this grain, India has to spend the equivalent of $600 million in foreign exchange. India borrowed nearly one-third of this huge sum from the United States, to be paid for over a period of thirty years starting in 1957.

So instead of being used to build railroads, steel mills, chemical industries, etc., a major part of India's foreign exchange must be spent to import the food required to enable her people to exist, and at relatively low standards of living. If India can raise enough food and cotton in the next few years, then this foreign exchange can be used to build steel mills, small motor industries, new transportation systems and for other basic development needs of the country.

That's why your Indian economic planners believe that improved agriculture is the first essential step and that industrial development should be the second step. And I think they are right.

BLITZ REPORTER: *Can it be that the U.S. Congress requires clearer evidence that, sooner or later, India would play up to the expectations of U.S. foreign policy, before larger sums of money could be voted for aid to India?*

MR. BOWLES: We couldn't buy a democratic country such as India if we tried, and we are not going to try. We want to help India meet her democratic objectives as a free people. We do not ask India in return to vote with us or agree with us. Sometimes she will, sometimes she won't.

There will be differences and some of these differences may even be good for both of us. We are primarily interested in seeing Indians grow and prosper in a society in which individual liberty and human freedom are fully protected. We think India will succeed in this.

BLITZ REPORTER: *You have sunk billions in Asia in recent years. Yet there is not a single country in the whole of Asia which has a sense of gratitude to the U.S. How do you explain this contradiction or fallacy?*

MR. BOWLES: Let me say again that we don't ask for gratitude in India or anywhere else. However, if you imply that Asian people are generally unfriendly to the United States, you should widen your circle of informants. I have found the Indian people warm, outgoing and friendly. I have sensed this friendliness everywhere, including the thirty Indian universities at which I have spoken.

I have also been in many villagers' homes in remote areas to talk and to have tea, where not many foreigners go. Everywhere I have had the warmest heartfelt reception from people, some educated but most of them not, who want for India and themselves precisely what we want in America—a rational, peaceful world in which people can work together in dignity.

We understand that the old colonial Asia for many, many generations was not treated fairly by the West. If I were an Asian, I would have resented the colonial rule under which most Asians worked and lived. But that attitude does not carry over in our present relationships. Come on a trip with me sometime and you will see for yourself.

BLITZ REPORTER: *Can you explain why the U.S. invariably finds allies among thoroughly unpopular reactionaries like Bao Dai who have absolutely no roots among their own people? Don't you agree that this has been the basic cause of American unpopularity in Asia?*

MR. BOWLES: We do not choose the leaders of other countries. They have been chosen by many methods, some good, some bad, some democratic and some quite undemocratic.

But let me add this: I don't believe that reactionaries of either the Fascist right or the Communist left can maintain themselves in the revolutionary world in which we are living. Reaction to the right is doomed and properly doomed. The Communist reaction of the left will eventually modify its policies or also fall apart of its own weight and inner contradictions.

Sometimes under the pressures of this unfortunate cold war struggle we find ourselves in difficult positions which require compromises which we do not like. But for the long haul the survival of the things in which we believe lies in a dynamic, liberal movement that rejects reactionaries of either left or right, that is dedicated to land reforms, minimum wages, higher living standards, broader social security, more adequate public health and greater opportunities for all people regardless of their race, creed, caste or color.

That is the kind of political movement in which most of us Americans deeply believe and which we will support here in India, and throughout Asia, Africa and Latin America. And eventually it will win.

══ 24

ASIA AND THE AMERICAN DREAM

*Following his return from India as United States Ambassador
in early 1953, Mr. Bowles spoke in forty-one states in behalf
of a new United States policy attuned to the new needs of
the awakening new Asia. Here, at the Community Church
in New York in May, 1953, he lists eight basic points for
a more constructive Asian policy.*

IN THE last decade we have laboriously hammered out an
American policy for Europe, a rational, practical policy, which today
the vast majority of us support. This policy recognizes the close relationship of the nations of the North Atlantic basin and the fact that we
can never allow any alien force to overrun or control Europe.

But let us face the blunt fact that eight years after the war America
still has no clear-cut policy for Asia. It is futile to argue about who is at
fault. There is ample blame to spread broadly across both political
parties. The important question now is: What are we going to do
about it?

Let me set down *eight basic points* on which I believe a constructive
Asian policy for America should be based.

First, we must understand that there is an Asian viewpoint.

I've heard this Asian viewpoint expressed in Lebanon, Ceylon, India, Burma, Indonesia, Vietnam, in the Philippines and in Japan, by

individuals who speak different languages and live many thousands of miles apart.

There is nothing "inscrutable" about it. It is simple, clean and understandable in the context of Asia.

Second, the future of Asia will eventually be determined by Asians.

We can encourage the positive elements and discourage those that are negative and destructive and this is important. But for better or for worse, the future of Asia will be decided, not in Washington by Americans, but in Tokyo, Djakarta, Rangoon, New Delhi and other Asian capitals by Asian leaders.

Third, the Asian revolution is a fact and not a theory.

This revolution is based on three powerful objectives rolled into one: the determination to be free of foreign domination; the determination to throw off the old feudal concepts of landlordism, moneylending and exploitation; and the determination that the colored peoples of the world must be accepted as the equals of the white people of the West. Asia's earnest, overwhelming desire for human dignity is both deep and dynamic.

Fourth, Asia looks at Communism quite differently than we do.

The average Asian leader *wrongly* looks at Communism today much as most Americans *wrongly* looked at Nazism in the 1930's—as an unpleasant, rather distant and vaguely dangerous force which fortunately is someone else's headache.

Fifth, the free Asian nations are struggling with immense economic problems which their people believe are not of their own making.

A moderate amount of U.S. economic assistance at this crucial time may well mean the difference between helping to build successful democracies in Asia or sitting idly by as confusion, chaos and finally Communism take over.

Specifically, we should offer both India and Pakistan the same bold assurance that we gave Turkey and Greece, and later the nations of Western Europe in 1947, i.e., that we will not allow their economies to fail in the next few years for lack of financial resources.

India has embarked on what many observers believe to be the boldest five-year plan ever undertaken by any democracy anywhere. She has already done as much through her own efforts, and until recently without any foreign assistance, as any nation on earth. If any free people deserve American support, it is the people of India.

But today the Indian Five-Year Plan faces a serious deficit. America should agree to meet that deficit without political strings.

Sixth, we should avoid doctrinaire thinking about Asia.

I know of no articulate American who has not been wrong an embarrassingly large number of times in the last ten years in his forecasting of future events. No one with a sense of humility will attempt to forecast the state of affairs in Asia or anywhere else ten years from today.

However, certain factors are already clear. For instance, we should recognize the fact that the greatest single disaster that could confront the Soviet Union would be the development of a more independent China. Today China seems tied tightly to the Soviet Union, but a United States foreign policy which assumes that such ties are permanent is almost certain to be proven wrong.

Seventh, the United Nations should be maintained as a forum of disagreement as well as agreement.

Let us therefore resist the temptation to turn it into a white, Western country club. In the traditions of Jefferson let us make the halls of the United Nations ring with clear statements of American opposition to colonialism, economic exploitation and discrimination of any kind based on race, creed or color.

Eighth, we cannot successfully promote democracy abroad unless we practice it more wholeheartedly at home.

It would be utter folly for us to weaken our military defenses at this crucial point in history. A weak America is positive *assurance* of a third world war under the most unfavorable possible conditions.

But we are faced, not only with a military threat, but with the threat of an explosive, dynamic idea in the hands of ruthless, bold and determined men. Such ideas cannot be destroyed with bombs. The sterile concepts of international Communism must be met and conquered by the contrasting concept of individual rights, democracy and a dynamic faith in individual human beings.

One hundred and seventy-seven years after the Declaration of Independence the American dream remains the most powerful idea on earth. Only we can destroy that idea and only we can put it to work.

25

A "MARSHALL PLAN" FOR ASIA?

The search for an effective means of channeling foreign aid led to this thought-provoking suggestion for a "Marshall Plan" for Asia, made at the Columbia University Institute of Arts and Sciences in October, 1953.

IT IS libelous to say that Asians will sell their souls cheaply for a bowl of rice. They have fought bravely for their freedom from colonial rule and they have successfully protected that freedom from local Communist attacks within their own borders.

Now they are insisting on bread and freedom too. Democracy in Asia must prove that it can provide both, or democracy in Asia is finished.

Primarily the leadership and resources for this crucial effort must come from the Asians themselves. The free Asian governments must carry out land reforms, establish fair systems of taxation and devise national plans for the harnessing of all available resources. Wherever they are now doing this, the people are rallying with enthusiasm.

Democratic Asia cannot squeeze its people with totalitarian ruthlessness. Therefore it must look to the West for assistance. Point Four has been a great step in the right direction. But our aid should provide capital as well as technical assistance, and the problem, as in Europe, should be tackled on a regional basis rather than piecemeal.

This can be best done if the resources of the whole free Asian region are harnessed through a joint plan.

There are many ways in which the free countries of Asia can help each other. Japan, with its rice yield per acre well above that of the United States and four times that of India, can provide technical assistance in intensive cultivation.

Indonesia, with its proven technique of growing large amounts of fish in the irrigation waters of the rice paddies, has something to offer the rice-growing nations of Asia. India, with its experience in malaria control, can send teams to malaria-infested countries like Indonesia. In training village development workers, India can offer much from her rich and successful experience.

Similarly, reciprocal trade among Asian nations can strengthen all their economies. South Asia can become a great market for Japan, and a source for some of the raw materials which Japan once got from China. Japanese small industries can become a model for decentralized industry in South Asia.

Our own aid programs will be more effective if channeled through an integrated regional program. At present there are the Point Four projects of the U.S. Government, the Colombo Plan of the British Commonwealth, the United Nations program of Technical Assistance as well as the work of a half-dozen other U.N. agencies such as the World Health Organization, the Food and Agricultural Organization and the Children's Fund, the aid projects of Norway, Switzerland and Sweden, and of private foundations and religious groups. All of these are doing important and valuable work. But all would profit by greater coordination.

Perhaps the present United Nations Economic Commission for Asia and the Far East (ECAFE), could serve as the nucleus for such a regional effort. If a practical over-all plan were developed, we should be prepared to give it our confidence and our support.

Is this not the time for the United States to invite the free Asian nations to take such an initiative, just as Secretary of State Marshall encouraged the Europeans in 1947? This is one way to help the rest of Asia keep from going the way of Communist China.

If we fail to take imaginative and sufficient action in time, the storm over why we failed in China will be small compared to that over a failure in all of South Asia. So far we have given India, Pakistan, Indonesia and Burma, who together comprise almost one-fourth of the human race, less than half as much help as we gave Chiang Kai-shek's China. We have given them together less than we gave Greece.

For centuries the Western world has taken profits out of Asia. From their Asian and African colonies, the European nations gained the wealth which made Western industrialization easier.

America, with its open frontier, did not depend on Asian colonies, but before World War I we did require a considerable amount of British capital—which was partially earned from colonial investments in Asia and Africa.

Indeed, the first major endowment of Yale University, from which I graduated, was presented by Elihu Yale, British Governor of the Province of Madras in Imperial India, in the form of five shiploads of textiles. I doubt that the powerless Indian men and women who were employed to make these fine cloths willingly gave their time and effort to help the sons of well-to-do American parents complete their education.

What a startling and wonderful turnabout in history if the West should now return with interest some of the wealth it took from Asia, to help make Asian development easier and Asian freedom secure. History now requires us Americans to act with imagination and sensitivity in a new kind of world.

26

BURMA AND VIETNAM: CONTRASTS AND LESSONS

Only nations that are wholly independent can be expected
successfully to defend their freedom, argues Mr. Bowles in this
prophetic piece on Southeast Asia. It appeared in the New
York Times Magazine, *June 13, 1954.*

IN EARLY December, 1946, in response to my questions
about colonial policy in Asia, a British Member of Parliament made a
prophecy: "You Americans have already freed the Philippines. Within
another year India, Pakistan, Ceylon, Burma, Indochina, Malaya and
Indonesia will also be free.

"But this new freedom cannot last long. The new governments will
be weak and inefficient. Their military power will be almost nil. Their
civil service, without Western direction, will soon fall to pieces. So
within another two or three years the Communists will take over China,
and that will be the end of freedom in Asia and the beginning of the
isolation of the West."

The first part of this grim prophecy has turned out to be true. In
1949 the Communists established their power throughout China. But
in another important respect the British M.P. was mistaken. In 1947
and 1948 the British had given up India, Pakistan and Ceylon, and
the Dutch had begun their withdrawal from Indonesia.

However, the presumably wobbly, newly independent nations,

which he predicted would fall early prey to Communism, did not fall.

The only places where Communism has made solid advances, with the exception of China, are the colonial areas dominated by white foreigners, where the Communists have been able to rally the people with the popular cry: "Throw the Western imperialists into the sea."

Is this mere coincidence? As we look closely at postwar developments in Southeast Asia, I think we shall see why it is not. The recent history of Burma and Vietnam provides some particularly pertinent lessons.

Superficially these two Southeast Asian nations have much in common. Each is rich in natural resources, with ample rainfall, good land and a rice surplus for export. Neither nation is overcrowded. Burma, larger than France, Belgium and Holland combined, has a population of nineteen million. Vietnam, roughly the size of Italy, has twenty-four million.

But the similarities are more than physical. Each of these nations has a long history of colonial occupation. French power was firmly established in Vietnam in the mid-nineteenth century, and the British wiped out the last vestiges of Burmese independence in 1886. During the Second World War each nation was occupied by the Japanese.

During that war anti-Japanese guerrilla movements developed in both countries with American and British support. Communist leaders were prominent among the guerrillas. When the Japanese were finally driven out, there was in both countries a similar and widespread demand for complete independence. In 1946, when the British Viceroy, Lord Louis Mountbatten, was negotiating with Gandhi and Nehru for India's freedom, U Nu, the present Prime Minister of Burma, was conducting similar negotiations with the British, and Vietnamese leaders were negotiating with the French.

But here the similarities between the two countries come to an abrupt end. In Burma, as well as in India, Pakistan and Ceylon, the British agreed to absolute independence. In Vietnam and the two associated states of Cambodia and Laos, the French hedged and hesitated, and the result has been an exhausting, eight-year civil war.

Today a French Union Army of 140,000 men is deeply involved, with an additional 150,000 of French-trained, French-equipped and French-led Vietnamese troops. French Union casualties total 38,000 dead, including 11,000 French soldiers, of whom a high percentage were experienced young officers and noncoms.

American military aid in support of this French effort now approaches two billion dollars—two or three times the total world-wide Point Four development program of the last five years. France herself has spent more on the Indochina war than she received from America under the entire Marshall Plan. And yet as this is written there is grave question whether the French forces can maintain even a foot-hold on the rich Red River Delta of northern Vietnam.

This military debacle has occurred because both the French and American governments have consistently underestimated the nature of the Asian revolution against colonialism. The French, defeated in the Second World War and deeply uncertain of their future, have been fearful that a colonial retreat in Asia would weaken their position in Morocco, Tunisia and elsewhere in French Africa. The Americans, aware of the need for French military support in Europe, have been reluctant to press for a clear declaration of complete independence for Vietnam, Cambodia and Laos, which alone could have created an effective basis for anti-Communist action.

As a result, Ho Chi Minh, an avowed Communist, has been able to pose as the patriotic leader of Vietnamese nationalism, while the anti-Communist leaders of Vietnam, many of them extremely able and dedicated men, have appeared to their countrymen as French stooges and apologists.

Although France has made substantial concessions toward a more independent Vietnam, particularly in the last few months, these con-cessions have invariably followed Communist victories over French Union troops, and hence have failed to achieve their objective of winning new support among the people.

Another reason for the inability of the French to rally mass sup-port has been their reluctance to support the most rudimentary village reforms. In 1952 the anti-Communist Vietnamese Prime Minister, Van Tam, told me that when the Communists captured a village, they an-nounced that all debts were canceled and that henceforth all land be-longed to the tillers.

When the French Union forces regained the area, they promptly re-established the landlords and moneylenders in their former posi-tions of power. "How can we beat the Communists in such a war?" he asked wearily.

Seven months later in his office in Saigon, Van Tam reported to me "great progress." "Now," he said, with a mock air of satisfaction, "when the French recapture a village, they let the peasants keep the land. So now the peasant hopes the Communists will capture him and give him land, and then he prays that the French will liberate him so he can keep the land."

This tragic Vietnamese tale of miscalculation, misunderstanding and stubborn disregard of the rising determination of Asians to be free is in striking contrast to the postwar story of Burma.

While the beginnings of armed opposition to the French were taking shape in Indochina in 1946, Burma was also on the verge of a civil war, with armed opposition to the British spreading rapidly. But in 1947 Burma, unlike Indochina, became free.

In 1948 the Communists, disappointed that British withdrawal had deprived them of the "down-with-colonialism" slogan which the French had provided in Vietnam, went into open, armed opposition to the new government. In 1949 they were followed by the Karens, a tough warlike people of eastern Burma who were determined to set up an independent state. By 1951 the fighting had spread throughout Burma, and the future of this Republic looked grim indeed.

By late 1951 the American Government had about decided the new government of Burma was doomed. At the same time the Chinese Communist Government, with a keener sense of the real sources of power in Asia, had written off the Burmese *Communists*.

At this time Chinese aid to the Communist-led forces in Vietnam was being rapidly stepped up. But in spite of the wobbly position of the new Burmese Republic, no Chinese arms or military equipment, so far as is known, were sent to the relief of the Communists in Burma. The Peking Government knew that such interference would enable the free Burmese to claim that the Communist insurgents were being financed by the Chinese, and thus awaken old fears of foreign domination.

Gradually Prime Minister U Nu and his associates succeeded in establishing the government on a relatively solid basis throughout Burma. By supporting economic and political reforms which were well timed and honest, they cut the ground out from under the Communists. The last Communist leader to surrender in early April of this year stated plaintively: "U Nu put through the village program which we Communists had been promising the people, and there was no way for us to gain their support."

Although clearly dedicated to democratic principles, Burma, like India, has stubbornly maintained a "neutralist" position in world affairs. In January, 1950, Burma became the first non-Communist nation to recognize Communist China. In 1953 the government, convinced that the Chinese Nationalist troops in north Burma had been armed and supplied from Formosa with American knowledge and consent, politely but firmly stated that it would accept no further economic aid from the United States.

Here, then, in capsule form are the stories of two Southeast Asian nations, so much alike in size and resources and yet so different in their political attitudes. What lessons have these nations to teach us as we grope our way toward a practical policy for security and survival in today's complex and divided world?

Does not the bloody story of Indochina emphasize beyond all question that colonialism in Asia, Africa and South America is a dying institution that America can no longer afford to support?

The French have said with obvious sincerity: "In Indochina we dare not show weakness, for this will encourage independence movements in Morocco, Tunisia and throughout French Africa."

But have 38,000 French lives and billions of French and American aid in Vietnam actually served to bolster French and American strength in Africa? On the contrary, may not young Tunisian, Moroccan, and Algerian revolutionaries logically assume from a study of the debacle in Vietnam that their own independence can only be achieved by bloodshed and with Communist support?

Another object lesson, I believe, concerns the nature of power in this revolutionary world. Can the effective weight of the free world be calculated by measuring the list of those nations which declare themselves with us against a list of those which are clearly opposed? Is the proper test of reliability subservience to America and willingness to accept our direction willy-nilly? Does diplomatic dependability assure us of military reliability?

If the dread day comes when the chips are finally down in democracy's struggle against expanding world Communism, can we count on all those who vote our way in the United Nations?

How about the "neutralist" Burmese, who have paid so dearly for their freedom and yet were the first to recognize Communist China? How about India with her 360 million people dedicated to the development of a dynamic democracy and yet unsure of American leadership? How about the "neutralist" Swedes and Swiss? Before we write them all off, let us remember that four million "neutralist" Finns once took on the whole Red Army.

American policy must recognize that power in today's revolutionary world is still vastly more complex than bullets and bombs or even votes in the United Nations. The French have learned it the hard way in Indochina. The Russians have learned it in East Germany, Poland and the Balkans. So have the Chinese in Korea.

Power is measured, to be sure, by many things. But the ultimate measure is people and the ideas that move them.

27

THE "BROWN MAN'S BURDEN" ANALYZED

As the need for mutual understanding between the newly independent nations and the West became critical, Mr. Bowles urged Asians and Africans to clear their own minds of anti-West prejudice and preconceptions. From the New York Times Magazine, *September 5, 1954.*

THE hypocrisy of the old-time "white man's burden" theme is obvious not only to Asians but to most thoughtful Westerners. But, as the West begins belatedly to seek a new basis for cooperation, it finds itself confronted with still another hurdle—an Asian state of mind that might be described as the "brown man's burden."

My admiration for the accomplishments of the new nations of Asia runs deep. My dislike of the classic Western viewpoint toward Asia is well established. However, to those Asians who throw stones with such abandon at the West, I cannot resist pointing out that they, too, live in a glass house. Perhaps a friendly look at Asia's glass house can help achieve some badly needed perspective.

Let us begin with the most basic question of all—colonialism. Asia's recent bitter experience with the Western variety tends to erase memories of non-Western imperialism conducted by Asians in Asia, of which Japanese aggression between 1931 and 1945 is a modern example.

A careful rereading of their own history will provide objective Asians with further proof that colonialism is not just a Western disease, but a possible stage in the development of any dynamic society, however unhappy it may be for the victims.

India, for instance, not only is proud of her antiquity but also boasts freely of her early colonialization in South Asia. From the time of Asoka until Western explorers filled the Eastern seas, India was a radiating center of culture, trade and conquest.

"Greater India" is the title of a chapter in the history text that my children studied in the New Delhi public schools. Its maps showed the Hindu colonies in Ceylon, Burma, Malaya, Java, Sumatra, Borneo, Bali and Cambodia. The authors assert that "the motive for this colonialization was not exploitation, or merely to find new markets for expanding trade."

On the contrary, Indian schoolchildren are taught that the Hindu colonists went to carry "the light of civilization and the blessings that depend upon it to the more backward regions." All of this may be true, but could that old apologist for European colonialism, Rudyard Kipling, have put it any better?

Nehru, in his *Discovery of India,* frankly places this historic Indian role within the realistic context of colonialism. He notes that Ceylon, South Burma and parts of Indonesia were conquered outright by the South India Chola empire. He says that even then the prize to be won in Malaya was the mining of tin.

Even today there are fears of a new Indian "imperialism" in neighboring Asian capitals, notably in Ceylon and Nepal. These fears seem as groundless to Indians as similar charges in regard to alleged United States ambitions against its neighbors seem to us. But the fact that these charges are frequently made and widely believed indicates that, with India's growing position of power and influence, her vulnerability to suspicion and criticism will increase correspondingly.

India's present relationship to Nepal, which stretches for five hundred miles along her northern border, is remarkably similar in its ups-and-downs to America's experience with some of her own allies and associates.

When Red China began to build roads across Tibet in 1951, India looked anxiously to her northern frontiers. In 1952, an Indian military mission was sent to Katmandu, Nepal's capital, to begin the reorganization and modernization of the Nepalese Army. Indian Army contingents were assigned to patrol duty side by side with Nepalese Gurkha units in the Himalayan passes on the Tibet-Nepal boundary.

A substantial economic development loan to the Nepalese Government soon followed. Then came a series of recommended economic and political reforms, accompanied by a large staff of able Indian Government experts to modernize Nepal's tax system, assist her road-building program and improve her governmental machinery.

This comprehensive and bold Indian effort, supported by a moderate amount of American Point Four aid, has given Nepal its chance for lasting democratic independence. Yet the popular Nepalese response to India's generous efforts has been no more cordial than that of most free nations to American aid.

There are other pertinent comparisons in the area of international conflict. Many Indians who are quick to criticize America's inability to find a basis for agreement with the Soviet Union and Red China seem unconcerned with the slow pace of an India-Pakistan *rapprochement*.

Yet these two peoples lived for centuries under the same government and for the most part speak the same languages. If they could adopt a reasonably coordinated policy toward the world, the outlook for peace in Asia would be immeasurably improved. Seven years after achieving their freedom, they remain antagonistic and reluctant to compromise.

Similarly, Asian teachings of tolerance, breadth and humanity constantly compete with Asia's own fierce divisions of caste, religion and nationalism, and we are puzzled in our turn and tempted to tell Asians to practice what they preach.

Surprisingly few Indians see any similarity between Negro segregation in America and the practice of caste segregation and discrimination in India, which is so deeply shocking to most Westerners. It is time that each tried to understand the other's problems, and assist, not carp at, the other's efforts to meet them.

Gandhi, who gave his life in opposing such passions, offered a kind of bridge between Asia's concepts of tolerance and relativity and the West's moral concepts of right and wrong. His approach was peaceful, but not at all passive or submissive. All living things were to be respected, but evil as one sees it was to be actively resisted.

He sought to reinforce the ancient Asian religious theme of peace and goodwill, but against him ran a countercurrent of violence. Subhas

Bose, the fiery leader of Bengal, who formed an "Indian National Army" to fight against the British, still has many millions of Asian admirers. India's immediate, bold and militant defense of Kashmir in 1946 thrilled millions of Gandhi's violence-hating supporters and won conditional, but sad, approval from the Mahatma himself.

Hence, even with the examples of Buddha, Asoka and Gandhi, Asia remains much like the rest of the world in her inability to abandon the ways of violence and war. When Pakistan strengthens her border guard, India does not know what to do other than to strengthen hers and vice versa. Arms races, with their vicious cycle of fear feeding on fear, have never been a monopoly of the West.

The developing new Asia's frank thirst for material progress is also evident everywhere. In Communist China vast reservoirs of human energy are being harnessed by violent, coercive and cruel measures. The leaders of democratic India who won freedom for their 360 million people by nonviolent means are throwing their energies into a five-year plan of development, designed to prove that poverty can be erased without dictatorship.

For better or worse and despite their heritage of other-worldliness, the Asian people are now in a hurry. It is haste for material growth, far more than for spiritual renunciation of Western ways, which now seems to be the common concern of the people and their parliaments.

Another question which honestly troubles many Westerners is the curious double standard that free Asian spokesmen so often seem to apply in forming their international judgments. From the beginning of time, Asia's great religious leaders have meticulously taught that even the most laudable ends can never justify evil means. This is the very core of Gandhi's teaching.

Nevertheless, free Asian leaders often seem selective in the evil means which they denounce. While holding the West strictly account-able for its every mistake, they have frequently appeared indifferent to the most blatant dishonesty and cruelty in the Communist countries.

Asians have a right to ask Westerners to cast aside their old arro-gant ways, to respect the views of others and to offer their assistance without political strings. Asians also have a right to demand of the West a higher standard of ethical behavior in international affairs, more flexibility in negotiations, less emphasis on bombs and brute power, and a deeper understanding of the political and economic forces which are setting the course of history.

But Americans and other Westerners in turn have an equal right to expect from non-Communist Asians a little more appreciation of the difficulties which we face; an understanding that peace is a two-way street which cannot become a reality until the Communists abandon their oft-stated objectives of world domination.

In the days of the "white man's burden," through all the hypocrisy there were many Westerners who sought with mixed success to bring the best of their civilization to Asia. Today, when the brown man assumes his increasing share of world responsibilities, it may be proper for the West, having learned its lessons, to urge Asia not to repeat our own mistakes.

Asia has a higher role than merely to add another source of dispute and name-calling to the confused international scene. Let us hope that she will deliver of her best to a world that sadly needs sustenance and hope.

This, I believe, is what Gandhi meant when he said to his followers: "Asia has a message for the whole world. . . . But for Asia to be not for Asia but for the whole world, it has to relearn the message of Buddha and deliver it to the world."

28

WHAT FUTURE FOR FREE ASIA?

*Convinced of the need for fresh thinking and proposals on
Asian policy, Mr. Bowles takes a searching and prophetic look
at the revolutionary forces at work there and suggests the
possibility of an Asian Monroe Doctrine.* From Foreign
Affairs, *October, 1954.*

HISTORIC parallels are often flimsy things. But the comparison is striking between the present-day viewpoint of "neutralist" Asia
and the attitudes which shaped our own foreign policy in the last
century.

The United States, like the newly independent nations of Asia, was
born in a period of revolutionary upheaval, with the French Revolution and the Napoleonic Wars in full swing. It was against this background that President Washington made a plea for an American policy
of neutrality and dynamic independence.

In 1814, after the collapse of Napoleon's armies at Waterloo,
American policy-makers were confronted with a totally new and un-
expected problem. At this time the United States lacked an army
of any consequence, and its navy was small. Its moral influence
throughout the world, however, was great, much like that of India's
today. And just as both blocs in the cold war now seek Indian friendship, so both the Russian-led Holy Alliance and the British Government sought American approval and support in 1820-23.

However, the Czar's Government in 1823 was as offensive to American believers in democracy as its Communist successor is to most of free Asia today. Its proposal was politely but firmly refused, just as the free nations of Asia have thus far declined to ally themselves with Communism.

British counterefforts to induce the United States to take a strong position in opposition to the encroachments of the Holy Alliance in South America were even more direct.

Monroe and his Secretary of State, John Adams, decided, however, in favor of a *unilateral* American declaration. On December 2, 1823, Monroe proposed his famous doctrine as part of his seventh annual message to Congress.

Thus early in its history the United States acted upon a basic axiom of world politics, one we often ignored later on: that neutrality and nonalignment are not achieved for the wishing; and that an ounce of timely, constructive, peaceful involvement may save many times that amount of tragic, bloody involvement later.

There are many obvious differences between India's position today and that of the United States in 1823; there are also striking similarities.

South America in 1823, like the Middle East and Southeast Asia today, was a power vacuum attracting like a magnet the ambitions of foreign powers. The essential question for India and free Asia now is the same as it was for the United States in 1823: how to keep the power struggle from exploding into a world war on its front doorstep, where military involvement would become a certainty.

Like the United States in 1823, India now considers herself geographically isolated from the major centers of conflict, is deeply concerned with the massive economic problems with which she is confronted, and with her own opportunities for development and advancement.

She is supremely suspicious of colonialism and anxious to support the independence of those nations which seek to throw off colonial domination. She is convinced that her best hope for peace and growing prosperity is to maintain correct relationships with all powers and to keep her people from becoming emotionally involved in current struggles.

How far will this parallel hold? Is India today, as was the United States in 1823, aware that an independent position can be maintained only by positive, imaginative action and by the assumption of some clear responsibilities?

As long as the present power vacuums continue to exist in the Middle East and Southeast Asia, Communism will be tempted to fill them, and any overt armed aggression by the Moscow-Peking bloc will be met head on by the United States even at the risk of a third world war.

Does India see that in the event of such a conflict, so disruptive of her essential sea communications, so very near her own borders, it would be impossible to maintain the neutrality which is now the bedrock of her foreign policy?

A defense system in Asia not supported by the Colombo powers* is a limited military expedient carrying obvious political liabilities.

During the coming years, the five Colombo powers have an alternative open to them which in the present complex situation offers the most practical hope for stability in Asia, and which is by no means out of the question.

While refusing to join a Western-supported military pact, they could sense the likelihood of future Chinese pressure and announce their determination vigorously to oppose any future aggression in South Asia from any source.

In this regard I believe it would be a serious mistake to consider the Indian-Chinese agreements in New Delhi as anything like a sweeping Communist victory. The Chou En-lai–Nehru statement issued in July proposed that the recent Indian-Chinese treaty on Tibet serve as a model for all of Asia. The preamble of this treaty lays down five principles for friendly relations: mutual respect for each other's territorial integrity and sovereignty; mutual nonaggression; mutual non-interference in each other's internal affairs; equality and mutual benefit; and peaceful coexistence.

The Indians cannot be unaware that China violated all five of these principles in taking over Tibet in 1951. Nor has anyone suggested that India has ever failed to live up to them in her conduct toward China. If the restatement of these principles now by Chou and Nehru means anything, it is a Chinese pledge to start living up to ideals which have been blatantly and recently violated by the Chinese themselves.

The Indians on their part are obviously hoping, as we of the West

* India, Pakistan, Burma, Ceylon, Indonesia.

so futilely hoped in the years following the war, that the Communist tiger, its appetite satisfied, will settle down to peace and harmony.

Arguments from Western sources, no matter how logical, will have little effect in persuading the skeptical Asians that they are hoping for the impossible. Only hard, bitter experience with broken Communist promises is likely to disillusion them.

For this reason the agreement between Nehru and Chou En-lai, instead of promoting closer Chinese-Indian relations, may prove to do the opposite. In any case it provides a clear test of Chinese intentions. If the Chinese follow the example of the Soviet Union in the 1920's and 1930's, and decide temporarily to relax their pressure and consolidate their revolution, India and other free Asian nations will be given a badly needed breathing spell in which to put their own economic and political houses in order.

If, as seems more likely, China disregards her new promises and embarks either directly or indirectly on further expansion, the real nature of Chinese Communism will become obvious to many Asians for the first time.

Such a development, following Chou's recent commitments in New Delhi and Rangoon, may provide free Asia with the kind of initial, psychological shock that the Communist *coup d'état* in Czechoslovakia and the death of Jan Masaryk gave the West in 1948.

India is the key to the situation. How far would she actually go in opposing a Chinese Communist advance in Asia? As things stand now, no one, probably including the Indians themselves, really knows. This doubt would have to be removed if the declaration by India and her neighbors of a Monroe Doctrine for Asia were to be meaningful.

The Ceylon Conference of April, 1954, made one thing clear. Although President Monroe could act unilaterally, without undue concern for the feelings of his wobbly neighbors in South America, Nehru cannot issue a unilateral "Nehru Doctrine" without risking the resentment of his proud neighbors in South Asia. An indigenous Asian Monroe Doctrine to be effective would have to be worked out on a multilateral basis, and this involves additional questions.

The obstacles to an indigenous Monroe Doctrine for free Asia are clear, numerous and formidable. It would be folly to predict whether, when and how such an approach may come into being. We can be sure that no such program will spring full-blown from the head of Zeus. Like all deep-rooted policies, it will develop out of a culmination of various ingredients of attitude, sympathy, choice, personality and power.

Recognizing this, we Americans would do well to submerge our craving for easy answers. There are none in Asia. The sooner we start to devote some dedicated attention to a longer view, the better will be our chances of contributing to the peace and stability which we so earnestly seek.

In the meantime, we should anticipate the possible future rivalries between the Soviet Union and Red China, and courageously resist domestic political pressures that would make it impossible for us to capitalize on them.

The ultimate objective is the development of free, confident, dynamic new nations between the Mediterranean and the South China Sea. Whether the Communist timetable will allow for such a development is itself open to question, despite what many free Asian leaders seem to think.

But the United States cannot create these conditions in Asia or anywhere else. They must grow—of themselves and by themselves. The most that we can do is to aid their growth by *friendly* and *unobtrusive* encouragement and support.

══ 29

ASIANS ARE ASKING HARD QUESTIONS

*In a double-edged dialogue suggested by countless conversations
with Asian critics, Mr. Bowles presents a Burmese professor
at odds with an American ambassador over America's
approach to Asia. From* Pocket Magazine, *November, 1954.*

IF WE are going to build some bridge of understanding with
the Asians, we must talk less and listen more. Sometimes we will not
like what we hear; we must listen, nevertheless.

A recent visit with a keen and persevering science professor in
Burma (who was as anti-Communist as he sounds unreasonably anti-
American) forms the basis for the following dialogue. It suggests
some of the bitter passions involved in the crucial and uneasy relationship between the free West and free Asia.

BURMESE PROFESSOR: It is tragic to see the mistakes you Americans have made in Asia. When World War II was over we expected
so much of you. Now we are disillusioned and discouraged.

AMERICAN DIPLOMAT: You probably expected too much. After
all, we are human beings like yourselves, with many limitations. We
are not international meddlers by nature. We avoided World War II
until 1941, when Pearl Harbor exploded us out of our isolationism.
As soon as the war was over, we disbanded our army only to find
that the Soviet Union kept theirs and spent billions in its modernization.

We haven't sought the position that we hold, and we want no advantages of any kind. We are neither isolationists nor imperialists. All we are really striving for is peace and security and some means of stopping Communism.

BURMESE PROFESSOR: I dislike Communism just as much as you do. Indeed, my nephew was killed by Communist guerrillas in August, 1951. Our government has been fighting the Communists for years and only recently has finally succeeded in defeating them. But you Americans have become so obsessed with your fears of Communism that you are out of touch with the realities of Asia.

AMERICAN DIPLOMAT: How can we be *too* obsessed with it? You forget that the Communists are trying to overrun the world. Lenin laid down the Communist party objective over thirty years ago, and every Communist leader of importance since then has echoed it.

BURMESE PROFESSOR: That's true enough. But you Americans seem to feel that you can stop Communism by dropping a bomb on it. Communism is not just an army or a place; it is an idea.

We have always assumed that you Americans had a better idea. Most of us educated Asians have read your Declaration of Independence; some of us know it by heart. Your Constitution has been a model for the democracies which we are attempting to create in Asia.

What concerns us is that you Americans now seem to be turning your backs on your own long tradition of freedom and your belief in humanity. In your efforts to destroy Communism in your own country you even seem ready to adopt the methods of Communism.

AMERICAN DIPLOMAT: How can you say that we have departed from our democratic traditions? Look at our record in Asia following World War II. During the war many hundreds of thousands of young Americans were killed in an effort to free Asia from Japanese imperialism.

President Roosevelt insisted that China be given a seat in the Security Council of the new United Nations as one of the five great powers. As soon as the war was over we gave the Philippines their freedom, just as we had said we would.

We supported the freedom of India and Indonesia, and we gave the Japanese more help and encouragement than any other victor ever gave a former enemy.

BURMESE PROFESSOR: I know. But we cannot forget that you are part of the West, which for generations took hundreds of millions of dollars of wealth each year from Asia to build up its cities, universities and high standards of living and left us poor, illiterate and close to the starvation line.

Even worse than the wealth the West took from Asia was the humiliation that we were made to feel. Because our skins were dark we were treated as second-class human beings.

AMERICAN DIPLOMAT: But again I ask, why do you include America in this? We have never held any such colonial position in Asia. And we ourselves were the first nation to fight our way free from the colonial domination of Europe.

BURMESE PROFESSOR: But what have you been doing in the last few years? For one thing, you have been propping up French colonialism in Indochina with hundreds of millions of dollars of military equipment. If you had taken a strong position in 1946, the French would have pulled out, as the British did in India, Pakistan, Burma and Ceylon, and Vietnam, Cambodia and Laos could have established their freedom without bloodshed.

AMERICAN DIPLOMAT: Yes, but Ho Chi Minh was a Communist and he would simply have turned over all three countries to the Communist Chinese.

BURMESE PROFESSOR: I admit that Ho Chi Minh is a Communist. But if he had attempted to sell out the newly won freedom of the Vietnamese to the Communist Chinese or the Russians or any other foreign power, he would have been swept aside by his people, who have always mistrusted the Chinese.

The French foolishly tried to destroy him with military power. You backed their efforts with many shiploads of machine guns, tanks, planes and equipment. So how can you honestly say that you have not supported imperialism in Asia?

AMERICAN DIPLOMAT: We don't like European colonialism any better than you do, and we agree that the French made mistakes in Indochina. But in Asia the colonialism that you are talking about is almost a thing of the past.

What you seem to ignore is the new *Communist* imperialism, supported by Moscow and Peking, which is infinitely more dangerous. While you Asians are arguing about the outworn *European* colonialism, the new twentieth-century Communist colonialism will gobble you up.

BURMESE PROFESSOR: If you will let us alone, we Asians can defend our independence against Communism a great deal better than you think. Just look at the record. In addition to the war in China, there have been six civil wars in Asia since the end of World War II, all fostered and organized by Communists.

Four of them were in countries which had recently won their independence—the Philippines, Indonesia, Burma and India—and in each of those four countries the Communists were crushed without any outside help. In the other two countries—Malaya and Indochina—the Communists succeeded in creating major trouble. In Indochina they have won a sweeping victory in spite of the combined military efforts of France and the United States.

Why? Simply because in Indochina and Malaya they were able to tell the people that they were leading an anti-imperialist war to drive the white colonial foreigners into the sea. But wherever they have had to cope with Asian nationalism they have failed.

Moreover, it is not only here in Asia that you Americans have supported colonialism. Your record in Africa is almost as bad. In spite of all the fine things you say about the right of all people to be free, you have consistently voted in the United Nations against the freedom movements in Tunisia and Morocco.

AMERICAN DIPLOMAT: We have had to compromise on French Africa because the French Army is essential to the defense of Europe. So we have had to keep on good terms with the French, who strongly opposed the freedom of Algeria, Tunisia and Morocco. This occasionally forced us to vote against our conscience.

BURMESE PROFESSOR: But what do you gain from such compromises? You have lost the confidence, not only of most of the people of Asia, but also of people throughout Africa.

The trouble with you Americans is that you seem to see everything in terms of military power in spite of the clear fact that military power is not the controlling factor in much of the world.

Why did the British leave India? Because they lacked military power? No. They were the third strongest military nation in the world. But they could have held India for only a very few years against the united will of the people led by Gandhi. Now in Indochina the French have discovered the same lesson at an infinitely greater cost.

When will you Americans learn that the problems of Asia are basically political and economic and that the military requirements are in a more subordinate position?

AMERICAN DIPLOMAT: But we have recognized this. Through our Point Four program we have tried to help Asian nations get on their feet and ease the poverty and disease and illiteracy.

BURMESE PROFESSOR: I agree that Point Four was one of the boldest ideas in the history of the world, and the American people are entitled to all kinds of credit for conceiving it. But if you are honest with yourselves, you will have to agree that so far the net result has been pitifully small.

AMERICAN DIPLOMAT: It is true that our Point Four program has been too limited, but we have political disagreements at home and many Americans are disturbed because they do not feel the peoples of other countries have been sufficiently aware of what we are doing to help them.

BURMESE PROFESSOR: Not sufficiently grateful? Is that the reason you give us assistance, on the theory that you can buy us as friends? Does it work that way in America? Can you buy friends there with money? I hope not.

As I see it, your American aid money should have one purpose and one purpose only, and that is to help people in the underdeveloped countries to help themselves. Once they begin to sense economic progress—to see their crops bigger, disease beginning to diminish and their children healthier and stronger, schools and roads being built —then they will have something to die for, if necessary. That, as I see it, is the only sensible reason for giving American aid, not to buy gratitude or friendship or votes in the United Nations.

Isn't a stable world enough for you? Does it also have to be a world subservient to American ideas and domination? If it were not for our noisy Communist minorities, you Americans would probably forget us and our poverty entirely.

AMERICAN DIPLOMAT: That's not fair. Look at all the money we spent trying to help China long before Chinese Communism became a real problem there. And now we end up with China our avowed enemy, spitting out hatred and false charges of germ warfare, trying to turn all Asia against us.

BURMESE PROFESSOR: I agree that the Chinese Communists are bitter and aggressive. They may turn out to be even more dangerous than the Russians. But again your policies are making the situation worse rather than better.

Whether we like it or not, Communist China is a fact. Why not deal with the Chinese directly instead of allowing the Russians to pose as their exclusive agent and interpreter?

AMERICAN DIPLOMAT: But how can we recognize Communist China after she killed thirty thousand American soldiers in Korea? It's time you looked at the record. Communist China is an aggressor nation.

BURMESE PROFESSOR: But you also call the Russians "aggressors," and the Russians are at least as Communist as the Chinese. Yet you recognized Red Russia twenty years ago and even fought side by side with them as allies during the war.

Many of us Asians have become convinced that the real reason why you refuse to recognize the Chinese is that they are colored and you are white. Don't you Americans consider colored people second-class citizens even in your own country? If you consider colored people the equals of white people, why did you drop the atomic bomb on the Japanese and not on the Germans during World War II?

AMERICAN DIPLOMAT: That, of course, is nonsense. The atomic bomb was not even developed until the war with Germany was ended.

BURMESE PROFESSOR: You will have great difficulty getting any Asian to believe that.

(And so on, far into the night.)

* * *

THIS RESENTFUL Asian offers arguments which represent the views of tens of millions of other Asians living between Teheran and Tokyo.

He has no liking for Communism. He earnestly wants to see democracy work. He wants to believe in America. He wants his own country to grow and develop toward new horizons of stability, prosperity and peace.

But he is troubled by an America that seems confused and out of touch with the people of the world who should be its friends. He is disturbed and also very much afraid.

His deep and often biased convictions will carry an enormous weight in the scales of history which may someday counterbalance all our weapons of war. We must listen to him, disagree with him when we think he is wrong, but listen.

════ 30

THE NEUTRAL NATIONS AND THE INDIAN SUCCESS STORY

Have we been overemphasizing the developing areas at the expense of our European allies? Mr. Bowles argues to the contrary and urges us to assist all those nations, neutral as well as allied, which properly use our assistance. This Month *magazine, July, 1962.*

MOST Americans have only recently become conscious of the so-called Afro-Asian bloc. This is natural, because a good many of the African and Asian nations that are now prominent in world affairs have achieved their independence in the last few years.

Fully half of the 104 nations now in the United Nations are from Asia and Africa. These new countries have been given an international sounding board in the world organization, and they have not hesitated to use it.

The attitudes expressed by the African and Asian countries in the U.N. harmonize with U.S. policy much more often than they do with the policy of the Soviet Union, but enough differences remain to make many Americans concerned.

In the past months these differences have seemed even more serious because important Asian and African leaders have been sharply critical of the U.S. while trying to maintain good relations with the Russians.

At the same time, the increasing complexity of foreign affairs, the absence of quick and simple answers to involved questions and the continuing danger of a nuclear miscalculation have given many Americans a sense of frustration and confusion.

This frustration has often expressed itself in impatient criticism of the neutral or uncommitted nations. Some of our more extreme critics charge that the U.S. has been paying too much attention to the Afro-Asians, that we are "courting" them unnecessarily, that our policies are not "practical."

Often these views are expressed by people who describe themselves as "hard-boiled realists." They consider those who take a more restrained view of world affairs "misty-minded idealists."

These self-styled realists represent an old and familiar school in foreign-policy-making, and I believe the record will show that in their impatience and insensitivity to world forces they are far more often wrong than right.

Immediately following World War I, for instance, the "realists' " attacks on Woodrow Wilson and his "visionary" concept of a League of Nations condemned us to a generation of isolationism and the world to a ghastly repeat performance of the "war to end all wars."

Their lack of vision about Asian and African questions has been equally costly. British members of the "hard-boiled realist" school of world affairs were persuaded that once they withdrew from India, Pakistan, Ceylon and Burma, and the "irresponsible natives" were left to handle their own affairs, these countries would promptly fall apart. More recently they argued that Egyptian natives could not possibly operate the Suez Canal without "experienced Europeans" to show them the way.

The results, of course, have been quite different. By and large these nations have proved remarkably competent to govern themselves and they are attacking with determination the tremendous problems that confront them.

After World War II the French chapter of the "hard-boiled realist" corps persuaded the French Government to adopt a policy of utter folly in Indochina. By attempting to maintain a colonial outpost in Asia under impossible geopolitical conditions, they pushed Asian anti-colonialists, nationalists and Communists together into a united front under Ho Chi Minh to wage the successful war of "national liberation" against the French.

Yet the disaster in Indochina taught the "realists" nothing. It was they who made it impossible for the French Government to negotiate a reasonable settlement with the Algerians for so many years. Only recently in Algeria the "hard-boiled" thinkers again threaten to lead the frustrated French *colons* down a road that could only result in another disaster.

Of the current crop of insensitive and often-blundering advocates of the "Let's not bother with Asia and Africa" policy, many, unconsciously or not, are charter members of a long and arrogant tradition that regards the white as the aristocrat of races. A few generations ago their ideological ancestors were calling for a "whiff of gunshot" whenever the "natives" appeared to be getting out of hand.

Had there been a little more patience and foresight in those days, and a little less "hard-boiled realism," the mountainous difficulties now being faced by the new governments in Asia and Africa might be somewhat less staggering. In an age when aristocracy in general is sliding rapidly toward extinction, this concept of a white-man aristocracy could be fatal.

In the past sixteen years, forty-four new countries, constituting roughly one-third of the population of the earth, have been created out of the old European colonial empires. Because these new countries are very touchy about their economic and political independence, they are unwilling to follow any policies, no matter how inherently sensible, that they feel are being imposed by foreigners. This attitude applies with quiet force to their dealings with both the Soviet and the U.S.

Our objective therefore becomes clear: to make sure each of these new countries is able to work out its own future in its own way, within its own cultural framework.

The capacity to stop Communism does not rest on the willingness of these new nations to adopt American ways or even on the ability of their citizens to shoot American guns. It depends on the ability of each new nation to develop its own natural and human resources and to fit its governmental institutions to its own sense of national purpose.

The building of present-day America took many generations, much work, much sacrifice and substantial help from investment. The Russians in three or four decades were also able to create a modern industrial state, but by methods that clash sharply with our concepts of freedom.

The spotlight has now switched to the underdeveloped countries of Asia and Africa. Here we see a fierce determination on the part of hundreds of millions of people to obtain a better life. Generations of poverty and colonialism have given them a tremendous sense of urgency and a determination to remain free.

Yet the Asian and African goal of prosperity through freedom can be met only if the more privileged free nations—Great Britain, the United States, France, Germany, Japan and others—provide the economic aid needed to speed up the development process.

If we fail to grant this aid, we can be absolutely sure that these dynamic new nations will not quietly slip back into the lethargy and hopelessness of the past. They have tasted the opportunities of the future and, one way or another, they are now determined to share them.

The situation calls for great patience and courage, for good judgment, understanding and sensitivity as well as money. Yet if we can help direct the tremendous political and social upheaval that is now taking place in Asia and Africa into peaceful channels of self-development, the gain for us, and for the new nations, will be great indeed.

The alternative is to stand by and watch the development of more Red Chinas, large and small, equally hungry, perhaps, but just as avowedly dedicated to our destruction.

Is this objective beyond our reach? I do not think so. As evidence, let us consider what has happened in a single underdeveloped country in less than one generation.

India is a nation of 450 million people, approximately the combined population of Africa and Latin America. On August 15, 1962, free, modern India will reach its fifteenth birthday. Thanks to the genius of Gandhi and the brilliant understanding of the British, India celebrates its independence with a great show of goodwill toward its former colonial ruler.

In the past ten years Indian national income has increased by 42 percent, food-grain production has gone up by 56 percent. In 1947 estimates indicated that 100 million cases of malaria developed annually; now this debilitating disease has nearly disappeared. Life expectancy in India in 1947 was twenty-seven years; it is now forty-two.

In a country that was only 10 percent literate fifteen years ago, 60 percent of all Indian children under twelve are now in school. Indian industrial production is expanding at the rate of 14 percent annually, one of the highest rates in the world.

In its first years of independence India developed a constitution that combined features of both the U.S. and British governments. Since then it has held three national elections—each the largest exercise of the democratic privilege in the world—in which a higher percentage of people voted than in the U.S.

India has freedom of speech, freedom of religion, freedom of the press and probably less government "interference" with private enterprise than does our own society.

India's success has been in large measure due to its own efforts. The Indian people have worked hard, developed able leadership, educated themselves and produced a sound civil service based on solid British training. But the outlook for the success of Indian democracy might not be quite so bright if it had not been for generous assistance from the U.S. In the last fifteen years we have granted India $3.8 billion in economic aid.

Approximately 55 percent of this assistance was in the form of "surplus" commodities—wheat, cotton, corn, etc. Another 42 percent was in dollars for the purchase of materials—steel, railroads and machinery, manufactured mostly in the U.S. and produced by U.S. workers. The remainder went for technical advice and instruction.

Despite our massive aid and India's devotion to democratic principles, India does not always agree with us. The close geographic proximity of the U.S.S.R. and mainland China and India's own past history have often given India a different perspective on world affairs, just as our own protected position behind two great oceans allowed us Americans to remain neutralists and isolationists for more than one hundred years, while British diplomacy and the British Navy kept the peace.

Yet the remarkable success of this Asian country is profoundly important to our own security. A free India with growing strength and confidence provides the all-important balance to Communist China in Asia. India demonstrates that democracy is more than a pleasant Western theory; it works admirably in practice.

So when we become annoyed and irritated by the criticisms of Asian and African spokesmen who do not fully accept our view of world affairs, let us consider the enormous boost that the success of India, Pakistan, the Philippines, and other new nations has given to the non-Communist world, and the unrelieved disaster that might have occurred if their efforts had turned out otherwise.

In the long run our national interest depends on the creation of a world community of such states—a community that shares an increasingly common view on human affairs. To such a world community Communism has no effective answer.

NEW TRENDS IN THE MIDDLE EAST

Will tensions decrease in this critical area as its volatile
inhabitants concentrate on developing their national resources?
Mr. Bowles expresses measured hope for a better atmosphere
in an address to the American Jewish Congress on April
12, 1962, in New York.

IN THE last decade the pendulum of American opinion on the Middle East has swung between high hopes and dire forebodings. Now it appears to be resting, momentarily at least, at some intermediate point.

To some extent our present estimate represents a scaling down of our high hopes for the rapid economic development and increasing political cohesiveness of the area. In another sense it reflects a realistic adjustment by our government, by the Soviet Union and by the Middle Eastern nations themselves to an enormously complex and difficult situation.

For hundreds of years the people of this crucial area were buffeted by wars and exploitation. World War I generated high hopes for independence, prosperity and a growing unity.

However, the political vacuum created by the collapse of the Ottoman Empire was soon filled by the British and French, and new conflicts replaced the old. In the wake of World War II came the final liquidation of European colonialism in the Arab world and the establishment of Israel as an independent new nation.

In this period of intense bitterness many Americans clung stubbornly to the hope that in the Middle East as elsewhere reason must somehow prevail, that the fast-growing oil revenues could be put to effective use throughout the entire region, that the Arab and Israeli peoples could learn to live and work together, and that such problems as water and refugees would be subject to growing cooperation.

A few years ago, when it began to be clear that these expectations were beyond our immediate grasp, we developed a more pessimistic view.

As we look at the Middle East today, it seems apparent that the situation has been improved in three important but unpublicized respects:

1. Communism as such is gradually losing its luster, and the Soviet Union is emerging as both a modern edition of czarist Russia and a major cut-rate oil competitor to boot.

2. The United States is much less tense in its relations with the nations of the Middle East and less inclined to expect immediate solutions to age-old conflicts.

3. The Middle Eastern nations themselves are becoming less focused on conflicts with their neighbors and more interested in their own internal development.

These three changes add up to a kind of quiet political and economic relaxation which, with a measure of good luck, may gradually make for lessening tensions and greater opportunities for all concerned. In our crisis-ridden world such relaxation doesn't make headlines, but it may write history.

Several years ago many Americans were concerned that Arab nationalism would become a captive to Communism. But in recent years we have seen how diametrically opposed these two political forces really are and what a powerful obstacle to foreign infiltration the dynamic effort of a developing new country can be.

One has only to look at Egypt, where President Nasser is accepting large-scale Soviet aid for the Aswan High Dam while developing his country along his own pragmatic lines. Far from controlling the United Arab Republic, Khrushchev cannot even persuade Nasser to tolerate the activities of the local Communist party.

At the same time our own government has recognized the limits of our influence in the Middle East and by trial and error has learned some of the basic facts of life in dealing with this explosive area. We have learned in particular that what we need in the Middle East is less than we thought we needed and that an emphasis on a maximum military security program is not necessarily the best way to protect our national interests.

What we really want is sufficient restraint to keep border conflicts and clashing ambitions from touching off a world-wide catastrophe and sufficient stability to insure orderly political and economic development. Above all, we want to see the nations of the Middle East grow as independent, self-respecting members of a free world community, developing their own economies and destinies in accord with their own national ideals.

In the process of our own education in the Middle East, we have learned to live with neutralism and varying forms of alignment as we have learned to live with it elsewhere.

The needs of the region are appallingly great. Generation after generation of invasions, plagues, massacres and revolutions have taken their toll on both the human and natural resources of the area. Ruins of great works of irrigation dot most of the deserts. Land once cleared of salt has been allowed to spoil. Drainage ditches have silted in. Irrigation terraces have been destroyed. In an area where almost everything must be wrested from nature it is a gigantic task simply to restore the economic foundations of the past.

In recent years a growing number of Middle Eastern leaders have come to see that overriding internal problems such as theirs cannot be solved by rhetoric. There has been increasing concern with the day-to-day problems of internal development such as maldistribution of land, lack of education and modern health services, and long-neglected social reforms.

Meanwhile, the United States, with a long record of successes and failures in the Middle East, has learned that it cannot mastermind the political and economic decisions of an entire subcontinent and that dollars alone will not assure a happy society. More particularly we are learning that a vital requirement for an effective U.S. policy in the Middle East, as elsewhere, is a more sensitive understanding of people —of their overriding desire for greater participation, for an increased sense of belonging, for a growing measure of individual justice and dignity.

Experience has taught us that when these human factors are overlooked, rapid economic development often becomes an instrument of frustration by encouraging men to hope for more than they can secure while at the same time disrupting old social relationships. Yet we also know that the developmental process cannot be stopped.

The challenge is a double one: to find means of meeting the essential economic goals, and to do so in a way that will provide an increasing measure of personal satisfaction for the individual.

By and large, the present mood in the Middle East is affirmative, and there is reason for measured confidence that this mood may continue and increase. If so, it will be a welcome break from the long record of destruction, of smashed cities, shifting causes and deeply rooted conflicts that has characterized the Middle East for so many years.

We must not underestimate, however, the continuing undercurrent of danger. A single, explosive accident could reverse the gradual progress that is now under way and plunge the whole region into bloody chaos. In the meantime the overriding regional problems remain largely untouched, and it would be folly to expect easy answers.

For instance, a sincere effort will be required on all sides if we are to ease the Jordan River and Arab refugee problems which have helped keep the entire Middle East in a state of permanent crisis.

Eventually, perhaps, we may see the emergence in the Middle East of a single dominant idea whose benefits are so important for all concerned that traditional differences may be forgotten, as the Common Market is now bridging similar differences in Europe. Until the essential new mood evolves, we must deal realistically with the day-to-day problems of economic and political adjustment.

Here Israel has a major role to play. In less than a generation Israel has achieved one of the most rapid rates of development in the world today, 8 percent annually. Her per capita gross national product is over $1,000 a year, far more than her Middle Eastern neighbors and higher than that of the Netherlands, Italy, Spain, Austria, Greece or Portugal.

In 1961 Israel's rate of industrial growth was 14 percent, one of the highest in the world. Her exports were up 25 percent and foreign exchange reserves up 65 percent over the previous year.

At the same time the Arab boycott has forced Israel to seek friends and markets outside the Middle East. One of the by-products is the ambitious Israeli foreign technical assistance program that is now reaching more than a score of nations in Africa, Asia and Latin America. Last year there were a thousand students from fifty-two countries studying in Israel and over two hundred Israeli technicians serving as advisers to underdeveloped countries abroad.

Israel's neighbors are not yet in a mood to appreciate and applaud these efforts. Israel's very success still generates an unreasoning antagonism. Yet even this may change as the Middle Eastern nations succeed in pushing forward their own national development plans and as a new confidence begins to breed tolerance and understanding.

In this context what are the basic ingredients for a realistic American Middle Eastern policy?

First, we must be prepared to help all the nations of the area maintain their independence. This requires an adequate and readily available United States deterrent to aggression from any source.

Second, we must use the instruments of the U.N. for the reduction of specific tensions and to prevent the Arab-Israeli dispute from developing into an open conflict that could rapidly spread.

Third, we can encourage all Middle Eastern nations to devote less time to angry propaganda debates with their neighbors and more to the solution of their own problems of internal development. We can also give special priority assistance to those countries which are genuinely concerned with improving the lot of *all* their citizens, not just a wealthy few.

Fourth, a persistent effort should be made to find some basis of cooperation between neighboring Middle Eastern nations, however tentative or restrictive the areas of cooperation may be.

There is no magic formula for stability in the Middle East or anywhere else. In spite of our vast military and industrial power, our capacity to shape events there, as elsewhere, is no more than marginal.

Yet a patient diplomacy, a firm willingness to stand against threats of aggression, a sensitive understanding of what motivates others and the wise use of our resources in assisting economic development may provide the margin between chaos on the one hand and growing political and economic stability on the other.

One thing at least is certain: Only through the creation of just societies, whose citizens have genuine independence, individual dignity and material welfare, can a permanent world peace be established.

In this regard the future course of events in the Middle East remains uncertain. But it is not without hope.

== 32

A TRAVELER IN AFRICA

*A six-week tour of sub-Sahara Africa with Mrs. Bowles in
the winter of 1955 is recorded in these penetrating notes
taken from informal letters to his family.*

BEFORE we came to Africa, many people had told us that
there was not one Africa, but at least a half-dozen. After only two
weeks on the African Continent, we have seen much that confirms this
advance notice.

At one extreme there is Moslem North Africa with its estimated 2.5
million French and Italian population. At the other extreme there is
South Africa with an equal number of stubborn whites. Portuguese
East and West Africa and British East Africa are similarly explosive
and for the same reason: white settlers who came, saw, were pleased
and dug in.

What a contrast is British West Africa, where the European settlers
are few, and where independence will be welcomed by Englishmen
eager to shed responsibility. Different again are French Africa south of
the Sahara, and the Belgian Congo, where the clear-cut plans of earnest colonial administrators still do not erase the heavy question mark
hanging over the future of these areas. And finally there is free Africa
—Liberia, Ethiopia, Egypt, Libya, and soon the Sudan—each of

which faces its own unique problems without a colonial whipping boy.

Some of these differences on the African scene may be apparent in these and subsequent notes on our African journey, dashed off roughly and at random and without the perspective that reflection and distance may later allow.

*   *   *

My impression of Africa is of an empty continent. It is particularly striking after Asia, and the difference constantly impresses me. Will not the relative scarcity of people in Africa have vast implications for the problem of economic development?

The Belgian Congo, for instance, is as rich in resources as India and nearly as large. Yet it has only twelve million people in comparison to India's 360 million. The Governor said to me, "If our population were five times as big as it is, our development would come twice as fast."

In Asia governments hesitate to encourage modern machinery. With so many people clamoring for work, wages and purchasing power rise with painful slowness. In Africa even now there is pressure to employ every labor-saving device. Thus as skills develop in Africa there is the opportunity for far higher wages and living standards. The political implications of this may be both complex and un-expected.

Today the factories of the Congo are more modern than those of India. A textile worker is paid two dollars a day plus a house, all med-ical expenses for himself and his family, and a food allowance.

*   *   *

I asked a British district officer who came to the Gold Coast in 1938 to describe his responsibilities at that time. "First, law and order," he said, "then communications and communicable diseases." (Commu-nicable diseases are those which Europeans are most likely to get.)

I asked him what his job is today. He answered without appearing to catch the significance of the change: "First, village roads and water.

Then schools, malaria control, village dispensaries, improving agricultural production."

It is not too much to say that the colonial *governments* have become interested in the people of Africa only since the war. Before the war these governments did things *to* the Africans. Now they do things *for* them. This is solid progress. But can essential partnerships be formed unless they do things *with* them?

*   *   *

A bitter African said to me in Accra: "The white man brought slavery to Africa in the name of Christ."

The missionaries have made their share of mistakes, but as I rode through the bush country I never ceased to marvel at their energy, courage and sense of purpose. Moreover, before any of us becomes impatient with the black man's demand for social justice, let us remember that it was through our own Christian teachings that he developed the faith and aspirations which now make him "hard to handle."

*   *   *

In the Gold Coast the British may be on their way to creating the same maladjusted educational system which is now turning out so many frustrated intellectuals in India.

When I suggested that this might be so to a highly intelligent Englishman, he said: "In India the system is weak because the standards have been allowed to deteriorate. Here in the Gold Coast we will see that the Oxford level is maintained."

"But isn't it possible," I suggested, "that an Oxford-Cambridge-Harvard-Yale education may not be precisely the best education for all able young Africans whose new society is in a hurry for technical skills?"

"No," he replied, "an Oxford education is the African's best hope." There were no ifs or ands about it, and we talked about something else.

Although it would be folly to downgrade the need of a liberal education for African leaders, I think that the extreme British view is unsound. At this stage if anything needs to be disproportionately stressed, it is the training of specialists.

Africa needs engineers, doctors and agricultural experts as well as capable political leadership. No one who has seen either Asia or Africa will dispute the statement that both could do with fewer lawyers and more down-to-earth, expert work in the field or, as I have learned to call it here, "the bush."

The contrast between colonial educational attitudes is fascinating. The British confidently rely on the benefits of a good education, preferably an Oxford-standard education, and believe that the more graduates, the better. Three thousand future citizens of the Gold Coast are now studying in English-language institutions abroad, and an Oxford-model university for one thousand is now going up outside Accra.

The Belgian officials, on the other hand, recoil in horror at the thought of the educated African. Eleven Congo students are now studying in Belgium, none elsewhere, and the barely begun university outside Léopoldville expects to graduate "no more than six or seven" each year for the foreseeable future.

The French are feeling their way somewhere between these extremes. There are three hundred Africans from French Equatorial Africa (half the size of the United States, but with a population of only four million) studying in France. The bulk of them are being guided into the specialized professions and away from the liberal arts.

The over-all education facilities in all colonial countries are growing fast. The usual guess is that 50 percent of the six-year-olds are in schools, which, if true, is higher than in India.

During my entire stay in French Equatorial Africa and the Belgian Congo, I have been introduced to only four Africans by name. All of them were tame and noncommittal. However, in Léopoldville, I asked three of them: "What do your people criticize most about the present system?" After a moment's hesitation, the answer came: "Not political discrimination so much as social discrimination. There is a black city and there is a white city, and after dark each is off bounds to the other."

* * *

The target of our U.S. information work in Central Africa is not the vast African majority who will shape the future, but the tiny European minority. At our library in Léopoldville 680 people have registered to take out books. Only twelve of them are Africans.

There are 4,300 books in all, only 280 of them in French. I asked how many people in Léopoldville can speak or read English. "Perhaps eighteen hundred, all but a handful of them Belgians," was the answer.

There must be wiser ways to spend our meager funds. If we can't speak our views frankly to the African majority, we should concentrate our efforts elsewhere.

Although there are two major daily newspapers in Léopoldville, only 1,600 copies are bought by the 300,000 Africans. Nervous Europeans find these figures immensely reassuring for they believe that they show that dangerous thoughts can be reduced to a minimum.

* * *

At the mine in Northern Rhodesia which we visited there are 9,000 African miners and 1,500 Europeans. Each has its own union.

The average monthly wage of the European miners is $294, plus a "copper bonus" of 60 percent, free medical care, a comfortable modern house, and for a nominal monthly fee membership in a most modern country club. Their wages are substantially above those of American copper miners although living costs are about half those in the United States.

The average monthly wage of the African miner below ground is $18 a month, plus a small but adequate house, a daily food ration and free medical care. Taking all factors into account the ratio is roughly twenty to one. These figures are from the December, 1954, edition of the *Monthly Digest of Statistics* published by the Federation government.

The Europeans, of course, do more skilled work than the Africans, in a ratio which might bring a three-to-two, or at most a two-to-one, differential in an American mine.

In Southern Rhodesia the average wages are about 30 percent less than in Northern Rhodesia. There is a legal minimum of $15 monthly and 70 percent of the Africans are at the minimum. In the entire Federation I was told that there are "no more than two dozen" Africans getting a higher wage than the lowest-paid European.

I asked what the African miners were demanding. "Eighteen pounds sterling [$48] monthly," was the answer, "obviously a proposal of the radical element for political purposes."

* * *

"I am puzzled," I said to a high official. "I understand that the African in the Gold Coast and the African in Southern Rhodesia are of identical Bantu stock. Yet four thousand Gold Coasters are going to college at home or abroad while here there are only fifty African college graduates in the entire Federation. Moreover, there are so many highly competent Africans in the government of the Gold Coast and none here. What is the explanation?"

The official looked uneasy, and agreed that it was strange indeed, but that he had never really thought much about it.

The answer is simple. In British East Africa every effort is being made by the colonial government to spread the progress of the Africans. Here in the Central Federation, where the Colonial Office has relatively little to say, there are 200,000 privileged Europeans lying like a great blanket over the hopes and aspirations of six million Africans. When will these frustrated hopes explode?

* * *

Let me add a few thoughts on the Congo in retrospect. The Belgians are embarked on a carefully planned, well-organized and logical development of this vast territory, from their point of view.

The weakness of their program appears to be their reluctance to allow the African to secure an advanced education—even a technical education—for fear that he will then demand a growing share of responsibility in the shaping of his own future.

The danger lies, not so much in the possibility that the Belgians will not compromise with the force of nationalism eventually, but that when they do compromise under pressure the Africans will be almost totally inexperienced in handling the responsibilities which they are certain to demand and eventually to get.

Although the British colonies appear a lot less politically calm than the Congo, this is because the British, except in Southern Rhodesia, are earnestly trying to give the African all the experience in government that he can absorb. As a result, when the nationalist forces finally take charge, the possibility of a relatively painless transition seems to me quite favorable.

*   *   *

We cannot exaggerate the hospitality and friendliness of the Europeans whom we met in Southern Rhodesia. For this reason I feel unhappy to express so bluntly my distress over their policies and attitudes. But one final example will suggest their remoteness from the facts of life, and the contrast to relatively race-free Uganda.

In Salisbury we were invited to three dinner parties in our honor, all "black tie." The last, given by the Governor General, was attended by sixteen people in addition to ourselves. Only two of the sixteen had no title—two young military aides who ushered us about. There were two "Lords," five "Sirs" and their ladies. At any of these three parties a "native" would have been nearly as out of place as a hyena.

In Uganda the situation was refreshingly different. The first night at dinner in the Governor's House on lovely Lake Victoria were the Indian Mayor of Kampala, several African officials, two American sociologists and their wives. The second night we were guests of honor at a buffet supper in Kampala, at which the Indians and Africans far outnumbered the Europeans. Another night there was a dinner for twenty at Government House, at which half the guests were Africans.

The last dinner, given in our honor by the Indian community of Uganda, was attended by both Africans and Europeans. None of these were "black tie" occasions "because that would be one more unnecessary expense for the Africans."

The difference is explained by the fact that the relatively few Europeans in Uganda are not dug in economically. There are only 6,000 Europeans in the entire colony out of a total population of 5.5 million. They own only one-half of one percent of the land and by law they can buy no more.

* * *

Today 95 percent of all the education in Africa is being administered by the Christian churches, usually through government subsidies. The Moslems have no comparable system, and hence it is the Moslems who are often most illiterate and backward.

If Christianity should fail in Africa, it will not be for lack of time or opportunity. Nor will it be because the teachings of Christ are any less invalid here. A large share of the blame may be placed on the relentless competition between the churches, and on a narrow application of Christianity by many missionaries of all denominations which often seems ludicrous and strange to the prospective converts.

Sometimes you can drive for miles without seeing a school. Then suddenly you see a large Catholic school and on a nearby hill, facing it, a competitive Protestant school. Who can blame the Africans for being mixed up?

* * *

Many Africans in Uganda fear industrial development and even the new hydroelectric project on the nearby Nile. "When the European discovers mineral resources or decides to start a factory, he brings in white experts to run it," they say. "Then they feel uneasy, and bring in white foremen and technicians to give themselves a firm grip. The next thing we know, we are held in a vise as tight as that of Kenya, the copper belt and South Africa."

* * *

Among the Europeans in Kenya we are impressed with the same extraordinary combination of decency, courage, charm and dedication, coupled with incredible ignorance about what is happening in the world and about the limitations of old-fashioned power, which we found so alarming in the Central Federation.

In Kenya there are 5.5 million Africans, 120,000 Asians (mostly Indians) and 40,000 Europeans (the African name for whites). The Europeans own most of the good land, the so-called "white highlands," only a fraction of which is cultivated. The remainder is simply denied to the Africans, who are crowded into limited areas of poorer soil.

"We do not deny the right of a good European farmer to the land he tills," an African leader said to me. "Even if he has five thousand acres, we do not object, *as long as he really farms it.* What we can't accept is what the European considers his divine right to possess the land whether he uses it or not—and to keep others from raising the food we need so badly."

On Sunday we drove to Nyeri ninety-five miles northeast of Nairobi on the slopes of Mount Kenya. The first thirty miles took us through rich, European-owned farmland, much of it untilled. The major crops seem to be coffee and sisal (for ropemaking). The Africans are prohibited from raising sisal, and their right to raise coffee is rigidly restricted.

As we moved into the sandy hills, the African farms began to appear. The corn crops were the poorest that we have seen in Africa.

Everywhere the Africans whom we have met appear reasonable and indeed quite conservative. We have yet to talk to any African or Asian who did not stress the importance of the European in Africa's future development.

If the Europeans cannot forge a partnership with these people, what possible hope exists for agreement with the radicals and demagogues who will surely follow?

33

AMERICA'S ROLE IN AFRICA

In 1955 America had no African policy, says Mr. Bowles as he suggests some basic principles on which a realistic policy should be based and which are now widely accepted.
Collier's *magazine, June 10, 1955.*

WITH all his other worries, most Americans are inclined to ask: "Why in the world should I worry about Africa? What can Africa mean to me?"

Africa is important to him for many reasons. Next to Asia it is the world's largest continent, covering one-fifth of the earth's surface. Although no one can tell the full extent of its resources, we know that they are fabulous.

Already we are looking to Africa for strategic uranium, rubber, cobalt, manganese, industrial diamonds, chromium, lead, zinc, iron ore and bauxite—and the surface of Africa's mineral wealth has barely been scratched. Seventy geological teams are said to be operating now in French Equatorial Africa alone, and surveys at least as extensive are under way in the Belgian Congo and British Africa.

But perhaps the most momentous development in Africa today is the awakening of its 200 or more million people. After a long night the African giant is stirring, blinking away his drowsiness and stretching his limbs with all the eager, impatient spirit of youth approaching manhood. In the next few years Africa will be bursting with explosive

173

problems, conflicts and headlines. We Americans will be worrying about them whether we want to or not.

It is not surprising that the new awakening has profound political implications. The day when the African will placidly accept the status of second-class citizen is rapidly coming to a close. He may reluctantly accept some delay, but there will be no fundamental compromises.

Everywhere Africans are starting to ask hard questions of the West. Many of these questions have racial overtones: "Why, when so much wealth is being taken out of Africa by white Europeans, do we black Africans remain so poor?" "Why, when the Christian religion considers all men to be brothers, do most Europeans and Americans continue to discriminate against us in economic, political and social affairs?"

To Americans in particular, Africans say: "Why, with your long history of anticolonialism, does your government now remain silent on the question of African freedom? Why do you consistently straddle this problem in the United Nations?"

What is our African policy? It is fair to say that at present we do not have one. We do not have one because for years we have told ourselves that Africa was simply a projection of Britain, France, Portugal and Belgium, and that a European policy would suffice. This same kind of disastrous reasoning in Asia led us to look upon Indochina as a French problem and not as an Asian problem. It can cost us even more heavily in Africa.

No responsible person will suggest that the development of a rational policy in regard to Africa is an easy matter. It is a subject on which European opinions are sensitive and easily aroused. It is highly complex, and wide-open for reckless, racial demagoguery. I suggest the following points to mark the direction which our efforts might take:

1. Let us start with the fact that we do not control Africa, that we have no desire to control it and that there is a strict limit to what we can do there.

2. Without pompously lecturing our European friends on their colonial policies, or making a demagogic play for the applause of the African gallery, let us privately and publicly place our influence behind every orderly and responsible proposal that moves toward freedom.

3. Africans themselves will eventually decide the pace of freedom. However, if America convinces the Africans that we honestly favor

their independence as rapidly as they can manage it, we shall be in a position to help moderate the demands of those Africans who now want more authority than they are qualified to use. Premature self-government would only lead to failures which would play into the hands of the bitter-enders.

4. If the Gold Coast and Nigeria, like India, develop as free nations in an orderly democratic way, those who are honestly convinced that the African cannot govern himself in the foreseeable future will be forced to modify their views.

Everything that America can do to help guarantee the success of these new, emerging, free West African governments will serve this constructive end. This means not only economic assistance from our government but vigorous, imaginative help from our private agencies, including foundations and churches.

5. For the same reason we should generously and intelligently assist those African nations which are already free—Egypt, Libya, Ethiopia, Liberia, and soon the Sudan. Their progress will help determine the pace for others.

6. Before agreeing to support any economic program in Africa, we should scrutinize it carefully to see that it offers full opportunity to people of all races. If we identify ourselves even indirectly with continuing foreign supremacy in Africa, our influence will vanish.

7. We should give Africa a far higher priority in State Department attention. Today we have only a handful of diplomatic missions in Africa. Although I was generally impressed with the ability and earnestness of the personnel, most of them are vastly overworked and responsible for areas far beyond their physical capacities.

8. We should also more clearly define our objectives. State Department and United States Information Agency people should be instructed that the primary purpose of their work is to develop close understanding and a working relationship with the Africans, not simply with the thin European ruling group at the top. Our information program in Africa should be stepped up materially and concentrated on contact with the Africans, rather than the whites.

9. In the United States itself there are now sixteen million Americans of African descent, many of whom are contributing vigorously to the development of our own democracy. In both private and official capacities, we can have no better ambassadors to Africa than those sons of America who are also great-great-grandsons of Africa. The

mere presence in Africa of able American Negroes as visiting lecturers, teachers, government employees and missionaries would do everyone concerned a world of good.

10. Africa should be given a much higher priority in American universities. The two centers of African studies which are already in operation in the United States should be strengthened, expanded and multiplied through foundation assistance and other means.

11. Through diplomatic channels we might suggest to our European friends the calling of a conference on Africa and the development of an African charter. Such a charter might lay down standards of self-government and emphatically restate the intentions of the European powers to press steadily and purposefully toward self-government.

If a partnership is effected between Europe's capital and scientific know-how and Africa's resources, natural and human, the future will be far more prosperous and satisfying for Africa and Europe as well.

A British official told me: "We must stay ahead of the demands of the Africans or we are finished. If we move too slowly, they will generate overwhelming explosive pressures that will force us into chaos. The wise thing to do is to anticipate their demands, and grant them in an orderly way before the pressures crystallize."

In this situation America has a historic role to play. By tactful, intelligent and forthright policies we can appeal to the best in Europe and the best in Africa. We can help to promote the essential partnership which will serve to enlarge the areas of freedom and material well-being for all men.

34

AFRICA'S CHALLENGE TO THE U.N.

*As the newly freed Congo exploded in the midsummer of
1960, the danger of a new and ominous battleground in Africa
prompted this unique proposal for U.N. initiative in developing a
"charter of conduct" for all non-African powers.* New York
Times Magazine, *August 21, 1960.*

THE RECENT explosion in the Congo, like a flare in a dark-
ened sky, shows up the extent and depth of Africa's problems and the
pressing need for bold American initiative in establishing a new relationship with that continent.

I believe the key lies in the capacity of the United Nations to take
the lead in filling the economic and political vacuum in Africa and in
the exceptional readiness of most Africans to accept the United Nations in such a role.

Thus the starting point for an affirmative new American policy in
Africa should be a dramatically expanded concept of the United Nations' contribution—a contribution that would include, not only internal and external security, but also economic progress and orderly
political transition.

This fresh approach could be dramatized effectively by the introduc-
tion of an American-sponsored resolution at the fall session of the
General Assembly proposing a charter of conduct for all non-African
powers in Africa.

Such a charter should be far more than a negative statement of what the great powers agree *not* to do in Africa. It would propose that all members of the United Nations agree to a broad-scale course of constructive economic and political action that will assure the independence of the new African nations, encourage their orderly political and economic development, and relieve them in large measure of the pulling and hauling of the cold war.

A commitment of this kind would enable the more developed nations to help meet Africa's vast and varied needs through the "neutral" machinery of the United Nations, rather than through the dangerously volatile competition of the power blocs, which has kept the world on the brink of war in the Middle East and in Southeast Asia.

Let us examine more precisely what some of those commitments might be.

1. A pledge by all nations to refrain from agitating propaganda within Africa and to end all efforts at direct or indirect subversion. The United Nations could be authorized to investigate all charges of violation and to report to the General Assembly.

2. A similar agreement not to feed the arms race in Africa. In present circumstances the actual military needs of the new African nations are modest. It is to our advantage and that of the Africans to keep them so.

3. An agreement by the great powers to channel the bulk of all economic, technical and educational assistance to Africa through the United Nations. The essential machinery already exists in the U.N. specialized agencies, the Technical Assistance Administration, the Special Fund, the World Bank and the new International Development Association.

What is needed now is the will to substitute this international machinery to the maximum possible extent for the well-worn path of bilateral aid, which inevitably introduces the competition of the cold war.

4. An imaginative and comprehensive effort through a newly created United Nations civil service to meet Africa's overriding need for experienced administrators, technicians, engineers, teachers and professional men of all sorts—outside the context of the cold war.

For a generation or more, non-African civil servants, working under African policy-makers, will be essential to the rapid economic and political development of the African nations. The essential question is:

Where will those non-Africans be recruited? To whom will they owe their first loyalties? Will they help bring the cold war to Africa? Or will they serve the cause of international cooperation and understanding?

5. The establishment of a permanent U.N. police force for use in Africa and elsewhere along the lines of that at present being shaped in the Congo. Such a force now represents the major hope of the new Congolese nation for internal security and national unity. Similar tensions are certain to develop in other areas, not only as an aftermath of the withdrawal of European control, but also as conflicts develop among the new African nations themselves.

A map of existing African loyalties superimposed on a map of national boundaries produces a crazy quilt of overlapping and intersecting lines. This situation has already led to considerable friction as various federations have been proposed, announced and dissolved.

It is not for the United Nations to decide the outcome of these matters, either to insure the status quo or to promote changes, however wise they may appear to be. This is a matter solely for the Africans themselves.

However, it is a proper and essential objective of the United Nations to prevent such situations from exploding into violence and particularly to prevent the great powers from intervening in behalf of one side or the other. The existence of an adequate U.N. police force, recruited largely by the African nations themselves, could do much to reduce the temptation for direct unilateral military intervention from outside.

6. The proposed African charter might also provide for the setting up of a special African court of justice, perhaps associated with the World Court, and specifically empowered to settle disputes between African nations and between African states and outside nations.

Such a court, with its members drawn largely, but not exclusively, from the African nations, would provide an additional barrier to outside intervention—provided the African powers could be induced to accept its jurisdiction without too many qualifications.

I do not suggest that the United Nations can successfully shoulder all the problems of the turbulent new Africa. However, I believe it can provide by all odds the most effective machinery through which to approach these problems while isolating them from the explosive antagonisms of the cold war.

Is our own government prepared to abandon our present inadequate and sterile approach to Africa and embark on a bold new effort in positive international cooperation there?

If we timidly turn our back on this opportunity, only one thing is certain: Africa will rapidly become an ominous new battleground of the cold war, with explosively uncertain results.

35

THE TIDE OF HOPE IN AFRICA

*In February, 1962, as Special Representative and Adviser to
the President on African, Asian and Latin-American Affairs,
Mr. Bowles outlines the Administration's new approach to
Africa before a predominantly African audience at a U.N.
Economic Commission for Africa gathering at Addis Ababa,
Ethiopia.*

WE ARE here to consider the immediate challenge of this
vast, dynamic African Continent, where 220 million people are awakening to the infinite promise of their land and their future.

Nowhere does the tide of hope run stronger or deeper than here in
Africa. Nowhere is there greater determination to use modern technical knowledge to create modern societies in which poverty, disease
and oppression will be replaced with prosperity, progress and justice.

Fifteen years ago how many of us could have foreseen twenty-eight
free African nations meeting here in Addis Ababa to discuss the economic and social future of their people?

How does the United States relate itself to Africa, and particularly
to Africa's future? What are our objectives here?

We begin with a sense of humility. We are profoundly embarrassed
by our long ignorance of Africa and by our lack of past contact with
your people. Our failure over the years to know you better reflects
our intense concentration on the development of our own country.

Paradoxically, the very vigor with which we attacked our own problems left us largely ignorant of the struggles of other peoples to obtain the same rights for which we fought in our own anticolonial revolution.

We also bring to Africa a sense of humility because of the racial conflicts that have troubled our own country. More than 10 percent of our people have their family roots in Africa. One hundred years ago in our great Civil War nearly one million white Americans died to end human servitude in the United States.

Since then the two races have been steadily creating a basis for cooperation and mutual respect. In the past few years, especially, we have made tremendous progress in eliminating discrimination on all fronts.

Although there are still some people in my country who have not yet accepted the great moral reality of human equality, the end of discrimination is now clearly in sight.

We see expression of our common objectives in the intense interest that thoughtful Americans of all races are now expressing in Africa. A growing flood of books, films, magazines and newspaper articles on Africa and Africans testifies to this interest.

In the area of international politics, one of our primary objectives is to keep the cold war out of Africa. It is in our interest as well as in your own that you be spared, insofar as possible, the bitterness, divisiveness and economic wastefulness of this tragic conflict.

We believe that our best hope of accomplishing this lies in a strong United Nations. That is why the United States pays nearly 50 percent of the United Nations costs in the Congo and vigorously supports United Nations programs everywhere.

In the area of economics, we are moving to create effective working relationships with many new nations of Africa. We know that what helps to strengthen your societies will help to strengthen our own.

We are encouraged by the direction in which most African nations are moving in regard to economic development. The following points appear particularly important:

First, although you appreciate the urgent need to promote industrial projects, you have not overlooked the importance of agriculture and rural development. As in Asia and Latin America, three-fourths of your people live in the villages. It is they who raise the food and eventually must provide the bulk of the purchasing power to buy the manufactured goods that are produced in the cities.

Without growing prosperity, literacy and justice in the villages, it will be impossible to create the solid economic, political and social foundations upon which an advanced economy must rest.

Second, we applaud your emphasis on the importance of human values and human relationships. Although economic progress is vital, it will have little effect on the political stability of a nation unless it is achieved with respect for the dignity and welfare of the people as individuals.

Third, we applaud your emphasis on the importance of education. The rapid development of your primary and secondary school system and the creation of forward-looking institutions of higher education reflect Africa's respect for and understanding of the key role education plays in creating a modern society.

Fourth, we are glad that many of you are preparing to look beyond government funds to the private capital which is available in many more developed countries. By far the largest proportion of our wealth is in the form of private capital, which represents the accumulated savings of our people.

The United States Government, however, is steadily increasing its assistance to Africa on both a bilateral and multilateral basis. In 1962 the total of our loans, grants, technical assistance, agricultural commodities sales and grants, and our contributions to United Nations programs in Africa will probably total more than $520 million.

Our programs of people-to-people cooperation are also growing. Through the Peace Corps, hundreds of American secondary school teachers are now at work, teaching in a number of your countries, with hundreds more on their way.

From this experience they will learn as much as they teach. There are also some three thousand African students now studying in the United States—and teaching us as they learn.

Our young people in particular see in Africa a continent where great new things are happening, where new frontiers, new hopes and new opportunities are opening. I know of this appeal to young Americans at first hand because for the last year and a half my own son and daughter-in-law have been teaching in a Nigerian secondary school as employees of the Nigerian Government. Through their letters I have had some insight into the minds of the young African leaders of tomorrow.

Finally, I want to applaud your increasing interest in the economic integration of Africa.

There are many different roads toward unity. It is for you to choose the one that appears best suited for you. One thing, however, is clear: The era of highly industrialized "mother" countries and their artificially maintained colonial markets is gone forever. This breakup has created some totally new economic realities. The development of regional economic groupings reflects these realities.

Yet formidable barriers to African regional cooperation and integration still remain. No continent, for instance, has so many independent sovereignties as does Africa, most of them carved out years ago by agreements among foreigners in faraway colonial capitals.

Today these entities have become national realities in which millions of people are rapidly and proudly developing their national future. Yet somehow a compromise must be reached between the surging new pride of independence and the regional cooperation that is required for faster economic growth. I know of no African country whose development could not be speeded if it were a vigorous member of a larger grouping.

You are well launched on a mighty adventure—the rebirth of what is perhaps the world's richest and most promising continent. I wish you Godspeed.

▬ 36

THE CRY FOR LAND IN LATIN AMERICA

Latin America's stormy reception of a visiting American
Vice President led to considerable uneasiness about U.S. policy
in that area. This article in the New York Times Magazine
in November, 1959, brings into focus one of the major social
and economic problems underlying popular unrest there
then and today.

LATIN America's nationalist leaders, most of them strongly anti-Communist, are out to end the poverty, illiteracy, perpetual indebtedness and fear which for generations have prevented all but a small minority from participating in the sound growth of their countries.

Inevitably, one of their principal weapons will be land reform to enable most farm families to own their own land. Inevitably, too, Latin-American Communists will increase their efforts to associate themselves with the movement.

The Communist version of land reform is only a first step toward a system of collectivization that makes every peasant a captive of the state. Yet it has a powerful appeal for naïve, landless peasants who see in it only the promise of freedom.

What are the issues involved? And what is the prospect of solving them by democratic means?

Today 1.5 percent of the people, those with fifteen thousand or more acres each, own half of all agricultural land in Latin America and even more of the best land. A heavy proportion of all Latin Americans are impoverished tenant farmers, deeply in debt to their landlords.

This land structure goes back to the original conquests and settlements by the Spaniards and Portuguese who brought with them their feudal institutions. When colonial ties were broken in the early nineteenth century, the dominant role of the large landholders was left mostly unchallenged.

If this antiquated rural system produced an adequate supply of food and fiber at reasonable prices, the social and economic injustices would be less apparent. Yet, because much of the land is set aside for cash crops such as coffee and sugar, which benefit only the few, and because farming methods are largely outdated, most Latin Americans continue to suffer diet deficiencies.

Meanwhile, a 2.5 percent annual population growth rate—among the highest in the world—exerts increasing pressure on the lagging food supply.

Throughout Latin America genuinely democratic elements recognize that a change in the land-tenure system is indispensable for the peace and stability of the region. Yet the landowning classes appear unable to understand their own profound stake in helping the peasants work out peaceful transitions by democratic means.

The excesses of the Mexican revolution a generation or two ago, and the even more terrifying lessons of the Russian and Chinese revolutions, appear to have been lost on them.

Latin-American land specialists emphasize that confiscation or nationalization of estates, no matter how equitably conducted, is not the only avenue for solving the problem. Each country presents its own type of challenge.

There is no doubt, however, that sweeping changes in Latin-American land-tenure systems are inevitable. Only one question remains to be answered: How will these changes come—by bloody revolution or by long-range democratic planning? Let us look at the lessons of some past experience:

In Mexico between 1916 and 1934, approximately 25 million acres of feudal land were expropriated and assigned to peasants. More than 900,000 peons received their own small farms in this opening phase of the system. Under President Cárdenas, who took office in 1934, an additional 50 million acres were expropriated and reassigned to eight million landless.

Some of the weaknesses in the early phases of Mexico's agrarian reform subsequently became apparent. The new landholding Indian, for all his will to work, found himself without good seeds, farm animals and tools. He had nowhere to turn for credit. He was unfamiliar with planning techniques and the profitable marketing of his crops. The result was a drop in agricultural production and a shortage of such Mexican staples as corn and beans.

Since then, the Mexican Government, with American private and public assistance, has taken steps to correct these weaknesses through a rural extension system that brings new methods directly to the peasants, and production is now mounting steadily.

In Venezuela, President Romulo Betancourt last July submitted to his Congress a bill vigorously tackling the problem of the country's outmoded agrarian structure. Profiting from such experiences as Mexico's, the Venezuelan program provides for liberal government credit for equipment, seeds and fertilizer, and for an agricultural extension service to advise new landowners what, where and how to plant.

It is Betancourt's second try. In 1948 his Acción Democrática party, in power for the first time as the result of the first free elections in Venezuelan history, passed an agrarian reform law which called for expropriation of land with compensation and redistribution to the landless. Thirty-six days later the military overthrew the reform government.

In Bolivia land reform was among the first acts of the revolutionary regime in 1952. Bolivian landlords had been notorious for the system of serfdom which allowed them to demand personal services from peons.

The revolutionary government planned to give each farmer between twenty-five and two thousand acres, depending upon soil productivity. But no soil survey of Bolivia ever had been made, and there were not even adequate maps of the farmlands available.

Impatient, machine-gun-carrying peasants ultimately took over. Today Bolivia's land reform remains chaotic. But one thing is certain: The Bolivian farm laborer will never again endure feudal servitude in silence.

Although responsible Latin-American leaders are anxious to legislate carefully planned land distribution programs before the restiveness of their people takes a similar ugly turn, the pressures favoring the status quo remain strong.

How long will history wait? Only four times in our century have large-scale land reforms been adopted by democratic governments; in Czechoslovakia in 1926, in postrevolutionary Mexico, in parts of India and in Puerto Rico, for which Congress in 1900 passed legislation limiting landownership by corporations to five hundred acres.

This situation challenges United States diplomacy throughout Latin America. United States citizens' private investments in the area amount to more than nine billion dollars. This is more than in any other region of the world, and not all of it is based on strictly legal arrangements. Although only part of this investment is in land, some American financial interests are certain to be seriously hurt by any legislation breaking up big estates.

This makes it likely that every attempt, however essential, democratic or reasonable, to overhaul the outmoded agrarian systems of Latin America will be misinterpreted as "Communist confiscation." The resulting pressures on Congress and the Department of State are likely to be great. Sooner or later these pressures may back the United States, with its long tradition of individual landownership, into a position of endorsing the very interests which are stifling the development of a region on which our own security depends.

The most radical land reform in modern history was launched under American auspices by General Douglas MacArthur in Japan immediately following the war. Before Pearl Harbor, two-thirds of all Japanese farmers were tenants. Today 92 percent of all Japanese rural families own their own land—and are producing record output per acre.

American influence, too, helped Chiang Kai-shek to put into effect on Taiwan a democratic system of landownership which, if it had been enacted on the mainland ten years earlier, almost certainly would have swung the peasants in his favor.

Under the Generalissimo's program, no farmer is allowed to own more than ten acres of land, nor is anyone allowed to own land which he does not till himself. Government officials in Taipei credit these reforms with much of the extraordinary increase in Taiwan's output of rice per acre.

Such was the strength of the opposition that these postwar reforms could be effected only by decree. General MacArthur's military government, in particular, rode roughshod over Japanese landlords.

Can United States diplomacy summon the tact, adaptability and persuasiveness to work with struggling Latin-American governments to bring about a peaceful revolution on the land?

Although our government cannot direct the course of events, it can often exert a constructive influence. For example:

We can reaffirm our traditional support for reasonable measures to assure the widespread ownership of land. We can draw on our world-wide experience to assist Latin-American governments in working out compensation plans which will provide fair payment to the landlords without unreasonably burdening the new owners.

We can adjust ourselves in advance to the certainty that reason will not always prevail, that injustices will almost surely occur and that the short-term price paid for long-term stability will often appear exorbitant.

Above all, let us not lose sight of the essential issue. The real choice in Latin America, as in Asia and Africa, is citizenship or serfdom, hope or despair, orderly political growth or bloody upheaval. Our failure to understand this choice, or to support the vital new elements which are striving to assert leadership, would be catastrophic.

═══ 37

WHAT IS THE ALLIANCE FOR PROGRESS?

*Under Secretary of State Bowles, speaking in Mexico City
to the Mexican-North American Cultural Institute in October,
1961, points out the historic implications of this long overdue
program for both the U.S. and Latin-American people, and
bluntly suggests the need for bold internal reforms.*

THE ALLIANCE for Progress is designed to strike at the
roots of poverty and injustice throughout Latin America and to enable the people and governments of our twenty-one nations to
strengthen their free institutions by peaceful democratic means.

As we consider the possibilities and pitfalls of this challenging new
partnership, we should, I believe, face certain hard facts.

For instance, we have learned by experience that there is a strict
limitation on what any foreign nation can do for others, regardless of
the extent of its resources and goodwill. Neither prosperity nor freedom can be bestowed on one people by another. They must be earned
by initiative, hard work and often through sacrifice.

Moreover, there must be a greater willingness among the privileged
minority in Latin America to forego some immediate gains in a common effort to create free societies which alone can assure political,
social and economic growth by peaceful means.

In many Latin-American nations the revolutionary process petered
out once the great liberators had broken the colonial ties. In spite of

the courageous and dedicated efforts of many democratic leaders since those early days, the economic and social reforms that alone can give depth and dignity to any society were often stifled or diverted.

And because the essential economic and social changes have not been forthcoming, great wealth often exists side by side with abject poverty.

The Alliance for Progress provides the basis for a partnership of nations designed to bring a fresh, democratic approach to the economic and social problems of the whole Western Hemisphere. How can such a partnership best be developed? How should the role of each partner be defined and understood?

In September, 1960, the Act of Bogotá stressed that economic and social development can only succeed if it is a two-way street.

"The success of a cooperative program of economic and social progress," it said, "will require maximum self-help efforts on the part of the American republics and, in many cases, the improvement of existing institutions and practices, particularly in the fields of taxation, the ownership and use of land, education and training, health and housing."

In August, 1961, at Punta del Este, the Declaration of the Peoples of America was even more precise. It condemned "unjust structures and systems of land tenure and use" and vigorously endorsed "programs of integrated agrarian reform in accordance with the characteristics of each country . . . to assure that the land will become for the man who works it the foundation of his increasing welfare and the guarantee of his freedom and dignity."

The Declaration called for "tax laws which demand more from those who have most, punishing tax evasion severely, and redistributing the national income in order to benefit those who are most in need, while at the same time, promoting saving and investment and reinvestment of capital."

The Declaration finally expressed the conviction that "these profound economic, social, and cultural changes can come about only through the self-help efforts of each country."

In early September the United States Congress passed economic aid legislation incorporating these principles and spelling out President Kennedy's responsibility in allocating the funds which were made available.

For instance, this new legislation states that in making loans and grants to developing nations the President shall "take into account the extent to which the recipient country shows a responsiveness to the vital economic, political, and social concerns of its people and demonstrates a clear determination to take effective self-help measures."

The legislation also stresses the need for comprehensive, well-thought-through plans which will guard against waste and corruption. It calls for special encouragement to integrated rural communities to help assure greater opportunity and justice to those who till the soil.

In its specific reference to Latin America, the new economic assistance program emphasizes that aid should be given "according to the principles of the Act of Bogotá."

These, then, are our clearly stated objectives. What about the program itself? Although techniques, standards and specific programs are still in the development stage, a few general points may be considered.

A challenge which requires particularly prompt and careful consideration lies in the rural areas, where 70 percent of the people of Latin America now live.

In dealing with this question we must look beyond the popular slogans which call vaguely for "land reform." Although individual or cooperative landownership is essential to the development of dynamic rural communities, it is not enough in itself.

If rural families are to achieve the increasing dignity and opportunity which they so urgently seek, government extension services must be created to promote modern farming methods and the more efficient use of resources. Such extension services should include carefully integrated programs for the development of health clinics, schools and roads.

Low-interest loans must also be made available and cooperatives formed so that whole communities may learn to work together to lift themselves up by their bootstraps. Where feasible, streams must be dammed and tube wells dug to provide water for irrigation.

By encouraging all able-bodied people in the community to volunteer their labor in building these new facilities, the extension worker can further increase their sense of individual pride and participation.

One overriding lesson has emerged from our recent experience in working with rural societies: Only when programs for rural betterment are carefully integrated are human energies fully released.

Let me suggest with particular emphasis that no country that aspires to economic development can say that it cannot afford to educate its children. It cannot afford *not* to educate its children. Nor can it afford not to conserve the health of its people.

Another essential form of self-help which was stressed in both the Act of Bogotá and the recent conference at Punta del Este is the graduated income tax. Such tax systems are needed to soak up idle profits, while offering dynamic incentives for capital investment in productive new enterprises.

Although we have no desire to interfere in the affairs of others, we know from hard experience that sharp and showy differences between rich and poor breed bitter unrest and frustration among the less privileged.

Another condition essential to increasing domestic investment and to successful development is a rational relationship between the currency of the developing nation and that of those with which it trades.

May I frankly add that I do not see why my government or any other capital contributor should be asked for loans or grants to replace runaway indigenous capital that could be kept at home by the same kind of curbs with which the British helped restore the soundness of their economy following the war.

Nor do I see why we should be expected to tax ourselves to help other nations which either fail to tax their own well-to-do people in relation to their ability to pay or wink at tax avoidance. In the United States we have been paying income taxes for half a century.

Now what precisely is the United States prepared to do to assist those nations which are taking the essential steps to help themselves in the spirit of the Act of Bogotá?

Each nation will present its own special needs and opportunities. However, substantial sums are available from a variety of agencies for loans and grants for development programs; also technical specialists for planning, operations and development; agricultural products such as wheat, maize, powdered milk and fats; and Peace Corps volunteers, largely recruited from our universities, to help in teaching, surveying and other projects.

Studies are also under way which we hope may lead to agreements that will provide assured fair prices for various commodities which are vital to the prosperity of Latin-American countries.

The issue before us can be bluntly stated: What we jointly pledged under the terms of the Act of Bogotá is no less than a continuing peaceful democratic revolution, reaching into every Latin-American community and calling in many cases for drastic change from the old ways.

How fully have we weighed the implications of this pronouncement? How clearly have we sensed the formidable difficulties which lie ahead?

They stem from several sources: from a sense of hopelessness among millions of impoverished peasants and slum dwellers, from the conviction among many important political leaders that constructive, peaceful change is impossible, and from the opposition of economic interests which are unwilling to face the hard realities of today's revolutionary world.

It would be folly for us to underestimate these difficulties. Yet we should take heart at the growing support among influential leaders and groups for the programs which will be required to meet our stated objectives.

To men of stout hearts and deep conviction, our age offers an exciting opportunity to lead and to participate in a great international effort for democratic development. The challenge is particularly great for younger men and women, who have so much to gain by the success of this movement and so much to lose by its failure.

This is no task for the timid or the doctrinaire. We must steer a pragmatic middle course between the naïve assumption that the world can be remade overnight and the panicky fear of ideological hobgoblins.

There is no time to waste. As President López Mateos recently said, "At Punta del Este, the door was open to the hopes of the people. A delay or inefficiency in the action agreed upon will produce a bitterness of total despair." This does not overstate the challenge.

Section IV

THE COMMUNIST CHALLENGE

Our diplomacy must be both resolute and profoundly alive to the revolutionary forces in the world which are shaping the future. It must be alert to seize and exploit internal contradictions in the far-flung Communist world. It must avoid the danger of becoming hypnotized into negation by the actions of Communist nations. It must support, to the absolute limit of practicability, the aspirations of all people to be free. Most important of all, it must maintain an attitude which our forefathers in the Declaration of Independence described as a "decent respect for the opinions of mankind."

February 28, 1954

IF MARX COULD RETURN

In 1952 Marxism was a widely accepted economic theory on Indian campuses even among non-Communist university students. To an audience of Indian political science students in New Delhi, in October of that year, Ambassador Bowles traces the basic fallacy in Marx's outdated views as applied to Indian economic and political development.

THE TEACHINGS of Karl Marx must be judged against the background of the times in which he lived and wrote. In 1848, when the *Communist Manifesto* was published, the Industrial Revolution was well under way in Europe, and for the average citizen there the world was a most unhappy one.

There was poverty on every side. Children eight, ten, and twelve years old worked long hours each day in the factories for a few annas a week. The few who were rich were very rich indeed and steadily becoming richer, while the poor saw no hope of relieving their poverty.

A never-ending supply of young peasants poured into the cities searching for jobs, pushing down wages, and thus creating new misery and bitterness. Colonial peoples were ruthlessly exploited and conflicts between the great European nations for raw materials created many tensions.

It was a world in which the few benefited and the many suffered. The art, culture, education which many of us associate with the nineteenth century were available only to a limited minority.

Marx, looking at this predominantly unhappy world of greed and exploitation in the mid-nineteenth century, came to a series of what seemed to him obvious and inevitable conclusions.

He reasoned that the capitalistic system must eventually be destroyed, that the "ruling classes" would be swept from power, and that "the masses" should then organize a "dictatorship of the proletariat." Eventually, according to Marx, this revolutionary government, its task complete, would begin to "wither away," the various classes of society would dissolve, and the peoples of the world could look forward to an expanding frontier of greater freedom and opportunity for all people.

In view of the background of poverty and exploitation against which Karl Marx wrote, these harsh conclusions are understandable. However, if Marx could return to our still imperfect world today, he would be in for some profound surprises.

For instance, Marx could not have visualized the dynamic expansion and industrial development, the steadily growing purchasing power, the steadily increasing opportunities for all people, which have been opened up under our American system of private ownership; or our American system of education which gives a free education to all boys and girls up to eighteen years of age; or our laws that prohibit people from going to work in the factories before they are sixteen; or the inheritance taxes; or old-age pensions starting from sixty-five; or medical insurance, unemployment insurance, public housing and free school lunches for children.

Those are new and truly revolutionary concepts. No one, not even a man of Marx's skill, could possibly have foreseen them. For more than a century a new kind of nonviolent revolution has been taking place in America, and it is still moving forward for the benefit of our people.

Moreover, these great twentieth-century advances were not confined to America. How could Karl Marx have foreseen the cooperatives of Sweden, Finland, Denmark and Norway where great industries are actually owned by the people who buy the products? How could he have foreseen the distributive cooperatives that have lowered still further the cost to the consumer?

How could Marx have foreseen government ownership that worked peacefully side by side and in competition with private ownership? How could he have foreseen a mixing of three different kinds of production economics—cooperative economics, private capital economics, socialist economics—working almost in competition with one another to see which could put out the best goods at the cheapest prices, which would pay labor the highest wages, which could offer people the best kind of future?

How could he have foreseen a labor government in England supporting the public ownership of steel mills and coal mines, but pledged to the maximum practical degree of private ownership?

What would he have thought if he sat in the British House of Commons and watched the members vote for freedom for the 500 million people of India, Pakistan, Burma and Ceylon? How could Marx have foreseen the great bloodless, nonviolent revolution of Gandhi?

And how could he have foreseen that the nations of the world would join together in the United Nations, which in spite of its imperfections has provided the world with its first global forum? How could he have foreseen the World Health Organization, UNESCO, the Food and Agricultural Organization and the Children's Fund?

Karl Marx could not have foreseen these revolutionary developments because he believed that the economic system which seemed so solidly established in the 1850's, and which he so properly criticized, would be unable to cure its ills, and that the world was certain to explode in bloody chaos.

Marx believed in economic inevitability. What he overlooked was the ability of human beings, working through democratic governments, to organize their lives and to control their environment, so that economic forces might be harnessed for the common good.

The theories of Malthus failed to foresee the growth of technology. The theories of Marx ignored the human factors in which Gandhi placed his faith.

What about Karl Marx and the Soviet Union? How would he react to the world Communist movement as it exists today?

I doubt that Karl Marx, newly returned to this earth, could even get through the Iron Curtain. But if he did manage to get visas for the Soviet Union and other satellite countries, he would surely be astonished at what he found there. The Communism which has been ballyhooed to the housetops bears little resemblance to the Communism for which Marx hoped and worked.

The first thing that would strike him would be the utter lack of personal freedom. In line with his writings, he would say, "This Communist Government has been in power for thirty-five years. Certainly by now it should be 'withering away.' The proletariat should be running their own affairs, with fewer and fewer state restrictions and greater freedom for each individual."

As Marx listened to the Voice of Moscow he might be momentarily reassured, for he would hear many familiar phrases. He would hear Soviet leaders prophesy that "capitalism" at long last is about to blow up of its own accord. He would hear that the so-called "capitalist" countries (which in Communist terminology now means any country opposed to Soviet expansion and aggression) will soon destroy themselves in a war which will split the "capitalist world" up the middle. But as Karl Marx studied the hard facts, those old familiar phrases would have a hollow ring.

To be sure, the world is divided as he prophesied it would be. But he would see that the conflict is not between "capitalism" and "Communism," but between those countries which are determined to remain free, regardless of their type of government, and those which seem bent on aggression by force.

In this unhappy modern conflict he would find the democratic socialism of Scandinavia and Britain standing shoulder to shoulder with the democratic private ownership of America and the independent Communist government of Yugoslavia.

Karl Marx would see that in this modern world the old conflict "Capitalism versus Socialism" is a make-believe conflict, and that the real struggle lies between the forces of freedom and independence and the forces of aggression and suppression.

═══ 39

WHAT THE SOVIET UNION FEARS MOST

The Korean War, ending in 1953, left bitter fears of further militant Communist aggression. Speaking at the YMCA in Hartford, Connecticut, in October of that year, Mr. Bowles tries to put such fears in perspective.

LET US consider for a moment, not what *we* Americans fear, but what the leaders of the Soviet Union fear as they consider the revolutionary world in which we are living.

Most of all, I believe, they fear that the democratic nations will provide such successful examples of democracy, and will cope so successfully with the world's problems, that the idea of democracy will become irresistible, even someday within the Soviet Union itself.

They fear that our positive actions will so strengthen the democratic world that internal Communist revolution will become impossible.

They fear that Point Four will be enlarged and boldly applied to the problem of economic development so that American aid will make it possible for free Asian, African and South American nations to develop without the ruthlessness of totalitarianism.

They fear we will give or loan these nations the capital and the technical assistance to succeed in their democratic efforts, instead of waiting until economic collapse has brought on chaos and its cousin, Communism.

They fear we will become acutely aware of the fact that the most crucial competition of Asia is really between Communist China and democratic India, the two poles of the underdeveloped world, and that we may give more effective support to India than Russia gives to China.

They fear we will come to accept and to respect the free Asian countries' determination to have independent foreign policies, not connected with any military alliances. They know that if the West thus respected Asian nationalism, only the Communists could be called the "agents of a foreign power."

They fear we will drop our present sterile "you must be for us or against us approach" which has irritated so many proud and friendly nations, and which runs so counter to the "neutralism" that we insisted on for ourselves for a full century before World War I.

They fear that American foreign policy will begin to champion national freedom and to oppose colonialism in Africa and in the few remaining colonial areas in Asia, so that the Kremlin's exclusive claims to be "anti-imperialist" will thus be exposed.

They fear that America will stop supporting undemocratic and unpopular governments which provide such an easy target for their Communist attacks.

They fear that we will begin to give special support to governments which carry out necessary land and social reforms and establish a fair system of taxation.

They fear we may even require such reforms as a condition to our economic aid, so that the people of the world will see that we are on their side.

They fear that we will support and strengthen the United Nations, not just for the purpose of collective resistance to aggression, but also for the purpose of meeting more of the world's economic problems.

They fear that through our tact and sensitivity we may help the U.N. become a rallying point for the allegiance of democratic peoples.

They fear that here in America we will be able to keep our economy going without a depression.

They fear that by confident new programs of national and international development we will continue to operate at full production and full employment, thus upsetting all their Marxist predictions.

They fear that we will not only continue the progress in racial relations of the last twenty years, but will make dramatic new strides toward full dignity and equality of rights for all our citizens.

They fear that Americans will become united in faith in their own free principles instead of divided by fears of Communists on many school boards and in many neighborhoods.

They fear that we will maintain our civil liberties in full force, even while fighting Communism, so that the democratic way stands proudly as an example to the world.

In short, they fear that the democratic world under the leadership of an awakened America, rededicated to the concepts of Thomas Jefferson, Abraham Lincoln, and Franklin Roosevelt, will undermine Communist hopes for world dominion by ending the conditions that make the spread of Communism possible.

══ 40

THE CRISIS THAT FACES US
WILL NOT WAIT

*In 1955, the shift of Soviet tactics away from open
aggression to the field of economic, political, and ideological
maneuver presented the U.S. with a new crisis and challenge,
which Mr. Bowles describes in this article in the November
27 issue of the* New York Times Magazine.

THE SUMMIT meeting of July, 1955, marked a realistic
agreement that nuclear war under present conditions would almost
certainly destroy both combatants, and hence that this kind of war
had become a practical impossibility. In this sense Geneva was historic. It did *not,* however, indicate that the Soviet Union had abandoned its long-term global objectives.

Khrushchev and Bulganin had previously grasped a point which
the more doctrinaire Stalin had stubbornly ignored: that for world
Communism, military aggression and threat of aggression, against the
background of a military stalemate, had become a dead end.

Even before the summit meeting, and with quickening tempo there-
after, the Soviet leaders boldly accepted the implications of the new
atomic power balance and proceeded to act upon them. In the last
several months they have skillfully switched the emphasis of Soviet
foreign policy into a totally different area of conflict—the field of po-

litical, economic, ideological and diplomatic maneuver.

Meantime, American policy appears committed to tactics which had already proved too narrow during the cold war and which in the new variety of competition seem even more inadequate. Today our policies in much of the world still rest largely on militarily oriented concepts of power. An inflexible diplomacy in many parts of Asia and in Africa still ties us to an outmoded, despised and doomed status quo.

If we should assume that nuclear war is more likely than not, long-range economic, ideological and political factors would be of secondary importance. But if the summit meeting at Geneva means anything, it means that as long as we maintain the present military atomic balance, a world war has been outmoded by the very frightfulness of modern weapons.

If such is the case, a foreign policy that gives almost automatic priority in every strategic or tactical situation to the military factors, and minimizes the political, economic and ideological forces which are now writing history, will almost certainly be inadequate.

Instead of fearing the new Soviet tactics, we should welcome them. Economic development, politics and ideas are part and parcel of our democratic system. Our adversary has shifted the competition to a testing ground where our strength has been proved. We can accept the new challenge with confidence.

To refocus Congressional and public opinion on the vastly broader challenge which now confronts America will call for bolder, more confident leadership and a new sense of enlightened, creative bipartisanship. The steps which will be required in 1956 and after to reverse the present trend may be no less radical and imaginative in concept than the moves which the bipartisan coalition took ten years ago to help keep Europe free.

Simply to list some items on the agenda which must be explored is to suggest the scope of the challenge:

1. A military defense program adequate to cope with whatever military threat may be developed by Moscow.

2. An economic development program substantial enough to do for Asia, Africa and South America what the Marshall Plan did for Europe.

3. The development of a German policy which concentrates on the actual problem: how to negotiate the Red Army back behind its own frontiers.

4. The encouragement of a European community which will create solid economic and political foundations under NATO and exert a steady Western pull on the satellite nations of Eastern Europe.

5. A colonial policy that will win the confidence of the Asian-African majority of mankind by placing us irrevocably on the side of freedom and yet encourage responsible, gradual action on the part of the remaining colonial peoples.

6. A Middle Eastern policy that is adequate for its essential objective: the encouragement of constructive indigenous forces and denial of this crucial area to Soviet penetration.

7. A new effort to achieve a realistic Far Eastern settlement that will assure a free Indochina, at least below the Seventeenth Parallel, a secure, independent Formosa, an economically viable Japan, with the prospect for more normal relations with Communist China.

8. An understanding of the crucial strategic importance of India and Japan in Asia. What India does or fails to do in these next ten years—together with developments in Japan—is likely to determine the future of non-Communist Asia. We must shake off our frustration over Indian neutralism and devise a positive, sophisticated, realistic course of action.

The key items are the first two. We must maintain our military strength but we must also counter the Communist offensives on the far-flung economic and political fronts.

There are some who still argue that we Americans cannot afford to meet the challenge of this new economic, political and ideological competition. The annual cost, no matter what it may be, will be no more than a fraction of the twelve-billion-dollar increase in our gross national income which we are adding in the single year 1955.

It cost America and her allies tens of thousands of lives and more than fifty billion dollars in equipment to keep the Communists out of South Korea. If we stumble now, we may be forced to pay a vastly higher price to keep them out of Europe, the Middle East, South Asia and Africa. The measure of our response should be its adequacy to the new Soviet challenge.

Let it not be said by future historians that in the second decade after World War II freedom throughout the world under the leadership of the United States died of a balanced budget.

▭ 41

A CONTEST WE CANNOT LOSE

On a visit to the Soviet Union in 1957, Mr. Bowles was
impressed by the eagerness of Russian young people to learn
more about America. One result was this protest against the then
current policy of stifling U.S.-Soviet cultural exchanges. From
the Saturday Review, *August 24, 1957.*

ON A recent trip to the U.S.S.R. I saw many signs of ferment
among Soviet youth. There was nothing that would indicate any
possibility of an effective rebellion against the system, but much that
suggested a softening of hard lines, a questioning of old dogma. Everywhere curious, friendly young people greeted us with warmth and
with questions.

The most disturbing question I came home with was whether we
are making good use of this tentative open-door policy of the post-
Stalin regime, or, more broadly, are we doing our part to encourage
the process of change and ferment which is certainly under way
throughout the Communist world?

In the U.S.S.R. I had heard much discussion of the forthcoming
Sixth World Youth Festival in Moscow to which thousands of young
people from all over the world had been invited. After my return to
this country in March I heard that several groups of particularly able
young students, sensing the opportunity to present their deeply demo-

cratic American views at this year's Festival, were tentatively planning to attend. Unhappily, they have been officially discouraged from doing so.

The timid position of our government was expressed in letters sent to all who inquired in the following terms: Your government will not deny you a passport, but this affair has been arranged by the Soviet Government for its own political purposes, and those Americans who attend will be furthering Communist ends.

As a result, the American delegation has been reduced to less than one hundred. Several of them are able, democratic spokesmen, capable of holding up their side in any argument. But most of those who are still planning to go are either politically naïve or out-and-out fellow travelers. With a handful of exceptions the young men and women who could have represented the American democratic view most competently were frightened by official disfavor into discreetly staying away.

Early reports of the Festival indicate that because of our timidity an unusual opportunity has been missed for the kind of person-to-person contacts in which young Americans are at their best. The total attendance was close to 220,000 young men and women from 102 countries. And the situation appears to have been made to order for articulate young Americans who understand the meaning of freedom.

In its most recent issue *Life* Magazine reported that: "The easy camaraderie permitted for the Festival left Russians breathless with a taste of forgotten freedom." Observing the easy social contacts and free-swinging political arguments, correspondent Flora Lewis was reminded that "smothered sparks of unrest began exploding in the Communist world" following the Warsaw Festival of 1955. In Moscow a Pole remarked to her, "I wonder if Khrushchev realizes what he is risking?"

This is by no means the only situation in which we have drawn back from the person-to-person contacts in which a free people is at its best. While I was in Moscow an international hockey competition was in progress. An American team had been invited, but had backed out at the last minute. "Why did your team decide not to come?" Soviet students at the University of Moscow asked me. "Was it because we beat you at the Olympics?"

I repeated as persuasively as I could what I had been told was our official explanation, i.e., that after the eruption in Hungary in October,

1956, we were calling off cultural exchanges with the Soviet Union in protest.

"In protest of what?" the Russian asked. At least this gave me an opportunity to present a view of the Hungarian Revolution which they had not yet heard. But such reverse-Iron Curtain "protests" are, to say the least, self-defeating.

If a protest is to be effective, those to whom the protest is directed should be aware of it. And the best way for Russians to understand what Americans think is to meet and talk to Americans—the very "cultural contact" which we have been timidly restricting.

Why not seize every reasonable opportunity to foster the awakening of Soviet young people which every qualified observer agrees is now in progress? What precisely is our government so afraid of?

Khrushchev's recent statements offer no hope that the Soviet Government is planning to relax its political position in the near future. But at least there has been a partial lifting of the Iron Curtain.

At the University of Moscow I was shown the student newspaper, which currently featured a letter from students at the University of Indiana proposing some kind of an exchange of information and students. The Russians were excited by the prospect.

American jazz tunes are played frequently on the university radio station. Indeed, Louis Armstrong's version of "Love, Oh, Love, Oh, Careless Love" was on the air when we visited the broadcasting room. When the students learned we had with us recent copies of the European edition of the *New York Times,* they begged to see them.

Everywhere I was deluged with questions about my own three college-age children. "What are they studying?" "What will they do when they graduate?" And over and over again: "Do they think that there will be peace?" Yet we seem to be holding back from the people-to-people contacts which should be our greatest strength with Russians of all ages.

Some months ago I was told that the Russians had agreed to let a group of enterprising American private citizens put on an agricultural fair in Moscow. We could have the choice of fairgrounds, present any exhibits we wanted and charge enough to make the show self-supporting. But our timid officials first took the project out of private American hands, and then quietly dropped it altogether.

What in the world are we Americans afraid of? How can we possibly lose in an open, free-wheeling competition between Communist ideas and our own? Certainly we cannot fear that Americans brought up in the tradition of freedom will come off second best in their contacts with Russians who have known only their own stagnant and discredited ideology.

After seeing the grim Soviet system at work and hearing the numbing, stilted, doctrinaire phrases which are so obviously boring this new generation of Soviet young people, I predict the opposite.

Why not ask the Kremlin to pick five hundred of its most trusted students to come to America, while we pick five hundred to go to the Soviet Union? The result could only be profoundly subversive of Communist dogma.

The Soviet students would return with their eyes opened to the dishonesty of their government's propaganda and new respect for the dynamic power of free institutions. The American students would undoubtedly develop human sympathy and personal liking for the Russian people. But this would be accompanied by an even keener awareness of how unpleasant life can be under an authoritarian government and an increased appreciation of our own accomplishments and our limitless democratic potential.

The Kremlin would not accept such a proposition. I am sure of that. But why shouldn't we propose it and thereby demonstrate to the world our faith in the vigor and persuasiveness of democratic ideas presented by American young people?

The Kremlin stills calls loudly over the Voice of Moscow for greater cultural contacts. Hasn't the time come to accept the challenge?

42

A CLOSE LOOK AT MAINLAND CHINA

China's uphill battle to increase food production under the commune system was beginning to run into trouble in 1959. In this article in the Saturday Evening Post *(April 4, 1959) Mr. Bowles considers the long-run dangers and significance of this struggle to feed China's millions.*

CAN COMMUNIST economics, which forced Russia into a modern industrial state in two generations, succeed in Asia, or do the totally different conditions which exist there doom Asian Communism to failure?

This question deserves urgent and thoughtful consideration by American policy-makers of both parties. On their answers may depend in large measure the nature of tomorrow's world.

The Chinese Communists face appalling problems which are now testing their political and economic theories under the most difficult conceivable conditions.

If the Peking Government goes through with its present plan for rapid industrialization on the Soviet model, it may place an impossible burden on the rural Chinese economy, which must feed 650 million people and provide "surplus" agricultural products to help pay for critically needed imports.

If it seeks to encourage increased food production by appeasing the peasants, it will almost certainly be forced to abandon its Communist political objectives. This, in a nutshell, is Peking's ultimate dilemma.

The system of pulling a whole nation up by its bootstraps, which worked in Russia at such heavy cost, may fail in China because the conditions there are almost totally different. The most important of these differences relate to land, food and people.

The Soviet Union sprawls for nearly ten thousand miles across two continents. Like our American West, the vast, rich expanse beyond the Urals was opened up only in the last two hundred years. It is still largely underdeveloped.

Before the coming of the Communists the Russian people had rarely known hunger. Indeed, before the outbreak of World War I czarist Russia exported some ten million tons of wheat each year.

Yet even with this massive, built-in agricultural advantage, the Soviet experiment nearly collapsed during the 1930's for lack of food. Speedy industrialization of the Soviet Union, Stalin saw, would require the diversion of enormous quantities of food to the cities to feed the growing industrial population.

Boldly scrapping Lenin's promises of independent landownership and increasing opportunity for each peasant family, Stalin moved to mobilize all of rural Russia along tightly regimented political lines.

For more than twenty years the Russian peasants were badgered and terrorized to increase their production. By setting low prices on agricultural products at the farm and charging high prices in the government-owned retail stores, huge profits were extracted from the peasants to produce more and still more capital for the rapid growth of industry.

Only a very small investment was made in rural development, and consumer goods were almost nonexistent. The Soviet Union lived precariously on its built-in food surplus, created not by Communism but by nature.

In long-term results, however, this fantastic gamble paid off. Although the cost in human misery was staggering, Stalin's determination and the limitless potential of the Russian land enabled the Soviet Government to create a powerful industrial state in less than two generations.

Now it is this Stalinist program that the Peking Government adopted as a blueprint for China's development. In doing so, under the infinitely more difficult Chinese conditions, it embarked on what is by all odds the most daring economic and political gamble of all time.

Mao, like Lenin, had based his revolution on the most dramatic promise that can be offered to any peasant people: "Down with the landlords. Land to the tiller." But when the time was ripe, Mao, like Stalin, did not hesitate to repudiate this promise and to press China's peasants into an economic and political system that had no place for private landownership.

By 1957 practically all Chinese rural families had been organized into 740,000 collectives. Then in 1958 Mao, as we have seen, went one giant step further. Henceforth all farm collectives, rural industry and local militia would be consolidated into communes. This was a step so breath-takingly radical and ruthless that even Stalin had not dared to attempt it.

Although it is now clear that the Peking Government has run into difficulty, it would be wishful thinking to assume that a change of direction is in the making. The goals of the commune program have been steadily re-emphasized.

The leaders of Communist China know that the success or failure of their efforts will be determined largely in the villages. Although the difficulties are admittedly great, they may argue persuasively that here at least they are far more experienced than were their Soviet counterparts.

The Russian Revolution was made by only 200,000 party members. They were mostly intellectuals and workers with their roots in the cities. Lenin's announcement of "all land to the tiller," skillfully timed to climax the revolutionary upheaval in Moscow and Leningrad, secured the cooperation of the Russian peasants. But they were never made to feel a part of the movement itself.

The Chinese Revolution, on the other hand, has always been deeply rooted in the villages. The five million party members who organized the countryside as a prelude to the advance of the Red Armies have now grown to thirteen million and most of them are of peasant stock. Under the direction of this rural-oriented Communist leadership and subleadership, many of China's one million villages have already known two decades of evolving discipline.

With these techniques the Communist leaders believe they can maintain a revolutionary enthusiasm which will carry China through this perilous period of development and create the capital for rapid industrialization.

In place of the uncertain but highly personal security rooted in close family relationships and ancient religious dogma, they have substituted a system that provides a dreary day-to-day sustenance in return for unswerving subservience to the will of the central government.

In place of the traditional economic incentive of increased consumer goods, they have substituted festivals, complete with booming brass gongs and sputtering firecrackers, dances, parades and mass condemnation of "enemies of the people."

Millions of official loudspeakers, supplemented by constant "study meetings," goad the people to greater effort, often by fanning the flames of external conflict. In this process the United States serves as a special target for vituperation unmatched even in this age of international mud-slinging.

But even with the near-total mobilization of human energies and the most favorable weather, food production in China, as elsewhere, faces certain harsh realities which cannot be exorcised by Communist slogans. The chief obstacle to the success of her effort is China's vast population, growing at the rate of sixteen million souls each year and crowded into her enormous but limited land area.

The present average is less than two acres for each rural family. With the exception of a few western areas, most of China's readily arable land is now under intensive cultivation. New acreage even there can be brought under cultivation only at a very high cost.

The fact that the people are already living largely on rice, wheat and vegetables means that there is little grain to be saved by reducing livestock consumption, as Stalin did. Furthermore, output per acre is already high. Long before China succumbed to Communism, the peasants were using better seeds, more abundant natural fertilizers and more skilled planting and harvesting techniques than in almost any other underdeveloped country.

Although Japanese output per acre has been almost twice as great, these levels appear beyond China's reach in the foreseeable future.

These, then, are the harsh social and economic realities of China's rural economy which must be considered side by side with Peking's boasts of a rapidly developing industrial base.

43

THE "CHINA PROBLEM" RECONSIDERED

*In this major analysis of the problem of China, and of
American policy in relation to both Formosa and the mainland,
published in the April, 1960, issue of* Foreign Affairs, Mr.
Bowles *suggests the guidelines for an effective new U.S.
position. These views have been strongly attacked by both
Mao Tse-tung in Peiping and the Nationalists in Taiwan.*

HAS THE time not come to face the fundamental realities of
our "China problem"? Until we do, we shall continue to be severely
hampered in our relations with all of Asia.

Under present conditions, debate over recognition of Communist
China by the United States echoes down a dead-end street. If we
should propose an exchange of ambassadors, Mao Tse-tung would
surely ask if our recognition extended to Communist sovereignty over
"the Province of Formosa." And when we replied that it did not, his
response would inevitably be a contemptuous refusal of our offer. A
similar outcome can be predicted if we proposed that "both Chinas"
be admitted to the United Nations. Chiang Kai-shek would also reject
such a proposal. The stalemate would persist.

This means that the two primary questions which have caused such
deep discord here in America are not at the moment solvable. At some
later stage we may find it useful to test the peaceful intentions of the

Chinese Communists by proposing that both sides accept a situation which neither we nor they can alter short of war. But until then, let us by-pass the question of formal relationships and focus on the immediate and, perhaps, obtainable.

If there were no other reason to seek a fresh perspective on Communist China, the crucial issue of disarmament would in itself be enough. For it is clear beyond doubt that no disarmament plan can have meaning without her participation. She possesses, not only the world's largest army, but a potential capacity for the production of nuclear weapons. Nor is there any reason to believe that we can hold the Soviet Union accountable for Peking on this matter. Either we must give up any thought of reaching an agreement on a safeguarded system of major world-wide disarmament or search for ways to influence the course of events in the China theater.

While we may be almost totally unable to affect short-term developments in Communist China, our capacity to influence other aspects of the China problem is greater than we seem to realize.

Formosa (Taiwan) offers a case in point. The island is rich and its economic development has been spectacular; yet its political position remains precarious, not only in regard to mainland China, but also in its relations with the whole arc of free Asia from India to Japan.

This is so because Formosa's political status is founded on a myth that Chiang Kai-shek, who was driven from the mainland eleven years ago, remains the ruler of 650 million Chinese. This myth—rejected by most Asians, by our NATO allies, by our closest friends the Canadians, and by a large number of Americans—is supported only by three or four Asian governments under heavy pressure from Washington, by our Department of State and by some members of Congress. Perpetuation of the myth will increasingly isolate Formosa at a time when its leaders should be striving in every way to identify their future with the mainstream of thought and action in free, non-Communist Asia.

Americans and Nationalist Chinese alike should strive to find a common ground with their allies and friends, and to relate their policies more rationally to the forces which will shape events in Asia during the next decade. Such policies, I believe, may be based on the following assumptions:

1. That the Peking Government, although beset with difficulties, is in firm control of mainland China.

2. That mainland China, with an inadequate resource base, spiral-

ing population, ruthless Communist leadership and intense nationalist spirit, will develop fiercely expansionist tendencies directed toward the weaker neighboring states to the south.

3. That a primary aim of American policy should be to prevent the armed expansion into Southeast Asia which Chinese Communist leaders may be tempted to undertake.

4. That any effective disarmament program will ultimately require Peking's participation.

5. That in the present circumstances no negotiation of our major differences with the Peking Government seems likely to be productive.

6. That the eight million Formosans and the two million mainland Chinese on Formosa have the right to a secure, independent existence and to cultural development outside the Communist orbit; and that such an evolution on Formosa is in the interests of the American people.

7. That for the time being Formosa's independence will continue to depend on American military guarantees and economic assistance.

8. That in the long run the security and prosperity of the people of Formosa will depend on the orderly political growth of the non-Communist nations of Asia, particularly India and Japan, and on their attitudes toward the Formosa Government.

9. That if ever it becomes practicable it will be in our national interest to restore our traditionally friendly ties with the Chinese people on the mainland.

Let us now examine, within the framework of these assumptions, the realities with which American policy must grapple.

*   *   *

TODAY political power in Formosa rests exclusively with the Generalissimo's authoritarian Nationalist Government. The two million mainlanders who fled with Chiang across the Formosa Straits in 1949 provide most of the central government's staff and account for two-thirds of his army of nearly 600,000 men. For a decade, American policy in regard to Formosa has largely focused on this Nationalist Chinese ruling minority. Yet in the long run it is the eight million native Formosans who will shape the island's fate. We hear very little about their wishes, hopes and fears. One of them, writing in *Foreign Affairs* recently, noted that there are no independent Formosan newspapers and no recognized Formosan political parties.*

For nearly two generations before 1945, Formosans knew only Japanese rule. Although most of them speak the Fukien dialect of southeast China, they were educated in Japanese schools. Because the island prospered, many of them had come to feel closer to Tokyo than to the mainland. But fifteen years of Nationalist rule has brought significant changes. Time, proximity and education are creating, among the younger groups in particular, a gradual amalgamation of the island's Chinese and Formosan communities. There may slowly be emerging a new national identity, predominantly Chinese by culture but Formosan in outlook.

Since 1949 the Nationalist Government has taken a series of constructive steps which it failed to take while it was on the mainland. Among the most important is its recognition of the decisive importance of the villagers who, as in all Asian nations, not only constitute the majority, but also control the food supply and hence provide the economic and political key to orderly growth.

Under Chiang's direction, a reform program which limits landownership to ten acres and substantially reduces rentals has been combined with a competent rural extension service, easy credit and an expanded fertilizer industry. The result has been a sharp increase in the output of rice and cotton per acre and an easier and more prosperous life for the peasants. Formosan living standards are now the second highest in Asia, surpassed only by Japan.

The internal political situation has also improved. To be sure, the national government is still run almost entirely by mainlanders. The Assembly has 1,576 members, of whom only 26 are Formosans. Yet there has been some progress toward democratic participation by Formosans. In the provincial assemblies and county administrations, for instance, the islanders hold large majorities through reasonably free elections. The mayors of most towns are also native Formosans.

For over thirty years, in victory and defeat, the Generalissimo has almost singlehandedly held the Kuomintang together. But he cannot rule forever; Formosa's future depends on the stability of the government which will survive his passing from the scene.

---

* Li Thian-hok, "The China Impasse: A Formosan View," *Foreign Affairs*, April, 1958.

As long as the United States maintains adequate sea and air power in East Asia, and the will to use it, there is only one way in which Mao Tse-tung can establish his sovereignty over Formosa and that is by a *coup d'état* which would depose Chiang or his successor and place in power a new island government prepared to come to terms with Peking.

On the mainland powerful totalitarian forces are reshaping Chinese society, remolding Chinese thought and rewriting Chinese history within the constricting framework of the Lenin-Stalin-Mao ideology.

An independent Sino-Formosan nation can offer the contrast of a modernized non-Communist Chinese society, free from mass regimentation, with an increasing measure of political liberty and with expanding economic opportunities for all citizens. In building such a society the younger generation of Taiwanese and Chinese can find a common sense of purpose and at the same time supply a cultural base for the thirteen million overseas Chinese.

* * *

HOW CAN we adjust our policy to foster such a development?

Let us accept the fact that Formosa's adoption of an affirmative new role in non-Communist Asia cannot be stage-managed by American policy-makers, however well supplied with goodwill and dollars. Nor can it be arbitrarily imposed on the Formosan majority by the Nationalist refugees from the mainland. Our role must be that of a genuine friend. The native Formosans, the Nationalist Chinese and the world generally must be convinced that our objective is not to create a military base for the invasion of the mainland, but to encourage the orderly growth of a new, independent nation.

In their present status they serve only to keep alive the myth that a Nationalist invasion of the mainland is imminent and thereby give Peking a handy excuse for "counter" hostilities. On the one hand, we should encourage the neutralization of the offshore islands immediately adjacent to the Chinese coast.

On the other hand, our assurance that we will offer all-out military opposition to a Communist attack on Formosa itself should be substantially strengthened and extended to include any measures necessary to deter a *coup d'état.* In the event of such a *coup,* we should institute an economic and naval blockade to deny the Peking Government effective occupation.

It might well take some time for Formosa's position in the United Nations as an independent nation to become accepted. Once this happened, its security would be backed by the organization's full guarantees. In the meantime, our unilateral military commitment to defend the island must be unequivocal. We can no more abandon the people of Formosa than we can those of West Berlin.

American policy and American funds should also be directed toward the development of Formosa as a cultural center for non-Communist Chinese everywhere. Substantially increased assistance to Formosan colleges from public and private American sources can be an important first step in that direction. Scholarships for overseas Chinese to study on Formosa as well as scholarships for both Chinese and Formosans to study in the United States should also be increased.

Similarly, more fellowships to enable talented American students to follow Chinese studies in Formosan institutions would help create the basis for a new partnership. Despite our long association with the Chinese, too many Americans are ignorant of their history and culture.

Finally, every effort should be made to persuade the Nationalist Government to adopt a more realistic approach to their non-Communist fellow Asians. Formosa's future as an independent nation is tied to the future of free Asia and particularly to those two great geographic and political anchors, India and Japan.

* * *

NOW WHAT of "the other China," the giant on the mainland? Here our field for creative action is inevitably restricted.

The Chinese Communist Government today is embarked upon a gigantic effort to industrialize its 650 million people on a resource base which is woefully inadequate. There seem to be three possible results of this experiment.

The Chinese Communists may be impelled by the harsh economic limitations of their position to modify their policies gradually, reduce their objectives and seek to relieve their food and other shortages through peaceful foreign trade. In view of their intense, deeply rooted and doctrinaire Communist nationalism, this development appears unlikely in the foreseeable future.

A second possibility is that they will seek to resettle part of their swelling population in the vast expanses of the Soviet Union bordering on China. But a large-scale development of these inner Asian regions of severe and uncertain climate would not be easy, and it is hard to imagine the conditions under which the Soviet Union would accept a great influx of Chinese settlers.

The third possibility is expansion into Southeast Asia, with its wealth of underpopulated, food-rich countryside, as well as the great reserves of oil, tin, rubber and other resources which China badly needs. Our objective must be to create a military, political and economic barrier sufficient to discourage any such attempt.

For us to indulge in threats of atomic war would merely frighten the non-Communist Asian nations and further feed the fires of aggressive Chinese nationalism. It is vital, however, that we make clear, in temperate language and through diplomatic channels, our total commitment to defend Southeast Asia against Chinese attack. And unlike an attack on Formosa, a Chinese thrust southward would also bring into play the existing guarantees in the United Nations Charter.

Ultimately, however, the fate of the non-Communist nations of South and Southeast Asia will be determined by two factors which we can influence only indirectly: by their own economic and political stability and their willingness to oppose any infringement on their sovereignty; and second, by the willingness of the two principal nations of the region, India and Pakistan, to add their weight more and more to the balance against Chinese aggression.

By wise and sensitive diplomacy we can contribute to this development. In the military sense, our role should be one of quiet readiness for any emergency, much as the British Fleet gave meaning to the Monroe Doctrine during our neutralist nineteenth century. Our direct economic assistance should give the highest priority to those nations which are willing and competent to help themselves and to devise programs to stabilize raw material prices at levels fair to the producers.

We undoubtedly have the strength to play our proper role in Asia; the question is whether we have the necessary tact, subtlety and flexibility. Let us, to begin with, put aside some of our own doctrinaire preconceptions and examine realistically the complex nature of the Sino-Soviet relationship.

Deep *potential* differences exist between Chinese and Russian Communism as a result of the radically different cultures, experiences and leaderships in the two countries. These are magnified by the fact that the two societies are at different stages of development—the one industrialized, with rich resources and an abundance of land; the other with a shortage in agriculture, inadequate resources and a burgeoning population.

No outsider can be sure of the present nature of future development of the Sino-Soviet alliance, but certainly it is an infinitely complex and delicate arrangement. The assumption that it is rigid, monolithic and unchangeable is out of date.

In view of this, recent efforts of State Department spokesmen to score debaters' points by depicting Mr. Khrushchev as "leader of the world Communist movement" and twitting him for not "keeping China in line" are naïve and self-defeating. Let us realize that Communist alliances as well as Communist nations are subject to the eroding effects of economics, nationalism and history.

Between 1919 and 1933 the United States had no diplomatic relations with the Soviet Union. Yet during that period thousands of Americans traveled in Russia and thereby increased both our knowledge of developments there and the Russian people's awareness and understanding of us. It seems to me that today we should be striving by all reasonable means to establish people-to-people contacts with mainland China. It may be useful as a first step to offer a fresh approach to the exchange of correspondents with Red China. We are badly in need of the facts and perspective that able American reporters can give us, and we have no reason to be embarrassed by what Chinese journalists may see in America.

Such a two-way exchange has been obstructed so far both by Peking and by our own government. It would be wishful thinking, of course, to assume that our attempts to reopen communications with the people of China will be welcomed by Peking.

In many ways, the Communists serve their own interests best by keeping us their Public Enemy. It is up to us, however, to remove all technical obstacles to the travel of correspondents still existing on our side so that responsibility for the continuing communications barrier will clearly rest with Peking.

But the freer flow of news is only the beginning. Educators, politicians, businessmen—all the many Americans who could profit by a firsthand understanding of the Chinese Revolution and who could transmit their understanding to the rest of us—should be allowed, in fact, encouraged by our government to visit China.

* * *

I N THE long perspective it seems clear that China's only practical alternative to an effort to seize the material and land resources of Southeast Asia by force is to embark on a greatly expanded trade program. Since world peace will depend on which road China ultimately chooses, this question deserves the most urgent attention of American policy-makers.

Only when we start to move off dead center in East Asia, beginning with the creation and implementation of imaginative policies based on the reality of two Chinas, will we start to exert a constructive influence on the shape of events to come. And as we do so, is it too much to hope that the sheer magnitude of the war danger in East Asia may gradually bring a degree of at least tacit cooperation between the United States and the Soviet Union in that area? Despite our profound ideological and political differences and aims, we seem to have a common interest in the development of a less precarious military, economic and political balance of power in Asia.

Nationalist extremists on Formosa will not be happy about the policies which I have suggested, and the Communists in Peking will denounce them violently. The patriotic but quite unrealistic Formosan Nationalists who demand that we push Chiang aside and help them to set up their own government will reject them also.

At this point, our policy should be directed toward proving these things to the Chinese Communist leaders:

1. We will oppose by all necessary means any movement of theirs into Southeast Asia.

2. We will not allow them to overrun Formosa either by direct attack or by subversion.

3. Our military installations on Formosa are not designed to aid or abet a Nationalist attack against the mainland.

4. Formosa is to remain a free entity and all its people should eventually be consulted as to its form of government.

If we adopt these objectives, it is possible that as the prosperity and stability of Formosa become evident the Peking Government may grudgingly come to accept the island's independence as one of the facts of life in non-Communist Asia.

═══ 44

WHY THE KREMLIN WILL NOT DISARM

In the New York Times Magazine *of April 19, 1959, Mr.
Bowles analyzes why the Soviets are reluctant to negotiate
an arms control agreement—and outlines his proposals for
an effective American position.*

DISCOURAGED and facing an apparent impasse, the world
wonders whether anything effective can still be done to escape from the
vicious circle of the arms race. On its face, the Soviet position suggests
that the Russian leaders do not want a workable agreement on arms
control.

Why do they not press for a sweeping disarmament program? There
are two potent reasons why they *should* do so: First, the Soviet Union
could divert military expenditures to consumer production with immediate advantage at home and abroad. Second, according to Kremlin
dogma, the capitalist West is largely dependent on its armament industries for continued prosperity.

As for the first reason, something like 22 percent of the Soviet
Union's productive energies is now allocated to the military. With a
gross national product of about $190 billion this is equivalent to some
$40 billion annually. A general disarmament agreement would enable
the Kremlin planners to divert most of this vast sum to other activities
that would enormously strengthen the Soviet position.

Inside the Soviet Union massive attacks could be launched on the grave housing shortage. Within ten or fifteen years urban and rural slums could be wiped out in much of the country. The production of Soviet Union automobiles and other consumer goods could be expanded rapidly.

Simultaneously, the Kremlin could launch a heavily subsidized export offensive to undercut the trading position of the capitalist powers in the underdeveloped continents and, indeed, in Europe itself. Typewriters, automobiles, trucks and other equipment could be priced to undersell American, British, French and German goods by 30, 40 and 50 percent. Communism, Mr. Khrushchev never ceases to tell us, would surely win any head-on test in peaceful competition.

As for the second reason for Russia to press for disarmament, the Communists assert that as American armament industries closed down, rapidly spreading depression would lead to bankruptcies, privation and bitter political differences which would hasten the collapse of capitalism and the coming of the Communist triumph.

Although this Marxist analysis greatly overstates our problem, even the most confirmed of us capitalists must agree that a major reduction in armament spending would create substantial difficulties for American industry.

True, if Congress cut taxes drastically, billions of dollars could be diverted from government armament purchases to family purchases or for job-creating expansion. Substantial sums could also be appropriated to meet the needs of the neglected areas of domestic national interest—housing, roads, urban renewal, hospitals, schools and many others. In addition, we could sharply expand our now inadequate economic aid programs to Asia, Africa and Latin America and thereby lay the basis for an expanding export trade.

Yet many months of difficult adjustment would have to pass before the effect of such measures was felt. In the meantime, our Soviet competitors, with the speed available only to a totalitarian system, would be opening up new markets, pushing us out of old ones and impressing millions of visitors from all over the world with the physical accomplishments of Communism.

On both these counts then, the Soviet Union appears to have every reason to work for a broad disarmament pact. The Russian leaders have issued broadsides, waved banners and released peace doves. Yet, on the negotiating level, they have failed consistently to come up with positive, workable proposals. Why?

The first answer is given by a group of Western observers, consisting largely of professional military men (but by no means representing a cross-section of military opinion), that takes a cataclysmic view of the future. This argument holds that the Soviet refusal to come to grips with the disarmament issue is proof that the single, unalterable objective of the Soviet Union is to dominate the world by force.

At the other extreme lies a second group that gives a different answer. Sensitive to our genuine shortcomings, idealistic to the point of being utopian, these people expect the best from all mankind, even from those who set Soviet policy. The Kremlin has not accepted disarmament, they hold, because we have not tried hard enough.

I suspect, however, that the real explanation is far more complicated. I am convinced that an explanation of present Soviet behavior must also include these factors:

1. A genuine fear among the Soviet leaders of the very forces which they themselves have brought into being: a resurgent, armed Germany, NATO and the world-wide American nuclear-base system.

2. Their 650 million dynamic, land-hungry Chinese neighbors, who seem likely sooner or later to bid for leadership of the Communist movement.

3. The extent to which the Soviet leaders themselves are victims of the Russian tradition of secrecy, and the relative advantages secrecy genuinely gives them in an armaments race with our more open society.

4. Policy hesitations and conflicting pressures—differences, for instance, within the Communist party and between it and the armed forces—which may limit the Kremlin's freedom of action as similar differences limit our own government's.

Finally, I would add my personal guess that one of the primary factors that may be causing the Kremlin second thoughts about disarmament can be summed up in the one word "Hungary." Following the relaxation in tensions after the Big Four meeting in Geneva in 1955, a sense of possibility spread throughout the Communist empire, erupting in the upheaval in Poland and the revolt in Hungary.

For the Soviet leaders, therefore, any genuine moderation of the cold war must be a terrifying thing, something that any totalitarian state would approach with supreme hesitation, for it would mean the abandonment of the unifying fears that have helped to hold the Soviet Union together.

Under the circumstances, what ought we to do? The answer is difficult. Since our estimates of Soviet intentions can be based only on guesswork, we must be prepared for any eventuality. To accomplish this, it seems to me, our policy must be threefold:

1. We must prepare for the worst. Those grim observers who assert that Soviet reluctance seriously to consider disarmament is proof that the Kremlin plans a war at a time and place of its own choosing may, in fact, be correct. We cannot afford to take chances.

2. At the same time, we should demonstrate convincingly to the world that a step-up in our military programming is no more than a logical response to an impasse created by the Kremlin and that we are genuinely willing and anxious to negotiate large-scale disarmament.

If our present government has a clear, dependable, negotiable policy in regard to such disarmament, no one knows what it is. The fact that the Soviet Union is unlikely to meet us halfway does not excuse our own failure to think through the admittedly difficult requirements and to develop a realistic, balanced peace program that we can press steadily and constructively before the world.

3. Finally, we must prepare for the best—the possibility of eventual Russian willingness to disarm.

This will call for a frank appraisal of the effect that any relaxation of the armament race might have on our own economy. Such a survey might be undertaken by the Joint Economic Committee of the Congress, or by an agency or committee expressly set up for the purpose. Teams of economic experts might be drawn from industry, the labor movement and our universities.

The study should consider, region by region, the extent of unemployment that would result from a cut in arms production, the nature and magnitude of corporate tax reduction that would be made possible, and the anticipated impact of these tax reductions on corporate investment and consumer buying.

It should explore the extent to which expanded urban development, housing, hospital, school and road-building programs and overseas investment programs could take up the slack, and the amount and type of unemployment compensation that would be required for the transition period.

Many Americans will recoil in dismay from an open discussion of the economic consequences of disarmament. But, Karl Marx to the contrary, I believe that their fears are grossly inflated.

In 1945, as a member of the War Production Board, I participated in planning our economic transition from war to peace. In a year and a half we successfully converted almost half of our industry from a wartime to a peace-time footing without a major depression and without serious unemployment, despite the sudden entrance of ten million veterans into the job arena.

Should a similar situation arise today, I have no doubt that we would be equally successful. A far smaller proportion of our total effort is devoted to armaments, and we have a tremendous backlog of needs in health, education, foreign aid and other fields to take up the slack.

To what extent, if at all, the Kremlin would be swayed by a new American initiative and a comprehensive American peace policy that considered the military, political and economic aspects no man can say. But this is a fast-moving age, and one of infinite possibilities. Changes within the Soviet Union have been considerable since Stalin's death.

At best, policy-making in our revolutionary century involves a delicate balancing of risks. Although there is no sure, no safe course, the policy of doing nothing as the arms race mounts in intensity may be the most dangerous of all. The creation of a sound, practical, imaginative American position on which we are prepared to stand is a national responsibility we cannot ignore or postpone.

45

DEFENSE, DISARMAMENT AND PEACE

*Mr. Bowles reviews the galloping new military technology
and the resulting explosive conflict between adequate armament
and a genuine effort at disarmament; he calls for a new attempt
to develop coordinated policies for both. From an address
before the Modern Forum in Los Angeles, March, 1960.*

THE WORLD today continues to spend over $100 billion a
year on arms. What is more, we do so with frighteningly inconclusive
results. The leading strategists of the very nations most involved in the
arms race are precisely those who are most preoccupied with spending
more.

As the arms race deepens, the intellectual and moral appreciation
of the urgency of disarmament deepens, too. But it has an inconclusive
air about it, and for practical purposes it is readily displaced by
the equally demonstrable necessity to regain a more stable and acceptable
defense posture.

For a host of understandable reasons, most men of affairs in Washington
and Moscow remain preoccupied with the challenge of armament,
not disarmament. On occasion they console themselves with the
sophisticated half-truth that more armaments will help promote disarmament
because, as Churchill once said, "We arm to parley."

But the side effects of the arms race are by no means all so positive.
It might seem absurd to keep telling ourselves that the best way

to promote peace is to speed up the arms race if the alternative—refusing to maintain effective deterrent strength against growing Soviet military capability—were not even more absurd.

Clearly peace is no longer—if it ever was—a simple, one-directional, pastoral proposition. It is an incredible maze of moral, military, economic and technological problems.

Today many of our most intelligent observers shrug their shoulders and conclude that it is impossible to bring any kind of ordered policy out of this chaos.

These pessimists may be wrong today. But if the increasing complexity of all these factors continues unabated, they will be right tomorrow. Year by year the problems of peace become inherently more difficult. This is especially true of the interlocking problems of defense and disarmament. The longer we let the problems grow, the less controllable they become. How, we may ask, can we get our bearings? Where can we take hold of the problem?

As the former AEC Commissioner, Thomas E. Murray, says: "Nuclear energy has to a certain extent developed according to a dialectic of its own. . . . Initially we were afraid to think of the ultimate consequences of integrating this boundless energy into a military strategy which already viewed the destruction of civilian populations as a normal objective of modern warfare. But we went ahead and integrated it anyway. In a fit of absent-mindedness we have allowed military technology to shape our strategic policy. . . . We have become caught in the grip of a technological runaway."

Khrushchev's speech before the Supreme Soviet on January 14, 1960, shows that the Pied Piper of technology has been sweeping everything before it in Russia, too. The character and speed of delivery of nuclear weapons now make it inevitable that technology on one side of the cold war will be challenged to work overtime and at forced draft to outwit technology on the other side. The premium is growing steadily on seizing a temporary advantage to forestall a new technological breakthrough from a probable opponent. The outlook is for an endless series of attempts to unbalance new temporary balances, with over-all costs in money and danger projecting upward geometrically.

Accompanying this trend is the growing gap between the rewards of offense and the penalties of defense. The disparity between the two has already become so great that perfectly sane and sober Soviet strategists may soon feel that a surprise nuclear attack on the United States would be a rational Soviet policy.

The perilous elements of surprise, speed, miscalculation and accident are inherent in the weapons technology of the decade we are entering. And if these factors were not enough, we can now add the deadly new picture of our cold war strategists psychoanalyzing one another's intentions across the Iron Curtain. It is hard to imagine a greater new element of instability.

Day after day the resources, energies, manpower and brainpower of this generation of Americans are increasingly concentrating on the prospects of bare survival against a cataclysmic, half-hour, nuclear holocaust. The displacement effect of our preoccupation with survival is awesome. Diplomacy, foreign aid and education alike become tails on the kite of this basic strategic effort.

Threatening and counterthreatening the extermination of tens of millions of people is the central feature of deterrence and counterdeterrence in the nuclear age, and we are advised that we must find new ways to make our threats ever "credible."

Yet because technology continues to triumph uncontrolled, the threats are losing credibility out of sheer frightfulness. The atomic bomb at Hiroshima was thousands of times more powerful than the biggest high-explosive bomb used in World War II. But some of the hydrogen bombs which we have since produced are one thousand times greater than the total explosive power dropped in World War II.

There is no mystery about what lies at the end of this road in the contest of nuclear technologies. If the contest continues unabated, the end of the road will be the end of the world. Someone has suggested that the planets around us may be unpopulated for a very good reason: their scientists were more advanced than our own.

*   *   *

WHEN WE talk about disarmament today, we must not lapse into the old habits of reference pertinent to the years before World War II, or to a prenuclear or even premissile age. The world of 1960 is a different world from all these, and we must look at it for what it is, discarding old dogmas when they are outgrown.

Ironically, Mr. Khrushchev seems at times to be freer in shedding his dogmas than his nondogmatic, democratic opponents have been. For instance, in his Kremlin office in February, 1957, I had occasion to ask Khrushchev if he were not in fact a deviationist from his own Marxist faith. We were discussing disarmament, and I had challenged his willingness to negotiate an effective disarmament agreement.

I mentioned that Marxist dogma stressed that the capitalist West was largely dependent on its armament industries for continued prosperity. That doctrine seemed to imply that disarmament would hasten the triumph of Communism. As American armament industries closed down, unemployment presumably would rise, purchasing power would dry up and spreading depression would lead to political upheaval and the collapse of capitalism.

Why, then, did Mr. Khrushchev not act on this Marxist premise and strive with everything he had to achieve a workable disarmament agreement, the prelude to capitalist collapse? Was his failure to act not tantamount to establishing him as a deviationist? Was he not concerned over the reactions of his more doctrinaire associates? His own smiling reaction indicated that he got the point and was unperturbed.

Here is one instance where we might prefer that modern Marxists keep their dogma and act upon it, rather than put it on the shelf.

Meanwhile, we Americans have our own dogmas to be overcome in the arms-control field. How often have we heard that the most intractable problems are, of course, the political ones—Berlin, Germany, the Middle East, Korea, Vietnam, the Formosa Straits—and how often has it been explained that these problems must be solved before arms control is possible?

There is a hollow ring to this repetition that arms are a symptom and not a cause. Arms control has taken on a significance all its own. Particularly in the light of the current non-negotiability, or doubtful negotiability, of many of the world's major substantive political problems, arms control indeed begins to take top priority.

At the heart of the problem lie two fundamental truths. The first is the fact that arms races throughout history have usually ended in war. The second is the fact that unpreparedness and unilateral or unsafeguarded disarmament have always ended in national catastrophe.

These two truths are equally basic and must be treated side by side. Some of our major difficulties stem from attempts to separate them in our thinking. Those whose principal emphasis is the perfection of our military defenses are often deeply suspicious of the advocates of arms control. Those whose emphasis is the achievement of safeguarded disarmament are equally suspicious of the military men.

Viewed from the defense perspective on survival, our problem is how to keep up with the arms race. Viewed from the human perspective on survival, our problem is how to curtail it.

Writing in *Foreign Affairs* for January, 1959, Mr. Albert Wohlstetter commented: "Relaxation of tension, which everyone thinks is good, is not easily distinguished from relaxing one's guard, which everyone thinks is bad."

The divergent perspectives of defense and disarmament converge on the inspection question. More reliable scientific preparation, in depth, might already have saved us much time, uncertainty and embarrassment. To the degree that forces within the governments involved desire to test regardless of whether tests can be detected, a solution for the detection problem would not end this controversy. But it would end a source of tremendous confusion and obstruction at Geneva.

In a field in which progress on all sides is difficult, it would be prudent not to neglect those areas where more accurate scientific information might tip the scales of policy. One obvious area for effort is to improve the scientific underpinning of the controversy over the detection of underground tests. Since we have not moved ahead with vigor to close this major technical gap in the past, it is essential that we do so now.

The controversy over the sharing of nuclear weapons is another major current example of how the different perspectives of defense and disarmament converge in the scientific and technical context of controls.

One view stresses the need for a wider sharing of nuclear weapons, arguing that denying our allies a capacity which our probable enemy already has is suicidal in an era of split-second strategy.

The other view stresses the equally realistic danger that a further proliferation of weapons increases the likelihood that they will never be brought under control, and that the dangers of the accidental or deliberate triggering of a nuclear war will be correspondingly enhanced.

But these divergent perspectives, under closer examination, may not be unalterably opposed. Once more, what chance there may be for reconciliation lies in the field of control systems. It is probably predicated on new procedural answers to this order of questions:

What specific steps, if any, are consistent with both defense and disarmament requirements? What new arrangements inside NATO can be made to present at one and the same time the steadiest deterrent and the least provocation to outside aggression? What system can maximize the dedication of nuclear technology to common purposes and minimize the sense of deprivation which now serves as an incentive for nonnuclear powers to become nuclear?

The answers are not likely to be found in the indiscriminate granting of nuclear weapons to our allies. By the same token the answer is not likely to be found in the simple satisfaction of hoarding our own nuclear weapons while refusing to consider the very real prospect of the spread of nuclear weapons over our objection and without our help.

Internal NATO involvement of nonnuclear members in control, supervision, observation and planning activities might help to divert the ambitions of some members to emulate France's independent course. Development of a credible, over-all NATO nuclear deterrent strategy itself could reduce the provocations of separate nuclear deterrents and even reassure the Russians. Joint scientific research, inside NATO, could be of great potential value in the fields of both arms and arms control.

Outside NATO the threatened spread of nuclear weapons is bound to have effects equally profound. There can be little private gratification in the Kremlin, for instance, over the prospect of an independent nuclear capability in Communist China or in restless East Germany. Out of mutual danger may come new opportunities for agreements based on mutual interest.

In its significant study on the "The U.S.S.R. and Eastern Europe," recently prepared for the Senate Foreign Relations Committee, the Columbia-Harvard Research Group may have had this in mind when it said: "In the long run, we may come to regard the Russians as our most conservative and responsible adversary, as we explore the possibilities of common interest in limiting certain aspects of the arms race." This may appear extraordinary to many Americans, but it is in no sense impossible.

* * *

THE INCREDIBLE fact is that we have delayed so long, and are still delaying, in giving the arms-control problem the priority it deserves. It is not that we have never been urged. Rather it is that urgings have fallen on deaf ears.

Thus, it was ten years ago last week, on March 1, 1950, when a distinguished Connecticut Senator, the late Brien McMahon, took the floor of the Senate to call for the kind of action which we have never had. He spoke with urgency then, and his message has great urgency now. Let me conclude, as he concluded, with these words, ten years old and still so new:

"With each swing of the pendulum the time to save civilization grows shorter. When shall we get about this business? Destiny will not grant us the gift of indifference. If we do not act, we may be profaned forever by the inheritors of a ravished planet.

"We will be reviled, not as fools—even a fool can sense the massive danger. We will be reviled as cowards—and rightly, for only a coward can flee the awesome facts that command us to act with fortitude. This time of supreme crisis is a time of supreme opportunity. The prize of atomic peace lies waiting to be won—and with it a wondrous new world."

46

THE MYTH OF SOVIET INFALLIBILITY

*In 1961 the new Administration initiated a series of regional
"briefing conferences" to discuss with top U.S. editors and
opinion leaders the problems and issues in U.S. foreign policy.
In the conference held in Dallas, Texas, in October, 1961,
Under Secretary of State Bowles suggests a fresh perspective
on Soviet maneuvers in the Cold War.*

A NATIONAL policy that fails to take account of Soviet
power and determination would be more than dangerous; it would be
suicidal. Yet let us keep our sense of proportion. Not all Russians are
ten feet tall.

What we often overlook, particularly in dealing with the new nations
of Asia, Africa and Latin America, is the clear fact that in the political
and economic field the Kremlin's mistakes have been both frequent and
serious and their own frustration correspondingly great.

To get the situation into focus, let us review the last fifteen years as
members of the Kremlin must see them in moments of cold, realistic
perspective. Such a review may help to clarify our own strengths and to
place the world-wide situations into better balance.

Following World War II a political and economic vacuum existed in
Europe. Most industries lay in ruins, and each nation's economy was
scarred by inflation and vast unemployment.

In the United States, meanwhile, there was a mad scramble, stimulated by thoughtless political leaders in both parties, to disband our victorious armies and to draw back into our shell.

With most of Eastern Europe already overrun by the Red Armies and nearly two hundred battle-tested Soviet divisions still under arms, Stalin was convinced that Communism would quickly fill the entire European vacuum. His techniques to achieve a Communist-dominated Europe combined the threat of military strength, Communist-controlled strikes, divisive propaganda and in Greece and elsewhere guerrilla operations.

Yet what was the result?

Soviet pressure toward the Mediterranean through Greece and Turkey in the classic tradition of the czars was forestalled by the prompt counteraction of massive American military and economic assistance under the Truman Doctrine, coupled with the Greek devotion to freedom.

Within months, Marshall Plan aid was provided to rebuild the war-torn economies of Western Europe; it was followed by NATO, which erected an effective military shield between our allies and the Communist world.

It is easy to forget that only fifteen years ago many Americans were grimly predicting that Western Europe would soon be in Communist hands. Yet, with the exception of Czechoslovakia, Soviet power has been unable to move beyond the areas conquered and seized by the Red Armies. By prompt, bold, united action, Europe's freedom was assured, and today it is stronger and more prosperous than at any time in its long history.

In 1948 the Soviet Union launched another cold war maneuver to seal off and suffocate Berlin. But here again American and British enterprise and ingenuity met this test. Through the fantastic Berlin airlift the Russian thrust was again curtailed; and the net result was an aroused Western awareness of the Communist threat.

It was also in 1948 that the Yugoslavs broke loose from the Soviet bloc; and thirteen years of Soviet threats and blandishments have failed to bring them back into the fold. This marked the first important rift in the presumably monolithic Soviet empire. Although they still call themselves Communists, the Yugoslavs are today building a relatively prosperous economy independent of Soviet control.

Nineteen forty-eight was indeed a busy year for Stalin and his overconfident supporters. In that same year in Asia six new Communist revolutions were launched by order of the Kremlin: in the Philippines, Indonesia, French Indochina, Malaya, Burma and India.

Five of these six nations were newly freed, relatively disorganized, presumably weak and divided. In the Kremlin's eyes they must have appeared to be easy targets for carefully organized, well-financed, indigenously led Communist revolutions. Yet in all five the effort was a resounding failure.

In the sixth area, Indochina, the Communists were able to focus their propaganda and their pressure against France, a white colonial power, and it was here alone that their forces were partially successful.

Again, only a few years ago all thoughtful observers were concerned about Soviet penetration into the Middle East. Many thought that Egypt, for example, was on the road to Soviet control. Yet today Nasser's nationalism fiercely combats internal Communism, and his relations with the U.S.S.R. grow increasingly cool. Although the situation in the Middle East remains unstable and unpredictable, the Soviet gains here run far behind their expectations.

In 1955 the Soviets launched a new Khrushchev-type political-economic program in India and Japan. All sorts of overtures and promises were made. And once again their efforts have fallen short of their goals.

India today with all its problems is a rapidly developing, increasingly confident, democratic nation. And postwar Japan appears gradually to be overcoming her internal conflicts and to be establishing an extraordinary record of economic and political success under a democratic government.

Now let us consider Africa—one of the highest priority targets for Soviet ambitions, and one on which they have set high hopes.

In the past ten years, twenty-four newly independent countries have emerged in Africa. As the Communists stepped up their efforts on that vast and chaotic continent, there was much talk of the inevitability of African Soviet "satellites."

Although there have been some irritating speeches from African capitals and some disturbingly wobbly relationships, African nationalism has thus far resisted Soviet blandishments.

The Soviets suffered a particularly dramatic setback in the Congo with the United Nations itself as its principal adversary. This setback led directly to the Kremlin's effort to destroy the effectiveness of the U.N. through the "Troika" proposal for a three-headed administrative unit to replace the single Secretary General. Not one nation outside the Soviet bloc has supported this proposal, and this constitutes another setback.

I do not suggest that everything is going our way in the United Nations. Yet the Soviet attempt to destroy or undermine this organization has thus far failed.

Even in Communist China, where the Soviets congratulated themselves on a startling victory for Communism, the Kremlin faces baffling pressures and unpredictable dangers. Today we see a bitter rivalry for the leadership of the world Communist movement, a rivalry expressed in the recurrent ideological disputes between Peking and Moscow.

Now let us consider one more dimension of the economic and political difficulties which the Kremlin must take into account. For several years now the Kremlin has been talking about "peaceful competition between the two kinds of systems." Yet haven't they experienced precisely such a competition on their very doorstep?

For fifteen years West Germany has been developing under one system, East Germany under another. And what has been the result? In West Germany we have one of the great economic, social and political success stories of modern times—a free, prosperous, dynamic society of enormous vigor and promise.

By contrast, the government of East Germany stands as a shoddy failure, economically depressed, intellectually sterile, and viewed with outspoken contempt by its own citizens. Indeed, the Soviet failure in East Germany has been so great that the Communists have had to build a wall backed by machine guns and tanks to keep the East Germans from moving en masse from the so-called "Communist Utopia" of East Germany to the "capitalist cesspool" of West Germany.

In this act of desperation the Communist leaders have made it clear to the world that the one way they can keep their people in is to lock them in. Although East Berlin creates new problems for the West, it stands as a monumental symbol of the utter bankruptcy of Soviet policy in Europe.

The Communist failure to win support of their own people extends not only to East Germany, but to Poland and Hungary, and indeed to all the rest of their unhappy satellite states. And this despite fifteen years of calculated, high-pressured, relentless indoctrination of the whole postwar generation through Communist schools, Communist radio and Communist books and newspapers.

The depth of the Soviet failure is dramatized by the urge for individual freedom and for national independence that has not hesitated to resist Soviet totalitarianism.

Twenty-five thousand young Hungarians proved it by giving their lives in the struggle against Soviet tanks in the streets of Budapest five years ago. Nearly four million East Germans, most of them under thirty years of age, have proved it by leaving their homes to seek security and freedom in the West.

Although we should never underestimate the material and military strength of the Soviet Union, the Soviet political and economic offensive has failed in Europe, failed in the Far East, failed in the Middle East and failed in Africa. With the single exception of Cuba, it has also failed in Latin America.

I submit that the Soviets have not been winning the cold war. They have been losing it.

47

THE WEAKENING OF COMMUNIST IDEOLOGY

The force of nationalism and the demonstrated success of Western society have outmoded the appeal of the Communist idea, says Mr. Bowles in this provocative article in Foreign Affairs *for July, 1962.*

IS COMMUNISM gaining strength as a world ideology destined to sweep new nations and old peoples before it with the force and inevitability that it still claims? Or has it unhinged itself from historical truth and modern reality, losing both relevance and momentum?

In recent travels on four continents I have become convinced that Communism as an ideological force is ebbing. The mounting contradictions between Communist doctrine and the hard economic and political realities of today are beginning to be understood more widely.

Even in the Soviet Union itself changes in practice are being reflected in publicly avowed changes in dogma. The simple fact is that the world is refusing to act as Communist ideology said it should.

By Marxian tenets, Communism should serve as an international beacon, around which the working classes of all nations would unite in a dedicated movement regardless of political boundaries. Thus Lenin had expected the Soviet Revolution to bring an internationally minded proletariat to power in a succession of key countries in Western Europe; he was bitterly disappointed that it did not happen.

241

When Stalin shifted his emphasis from world revolution to the doctrine of "socialism in one country," he was embarking on a primarily defensive gambit, designed to give the Soviet Union the time and means to prepare for whatever next step to world domination might prove practicable.

The time arrived following World War II when the Red Armies overran Eastern Europe. The means had been developed by expanding the programs of education and industrial growth within the Soviet Union. Almost at once Communist pressure was felt in war-stricken Western Europe. Here again Soviet plans were blocked, this time by the rapid economic recovery of the European nations, buttressed by the Marshall Plan and then shielded by NATO.

Stalin then turned toward Asia and Africa. In 1948 six Communist-led revolutions were launched in Asia—in addition to the unique and long-developing Chinese Communist Revolution—under what appeared to be extraordinarily favorable conditions. In newly independent India, Indonesia, Burma, Malaya and in the Philippines these revolutions failed; only in Indochina, where the French tried to maintain an impossible colonial position, was there substantial success.

Since then, the difficulties encountered by the Communist drive in Asia and Africa have multiplied. Evidence of this can be seen in the contradictions in Communist propaganda, in the disagreements between Moscow and many native Communist parties, in the splits within the local parties, and in the constant shifts and experimentation which mark Moscow's effort to establish satisfactory working relationships.

A striking aspect of this Communist drive is that its propagandists seem reluctant to cite Communism's supposed economic or social merits. Instead, they present Communism as an ally of the forces of nationalism.

This in turn creates considerable ideological confusion. For one thing, the Soviet Union's anti-national practices in its East European satellites are now well known. Moreover, in giving lip service to nationalism the Soviets are championing a force which is incompatible, not only with Communist doctrine, but also with their own long-run objectives.

In South Vietnam today, for example, Communist propaganda finds it more effective to warn against intervention by white foreigners than to call in Marxist terms for an uprising of the "proletariat" and the "toiling masses."

In other nations, propaganda extolling the merits of Communism is apparently judged a positive handicap and therefore abandoned in order more effectively to promote traditional Russian objectives. In Afghanistan, for instance, no Communist posters, no demonstrations, no slogans, no overt Communist propaganda can be seen or heard. Instead of acting in the Marxist tradition to stir up antagonism among students, workers or peasants against the Afghan royal family, the Soviet line, at least for the present, is to persuade both the rulers and the ruled that economic aid and technical guidance from the neighborly U.S.S.R.—allegedly free from ideological connotations— provide the best means of bringing Afghanistan rapidly into the twentieth century.

Out-and-out contradictions between Soviet policy and the interests of Communist ideology are seen in many other places. In Algeria, for instance, Moscow was so anxious to please the de Gaulle Government, for reasons strictly in Russia's nationalist interest, that it missed a promising ideological opportunity by not recognizing the Algerian Provisional Government until after the cease-fire.

Similarly, the Soviet Union is aggressively selling its own oil anywhere it can find a market, regardless of the adverse impact on the Communist movement in the oil-producing states of the Middle East.

Meanwhile, Communist parties have been suppressed by either decree or statute in some forty-five nations. And this does not count the many new nations in Africa where the Communist party has failed even to get a start. It is now operating legally in only two African states: Tunisia, where it is unimportant, and Madagascar, where the Communists call themselves "Titoists."

Even where Communists are tolerated in one of their many guises their effectiveness has usually been limited. Where they have merged successfully with other parties they have lost their identity; where they have failed to merge they have often found themselves in jail.

Guinea illustrates the difficulties which the Communist ideology faces in the relatively classless and intensely nationalistic new African societies. In order to gain status within the one-party Guinean state, the Communists have had to subordinate their interests to the dynamic nationalist aims of the government. Last December when they neglected to do so, the Soviet Ambassador was invited to leave the country.

In India the Communist party remains legal, but the disarray within the organization reflects the same sort of dilemma that besets the Communists in several other developing nations. In order to maintain their voting strength, the Indian Communists have been forced to play down their doctrinaire appeal and to emphasize their support for such nationalist causes as Goa and Kashmir. And within the party itself the pro-Moscow and pro-Peking factions are waging fierce and destructive ideological warfare.

In almost none of the developing countries does one find the local Communist leadership acting today as the primary and overt agent of Soviet aims. Where it has not been curbed or where it is not ignored as of little importance, it has been left to play an expendable role of diversion and troublemaking.

An important exception is Indonesia, which boasts the largest Communist party in any country outside the Soviet bloc. Yet a major explanation of the Communist party's strength there lies in its identification with nationalist forces on the one remaining "colonialist" issue in Indonesian politics, the question of West New Guinea. If that issue can be resolved peacefully, and an intensified effort is made to achieve economic development, the present strength of Indonesian Communism may be expected to decline.

*   *   *

SINCE it found that Communist ideology was becoming less appealing in the newly developing nations, the Soviet Union has turned increasingly to two other weapons of political penetration: subversion and foreign aid.

In South Vietnam and Laos the geographical conditions were ideal for Communist infiltration and subversion. But in situations less exposed to direct Communist pressure the attempts at subversion by both Moscow and Peking have usually aroused popular distaste or hostility and in many cases have led to effective official countermeasures.

I found this particularly so on recent trips to Latin America. Either because or in spite of spending large sums and much effort on espionage, propaganda and agitation, Castro has thus far lost diplomatic representation in fourteen Latin-American nations. Partly at least in an effort to counter his political slippage outside Cuba, he has recently disavowed the more doctrinaire Communist elements in his own house.

As a second means of forwarding their political aims, the Communist governments have gone increasingly into programs of foreign aid. From 1955 to 1961 the Sino-Soviet bloc extended about $4.4 billion in economic grants and credits, mostly the latter, to twenty-eight nations outside the Iron Curtain. The Soviet Union supplied about three-fourths of the total. At the end of 1961, some 8,500 Communist-bloc technicians were in the field.

In many cases such assistance has gone to nations which have taken openly anti-Communist positions. Whatever may be the political effect of this effort to offset American and European foreign aid programs, it bears no ideological relationship to the concepts of Marxism-Leninism.

On the crucial question of arms control, Communist ideology has again come into conflict with the assumed interests of Russian nationalism.

According to Marx, the capitalistic economies are sustained either by war or by the threat of war. If the Soviet leadership really believed its own dogma, it would sponsor a vigorous and realistic program to reduce the armament load, confident that if the United States agreed to lower its defense budget it would face unmanageable unemployment, and that if it refused it would face a unanimously indignant world opinion. Yet the traditional Russian nationalist obsession with secrecy has made the Kremlin unwilling to accept any practicable version of the principle of inspection which would make arms control a reality, Karl Marx notwithstanding.

The instances I have cited suggest that whether in Communist propaganda, political action, subversion or foreign aid, Communist ideology has proved to be either an ineffective servant of Soviet foreign policy or an actual handicap to its operations; and that as Soviet experience has made this or that maneuver or adjustment to the practical realities expedient or necessary, the ideology itself has become increasingly twisted and confused or in many cases has been outright ignored.

Communist ideology has even failed to provide a reliable cement to bind together the nations which claim to believe in it. Indeed, one might say that the main importance of Communist doctrine today is found in disputes within the Communist bloc itself—above all, of course, in the ideological controversies between Moscow and Peking. These controversies damage the whole Marxist concept of a single political and economic orthodoxy and create havoc with Moscow's effort to interpret it to suit the Soviet Union's particular experience and national priorities.

Nationalism itself runs counter to Marxist-Leninist concepts of a world structured by classes, for it switches the basis of change from the supposedly inevitable tides of economics and history to the interpretations and imperatives of a particular man or group of men. This is markedly present, of course, in the disagreements among Moscow, Peking, Belgrade, Tirana and the satellite capitals of Eastern Europe.

The fact that the Communist nations with so much at stake are unable to create and maintain a common front affects not only their political future as the "socialist camp," but the power which the Marxist concept is assumed to wield in the world as a result of its alleged unbreakable unity.

I have suggested that Communist ideology is declining in relevance to the tasks of the modern world and that the Communists themselves are finding it of declining value as a political tool, an economic panacea and an instrument of diplomacy.

Although this tendency may work to our advantage in the long run, I must point out with the greatest possible emphasis that it in no way lessens the short-range challenge that the Soviet Union poses to the American people and their policy-makers.

As Soviet leaders are increasingly liberated from their own dogma, they may be encouraged to apply their great powers more constructively. Or the result may be something of a crisis of faith within the Soviet Union itself, a confrontation of the "believers" and the "realists." This in turn might release frustrations and hostilities in the Communist world that could have dangerous results for world peace.

We can only pray that the waning of doctrinaire zeal and the replacement of it by nationalist aims among the Communist countries will not have this result, but that on the contrary it may in time offer new grounds for successful negotiation and even peaceful accommodation with us and our friends.

The question remains: What of America itself? Even if it is true that Communism is gradually losing much of its significance as a global ideology, this will not be of great importance to our grandchildren unless the democratic faith as we aim to practice it can be made relevant to the world of the future.

If this is to happen, the American people will have to adopt a role which no prosperous and powerful nation has ever undertaken to play in the long history of mankind. It will have to identify itself boldly with the social, economic and political revolution that is now beginning to transform the lives of hundreds of millions of human beings in all parts of the globe.

The obstacles to our playing such a role are appallingly large. Yet the possibilities for us and for mankind are very nearly infinite.

══ 48

THE THREE FRONTIERS THAT DIVIDE THE COMMUNIST WORLD FROM OUR OWN

Mr. Bowles argues for a policy of "maximum maneuverability" instead of "maximum rigidity" on the economic and cultural frontiers while we maintain our power to safeguard the military frontier. Address at the University of Nebraska on June 21, 1962.

DOES a national consensus on foreign policy exist in America today? On three key aspects of foreign policy I believe that the answer is affirmative:

1. The need for powerful armed forces and the will to use them if necessary to oppose aggression.

2. The fact that nuclear weapons have brought a new dimension into the military situation, and that any war can quickly become an exercise in mutual annihilation.

3. The importance of the political and economic forces which in less than twenty years have so dramatically reshaped maps of the world and altered the lives of hundreds of millions of Asians and Africans.

The remaining differences among us relate to questions of method and priority; more specifically, to our dealings with the Communist nations and with the unaligned nations. These differences should be discussed frankly so that we may close the gap and establish a framework of national agreement within which our government can act with confidence.

In their approach to these questions, most Americans fall into one of two groups, each committed to a peaceful, more orderly world, each aware that no panaceas are available to us, but with sharply divergent views on the nonmilitary aspects of American foreign policy.

In this regard one group may be said to advocate a policy of "maximum rigidity"; the other a policy of "maximum maneuverability."

Those who support the "maximum rigidity" approach hold, in essence, to the old aphorism that he who is not with us is against us. They believe that the lines of conflict must be tightly drawn everywhere. They hold that there is no basis for cooperation with those who do not share our interpretation of the world, and that eventually the Communist side or the democratic side will emerge as the dominant world force.

The application of this "maximum rigidity" approach to specific questions of foreign policy is illustrated by recent actions of the United States Senate when it first voted to reduce our support for India and then to eliminate United States assistance to Poland and Yugoslavia. Although these provisions were subsequently removed from the bill in conference, the Senate action was symptomatic of the pervasiveness of this school of thought.

The advocates of the opposing policy of "maximum maneuverability" stress that the balance of forces within the Communist world is in a constant state of flux, and that this flux creates increasing pressures for change within each country and in their relations to one another. Our policies, they believe, should be designed to encourage this process.

While aware of the hard military requirements, their definition of "power" goes beyond military weapons and industrial capacity to include people and the ideas that move them. Thus they attach special importance to the yearnings for justice, dignity, and progress which shape the views and policies of the developing nations.

Against this background, let us explore these two approaches—one of rigidity, the other of maneuverability—as they affect the three frontiers that lie between Communist interests and our own: the military, economic, and cultural frontiers.

Although the character and significance of the three frontiers vary greatly, advocates of "maximum rigidity" would largely ignore these differences. In their view, each frontier is a barrier to be relentlessly held, not simply against tanks, but against trade, aid, people, and ideas.

In contrast, the advocates of "maximum maneuverability" believe that the differences among these three frontiers are the decisive key to an effective foreign policy in the nuclear age. What are these differences?

The military frontier extends from the Baltic along the Iron Curtain to the Bosphoros, where Soviet and NATO troops, tanks, and planes confront each other across a barrier of barbed wire, watchtowers, and mined areas.

Through CENTO, SEATO, and a variety of other multilateral and bilateral military pacts, it continues with varying effectiveness to the South China Sea. Behind this complex of troops and alliances stands the awesome nuclear capacity of the two opposing power blocs.

In respect to this *military* frontier our national foreign policy consensus is clearly established. Both the "maximum rigidity" and "maximum maneuverability" schools agree that weakness in the face of armed aggression or threatened aggression would lead to more aggression, and therefore cannot be accepted.

But at that point agreement comes to an abrupt end. Advocates of a rigid approach would treat the *economic* frontier in the same inflexible terms as the military frontier. They would maintain a barrier not only to troops but to trade, technicians, and capital.

The advocates of greater maneuverability disagree. They look at the economic frontier as an opportunity for boldness, flexibility, and initiative.

The differences between the two schools are brought into clear focus by their views on the question of economic assistance to Yugoslavia. Advocates of a rigid approach believe that this assistance has merely strengthened a potential adversary. Advocates of a policy of maximum maneuverability believe that such aid has been wise and productive.

Let us briefly review the conditions which existed in early 1948 when the Yugoslav question first came under discussion.

At that time the Greek civil war was in full swing, with Soviet-directed Communist guerrillas pressing their efforts to destroy Greek democracy from bases in southern Yugoslavia.

In Italy a bitter election campaign was moving toward its climax. Because of widespread poverty, war-weariness, and political frustration, many observers feared that the Communists might win their first genuine success in the history of free elections. On the other side of the world a sweeping victory for the Communists in the Chinese civil war appeared imminent.

Thus we faced the prospect of a monolithic Communist empire stretching all the way from the borders of France to the Sea of Japan. The impact of such a development on the war-devastated nations of Europe and the newly liberated nations of Asia was difficult to exaggerate.

In February and March of this fateful year, Tito's long-smoldering disagreements with Stalin first became evident. In June, Yugoslavia courageously announced its independence of Soviet control and appealed to us for assistance.

President Truman and the Republican Congress under the leadership of Arthur Vandenberg were thereby faced with a dilemma of historic importance. During the war the Yugoslavs had stubbornly pinned down some thirty Nazi divisions. More recently, however, Yugoslavia had been one of the most anti-Western members of the Communist bloc, and American public opinion had become increasingly embittered.

Yet if we failed to support Tito in his new effort to establish national independence, Yugoslavia would be forced back into the Stalinist orbit, and the first crack in the Communist empire would be effectively sealed.

After much soul-searching, a bipartisan agreement was reached that American interests would best be served by vigorous support for Yugoslav independence. Substantial shipments of military and economic equipment were soon on their way. Following his election in 1952, President Eisenhower announced his intention of continuing this policy. President Kennedy did likewise eight years later.

The immediate results of this aid program were dramatically favorable. In April, 1948, democratic forces in Italy, encouraged by rumors of the defection of Yugoslavia, had won a decisive victory at the polls. A year later Communist guerrillas in Greece, deprived of their former base of operations in Yugoslavia, were overcome.

Since then substantial changes have occurred within Yugoslavia itself. For instance, Soviet-type rural collectives have been largely abandoned; nine out of ten peasants now own their own farms. Communist dogma in regard to industrial development has been greatly modified. Seventy percent of Yugoslavia's foreign trade is now with the non-Communist nations. This has led some foreign wits even to say that "the only people who are still persuaded that Yugoslavia is a Communist State are the Americans and the Yugoslavs."

On political questions in the United Nations the Yugoslavs still vote more often than not with the U.S.S.R., and their leaders frequently take positions with which most Americans profoundly disagree.

Yet Yugoslavia can hardly be described as a Soviet satellite. Yugoslav delegates supported the United States and opposed the U.S.S.R. on the key issue of a single Secretary General versus the so-called Troika plan, on the financing of U.N. forces in the Congo, and on the Soviet explosion of the fifty-megaton H-bomb last October. Yugoslav opposition to Communist China has been bitter and persistent.

Within the Communist bloc itself Yugoslavia's independent example has also had a powerful effect. For instance, most observers believe that it has encouraged Poland to abandon many doctrinaire Communist techniques such as land collectivization.

In dealing with foreign policy questions, Poland—caught between Red Army units in East Germany and the Soviet Union—consistently supports the Kremlin. Yet modest economic assistance from the United States across the military frontier has helped create a new sense of confidence and independence among the Polish people. Forty-two percent of Polish foreign trade is now with the non-Communist nations.

From its beginning the objective of our aid effort in Yugoslavia has been to assure the government freedom to make its own basic choices and to encourage a similar sense of independence among the peoples of other Communist nations. By and large, it seems to me, this objective has been attained.

Let us now consider another key sector of the economic frontier where the argument between the two schools continues: the new and emerging nations of Africa, Asia, and Latin America.

Here the advocates of "maximum rigidity" would assist only those peoples whose governments support the policies of the United States. The advocates of "maximum maneuverability" believe that this "either or" approach would force the new developing nations to choose between subservience to either Moscow or Washington on the one hand, or chaos and continued misery on the other.

The issue may fall in clearer perspective if we examine the situation we now face in the developing continents.

The emerging nations of Asia, Africa, and Latin America are wrestling with awesome problems of illiteracy, ill health, poverty, and injustice. Unless their people can be convinced that reasonable progress is being made toward the elimination of these evils, orderly political growth will be impossible.

United States efforts to help these new nations have been complicated by the cantankerous political attitudes of many Asian, African, and Latin-American leaders, who have been embittered by their own past experience with the economically privileged and, in some cases, race-conscious colonial nations of the West.

When these Afro-Asian spokesmen criticize United States policies in the United Nations and elsewhere, editorial writers chastise them as "ungrateful Communist dupes," and members of Congress rise to demand that our aid programs to such "uncooperative" nations be terminated forthwith.

Although such reactions are understandable in terms of our own jangled nerves and frustrations, they will not cause the complex realities of our world to disappear.

A key Communist objective is control of the resources and markets of Africa, Asia, and Latin America, on which the industrialized nations of the West are heavily dependent. A primary task of United States foreign policy is to block this effort and to help the developing nations fully to establish their independence with an increasing measure of political stability and economic progress.

However unpredictable they may appear to us, the new nations have no desire to exchange British, French, Belgian, and Dutch rule, from which many of them have recently emerged, for the more ruthless domination of the Russians. Moreover, their own cultures and history encourage a deeply rooted diversity that does not easily succumb to foreign pressures and ideologies.

As the Kremlin strategists are discovering by harsh experience, these indigenous counterforces provide formidable barriers to the Leninist objective of a Soviet-dominated world.

Advocates of a policy of "maximum maneuverability" believe that a flexible, well-administered, sensitive economic assistance program can further strengthen these built-in barriers. They stress, however, that our minds must be clear as to the purposes and limitations of this effort.

Our objective is not to control the utterances and policies of the developing nations, to win a global popularity contest with the U.S.S.R., or to purchase votes in the United Nations.

Governments that can be "bought" with American dollars can no more be counted on to *stay* bought than can individuals purchased in the same manner. Nor can nations as wealthy as ours expect to be loved by those which are less fortunate; the best we can expect on that score is respect.

Our true objectives, therefore, should be twofold: First, to help increase and spread economic progress in those developing nations which are genuinely anxious to help themselves. And, second, to do so in a way that encourages broader participation among their people and gives each family an increasing personal stake in national independence.

With these two objectives in mind, let us briefly consider the application of the two contrasting approaches—one of rigidity and one of maneuverability—to the Republic of India, the largest and most crucial of the new independent nations.

For more than a decade we have been witnessing a dramatic and portentous development between the two most heavily populated nations in the world, India and China, one using totalitarian techniques, the other committed to democracy.

In the last year or two the results have become clear. While India has been proving that a competent democratic government can provide an increasing measure of bread, freedom, and opportunity, Communist China has fallen under an avalanche of internal troubles.

Yet today, just as the implications of this outcome are becoming understood, American advocates of a policy of "maximum rigidity" propose that our crucially important aid to India should be substantially reduced.

This proposal may be explicable in terms of irritation over what most Americans believe to be misguided actions by the Indian Government and by Indian sensitivity to any criticism from others. To those who write the history of our era, however, it will appear fantastic.

The economic frontier between the Communist world and our own is thus a complex one. By keeping this frontier open, in line with the policy of "maximum maneuverability," we have been making steady progress.

What now of the third frontier between East and West—the *cultural* frontier?

The "maximum rigidity" school argues that, except for radio propaganda, the cultural frontier, like the economic frontier, should be as tightly closed as the military frontier. The "maximum maneuverability" school once again favors flexibility and initiative. Which is the wiser course?

Since the Geneva Conference of 1955, there has been a steady flow of scholars, students, artists, musicians, farmers, and scientists across the military frontier that separates the Soviet and the Western worlds.

To those who subscribe to the philosophy of "maximum rigidity," this two-way cultural exchange seems dangerous and even immoral. Advocates of a flexible program of maneuverability, on the other hand, argue that it is helping to establish people-to-people understanding and to give the citizens of each world a clearer appreciation of the other.

If the conflicts that now separate East and West are eventually eased, they assert, it will only be as a result of understanding which has slowly and painfully been cultivated on both sides of the military frontier.

To some extent we are all the prisoners of stereotypes; we see each other in terms of distorted and oversimplified images. Better communication in the realm of ideas, of the arts, and of science can help refashion these false images. And by seeing more clearly we may act more wisely.

In my mind, the choice between these two positions is clear. Why should we, a free people, be afraid of ideas? Isn't it the Communists who should fear them?

*   *   *

WHAT ARE the prospects for the future?

Although the nuclear impasse is dangerous, our position on the military frontier is strong. Russian deadlines have come and gone; but West Berlin, an outpost of that frontier, still stands as a shining example of the determination of free men to defend their freedom.

In the last two years, our military power generally has become better balanced, more mobile, and hence more effective in defending the military frontier. Meanwhile, we must continue to hope that the Soviet leaders will ultimately recognize the folly of a continuing, escalating contest between the two greatest industrial powers of all time to see which can develop the greater capacity to destroy the other.

On the economic and cultural frontiers, the prospects for continuing progress and change appear more promising.

The non-Communist world is poised on the threshold of more rapid economic growth than ever before. As we build a more prosperous, more interrelated society of free men, the Soviets may be forced to modify even further the sterile rigidities of their own system.

In the meantime, the burgeoning flow of trade, capital, technicians, Peace Corps volunteers, wheat, cotton, orchestras, and ideas across the economic and cultural frontiers will continue to open up minds, undercut dogma, and encourage diversity.

We Americans have always prided ourselves on our eagerness to experiment, our adaptability to new situations, and our imagination in devising new courses of action. Within a framework of unflinching dedication to democratic principles, we have grown strong precisely because we have preferred creative, responsible action to the rigidities of the status quo.

Why should we abandon this traditional concept now as we seek the basis for a rational peace? And why should we, of all people, expect the proud new developing nations to see the world precisely as we see it? Was any new nation ever more outspoken, independent and unaligned than the young America of Jefferson, Jackson, and Lincoln?

* * *

THE BASIC question remains: Can a democratic government create and administer a foreign policy that is adequate to the complexities of today's world?

The answer depends on our capacity to create a national consensus that will provide the President with a solid foundation from which to exercise world leadership.

Since the war we have taken long strides toward the creation of such a consensus. The nagging differences that remain involve our approach to the satellites on the one hand and our relationship to the unaligned new nations of Asia and Africa on the other.

This gap threatens to undercut the effectiveness of American foreign policy at a critical moment in history. It can be closed only by forthright and responsible public debate. The views which I have expressed here are one man's contribution to that debate.

BOOK II

REALIZING THE AMERICAN DREAM

▬ *A Personal Note on Book II*

The effectiveness with which we deal with the world problems discussed in Book I will ultimately be determined by the nature of American society itself. This will be shaped by three factors:
—the strength and dynamism of our domestic economy;
—the responsiveness, flexibility and balance of our federal-state and Executive-Legislative-Judicial political systems;
—the depth of our moral commitment to provide a full measure of dignity, opportunity, and justice for all our fellow Americans.
If we fail in these three respects, the United States will lack the productivity to meet the world-wide economic challenge, the resilience to cope with political crises abroad, and the national integrity to win the respect of other peoples.
Book II contains articles and speeches dealing with each of these factors, written over a span of seventeen years. As I reread this material I am impressed with our progress on some of the key issues raised and concerned with our lack of it on others.
Our continuing residue of unemployment, segregation, and corruption, of unbuilt schools, unbuilt homes, and shabby cities, of imbalanced representation in our state legislatures, and governmental roadblocks in Washington, remains a burden on our national conscience, confidence, and competence.
For example, the issues with which I grappled as Governor of Connecticut a decade ago remain at the heart of the national legislative deadlock of 1962; while political leaders who speak most eloquently of states' rights are often in the forefront of those who reject state responsibilities.
The bipartisan consensus which has been achieved in regard to many of our world objectives has not been matched by similar agreement on the nature and thrust of our own society. The gap that remains is a dangerous one.

CHESTER BOWLES

Section I

TOWARD A
MORE ABUNDANT SOCIETY

It is my conviction that the only way we shall know true economic freedom in this country, and develop the life of the individual according to our American traditions, is in an atmosphere of full production and full employment, with good profits for business, good jobs and steady wages for workers and high incomes for farmers. Only then are we released from the trammels of fear and insecurity which in the past have rendered millions of us incapable of imaginative and courageous thinking.

September 1, 1945

PEACE AND FULL EMPLOYMENT

Three weeks after V-J Day, the Senate Banking and Currency
Committee held hearings on a Full Employment Bill designed to
meet the major problem of reconversion—providing jobs for
all in the postwar economy. Mr. Bowles, then head of the
Office of Price Administration, testified on September 1, 1945.

WITH the coming peace the American people are on the threshold of a whole new world of peace, prosperity and plenty.

During the war years we have seen at first hand the tremendous production of which our industrial machine is capable. There are few of us who do not sense what this same industrial machine, turned from the production for war to production for peace, now can create in the way of a vastly higher standard of living, modern homes, good educations, and far higher standards of health, recreation and leisure.

The Murray-Patman Bill, which is now before your committee, states that it shall be the national policy of Americans to achieve this kind of prosperity—sustained prosperity under a system of free enterprise.

There are many who view this bill with grave alarm.

Some oppose it because they dislike and distrust all government, and fear the limited government planning which this bill calls for.

Do they really think that we would again be able to go through another depression even approaching the intensity of 1932 without

265

government controls carried far beyond any proposal outlined here?

Others oppose this bill because they claim it will bankrupt the federal government. But who can seriously assume that with a faltering national production and with millions of men again walking the streets in search of jobs we could raise the necessary money to meet our federal commitments within the bounds of a balanced budget?

Still others oppose the bill in a spirit of general defeatism. It is their belief that freedom and security are somehow incompatible. If we are to maintain our free enterprise system, they say, we are doomed to the cycle of booms and depressions. They point out that we have gone through this cycle many times before and in spite of it our country has grown great.

Through our system of private initiative we have developed the greatest industrial machine and the highest standard of living of any country on earth and we have achieved this without the sacrifice of individual freedom.

Yet in spite of the great achievements of the free enterprise system in the past and the unlimited contributions it can make to our future, these boom-and-bust cycles, if permitted to continue, may eventually destroy it.

Isn't our real goal the personal freedom of the individual? Aren't we anxious above all to protect the right of any young man and woman freely to enter any field of activity?

Except for those who look on our economic system as an end in itself rather than as a *means* to an end, I do not believe there are many who claim that there was any great sense of individual freedom and opportunity during the depression days of a decade ago.

It is my conviction that the only way we shall know true economic freedom in this country, and develop the life of the individual according to our American traditions, is in an atmosphere of full production and full employment, with good profits for business, good jobs and steady wages for workers and high incomes for farmers. Only then are we released from the trammels of fear and insecurity which in the past have rendered millions of us incapable of imaginative and courageous thinking.

The passage of this bill will be a long step forward in our efforts to achieve full peacetime production with full employment. But the bill in itself is not a program. It merely states a national policy and calls for the development of a program to achieve it.

As a private citizen, I sincerely hope that a program will be developed during the coming months which will include social security covering all our working groups, more adequate minimum-wage legislation, an adequate compensation program for temporary and unavoidable unemployment, a broad health insurance program as part of social security, and a farm program which will develop as a national policy the maintenance of a high farm income with ample food reserves for shipment overseas.

These steps should be taken courageously and promptly.

America has come through this greatest of wars as the strongest nation on earth. As we turn to peace, we must face the fact that it is in America and only in America that there is worry about too much capital, too many workers, too many machines, and too much food.

For the sake of ourselves and for the sake of all those throughout the world who love democracy, we must put aside defeatism and apply ourselves to the building of the future of which we are so fully capable.

═ 2

BLUEPRINTS FOR A CHANGING AMERICA

As a former businessman Mr. Bowles challenges other
businessmen to a more realistic view of the workings of the
private enterprise system and the urgent postwar need for
sustained full production and employment. From Saving
American Capitalism, *edited by Seymour E. Harris.*

WORLD War II has left a legacy of destruction almost beyond human comprehension. It has destroyed cities, factories, dams,
power plants and railroads. Worse still, it has sapped the vitality,
hopes and capacities of hundreds of millions of human beings upon
whom world recovery must depend.

Against this background of world devastation America appears as
an economic dream world; physically untouched by war, her resources
undamaged, her people largely prosperous and united.

And yet, today, throughout America there is uneasiness about our
economic future. As we look abroad at the chaos of Europe and Asia,
many wonder if we can prosper on an island of plenty in the midst
of a world of want.

In the 1930's our economic development had been seriously hampered by a philosophy of economic scarcity. A month after Pearl
Harbor, when President Roosevelt called for the annual production
of fifty thousand planes and five million tons of shipping, many Americans were certain that he was asking the impossible.

But the timid thinkers were wrong. As the months wore on, our country hummed again with all the full power of its huge industrial capacity. We met the President's goal of fifty thousand planes and went on to double it. We quadrupled his estimate of five million tons of shipping annually. Our farmers, with 10 percent fewer workers, produced 30 percent more farm products. In 1942, 1943 and 1944, the records show that we produced more civilian goods than in any previous period of our history. And, on top of that, at the peak of the war effort we achieved an annual production rate of $100 billion worth of military equipment and services.

Our wartime production record re-established our faith in what our industrial machine could provide for our people. As we saw our war factories working day and night, we began to sense the torrent of consumer goods which these factories could produce for all of us in peacetime. And so the conviction developed that depressions must not be accepted as inevitable; that we must put outworn economic theories behind us; that somehow, and without loss of our individual freedom, we must keep our factories and our farms fully at work turning out the goods and services which our people—indeed, the whole world— so badly needed.

How can we keep our wartime momentum? The principle on which a full-employment, full-production economy must be built can be stated simply: For every dollar's worth of production of goods or services, there is created one dollar of potential purchasing power.

If the level of production is to be maintained and increased, all this money must be spent currently by individuals, groups and institutions. Otherwise, goods and services will remain unpurchased and our production will be decreased by a similar amount.

This, in turn, will lead to the canceling of orders for new equipment and new plants, to increasing layoffs and unemployment. Purchasing power will shrink and we will begin to go downhill toward a depression, with each reduction of employment and each drop in purchasing power feeding on itself.

There are three groups which *together* are in a position to spend all the money represented by our total purchasing power and thereby assure a prosperous expanding economy. One of these groups is business. Each year, this group spends a vast but varying amount of money on industrial expansion, inventories, new equipment and buildings.

The second of our three groups of spenders is government—federal, state and local. Each year, and in varying amounts, our governmental institutions spend money on schools, hospitals, roads, bridges, irrigation projects, police and fire departments, and on military and naval establishments.

The third of our three groups of spenders is the American people themselves. Each year, and again in varying amounts, we as consumers spend our wages, salaries and dividends for food, clothing, travel, movies, washing machines, vacuum cleaners, books, houses and hair-dos.

Although each of these three groups will change its pattern of expenditures from year to year, the total spent by *all three* must add up to the total income earned by everyone in the production of goods and services—otherwise we will face increasing unemployment.

The problem, therefore, becomes clear. In some way, a balance must be maintained between these three groups so that there will be a market for all the goods and services which we produce; so that production and employment can be maintained at a high level, a level which increases as our productive power increases.

The government's role in maintaining our total purchasing power is of vital importance because of the impact of our present governmental budgets on our economy as a whole. It is doubly important because the percentage of our total purchasing power, which is supported by government expenditures, can be varied within reasonable limits each year in line with our total needs.

As we examine what government must and can accomplish, we are faced with many inhibitions and prejudices. Americans over forty years of age came to manhood in an age when government's primary responsibilities were largely to keep down crime, to see to it that we had the nucleus of an army and navy, to keep up the roads and to levy a minimum of taxes to pay for these limited services.

We were told that any expansion of government represented an encroachment upon individual liberties to be resisted to one's utmost and that even the necessary minimum of government was to be condoned rather than admired. The cartoons of our childhood presented public servants as fat politicians with well-chewed cigars, derby hats and thousand-dollar bills labeled "graft" dropping from their pockets.

Since the collapse of 1929, this shopworn view has been harder and harder to take. With the development of the country, it has become increasingly clear that our government must grow up to larger responsibilities. As our economic and social system evolved and took on new complications, a revision of the older attitude toward government was inescapable. Without such a revision, how could we expect government, forced by implacable events into new responsibilities, to discharge them efficiently, adequately and without destroying our liberties?

There is one critical point which we can never afford to ignore: If the American people are unprepared to accept enough government, we will end up with too much. It may be paradoxical, but it is true. If we are reluctant to grant our government enough power to meet its essential tasks, the unsolved tasks will overtake us, and in the ensuing crisis we will be obliged to go far beyond what would have been necessary in government control had we taken adequate steps sooner.

* * *

THE GOVERNMENT, as I see it, has six fundamental roles. Its first responsibility is a traditional one: the maintenance of an efficient post office system and other fundamental government services. On this there can be but little disagreement.

The second role of government is to act as an umpire between the four major groups which make up our economy: business, labor, the farmer and all of us as consumers. In the early days of our economic history this role was relatively unimportant.

But the growth of Big Business led to Big Farming and Big Labor. This, in turn, has led us toward Big Government, government strong enough to protect the interests and rights of 140 million citizens, who otherwise would be at the mercy of the highly organized groups representing business, labor and the farmer.

One of the major responsibilities of government in this field is the curbing of economic monopoly from any source. Restricted industrial production has its counterpart in the labor movement in featherbedding and other make-work practices. Both of these evils grow out of the concept that we dare not use all our resources, both industrial and human, because there is not enough work to go around.

A third responsibility of government is to provide those services which we cannot reasonably expect to be created by individuals operating on a profit-and-loss basis. We could not reasonably expect, for instance, that the Tennessee Valley Authority, calling for an investment of more than one billion dollars, could be created by private capital. Nor can we expect adequately to control the waters of the Missouri, Arkansas, Columbia, St. Lawrence and other major river waterways with private funds.

For the same reason, we cannot expect private investors to finance the elimination of our slums, the building of modern parks and hospitals and recreation areas. There are many services in this broad field to which the American people are entitled and which are not yet fully available to them. It is the responsibility of our modern democratic government to proceed aggressively to provide them.

The fourth responsibility of government under our private enterprise system must be to assure reasonable equality of opportunity to every citizen, regardless of race, creed or color. Throughout our history, we have pointed with pride to those among us who have risen from poverty to positions of responsibility in government, business and the law.

And yet any objective observer must admit that we are still a long way from our ideal. The son or daughter of wealthy parents has opportunities in education, health, recreation and general development which are denied to the children of the lower-income groups.

It is the responsibility of the federal government to see that a high standard of education is available to every boy and girl in the United States, regardless of the income of their parents.

We should also establish a minimum standard of public health and this minimum should be a high one. A comprehensive medical insurance program will call for the building of many thousands of hospitals and the training of tens of thousands of doctors, dentists and nurses. But we are a rich nation, and we cannot afford to shrink from this responsibility.

Our government must also act as the spearhead in the fight to provide decent housing for all our people. It was estimated before the war that more than one-third of all American families were living in dwellings which were grossly inadequate. The monopoly-ridden housing industry, with its featherbedding and politically instigated building codes, has fallen down miserably on its public responsibilities.

The fifth responsibility of our government is to so integrate our export and import program that the work of relief and rehabilitation throughout the world will be pushed steadily forward.

Ours is the only major nation in the world untouched by war. We are rich in natural resources, in human skills and in productive capacity. The world in which we live keeps growing smaller. There are some among us who still say that we have no responsibilities to the rest of the world and that our efforts should be concentrated solely on increasing the wealth of our own people. It is essential to our own welfare and to that of the world that this viewpoint should be rejected.

We cannot successfully build a palace for Americans in the midst of a world slum. Unless the standard of living is raised steadily for all peoples, there can be no peace or security for ourselves or for our children.

If we are to raise the world's productive power and with it the security of the world's people, we must help modernize world agriculture. This is a fundamental challenge for the next generation. We must also help to build modern transportation systems, power developments and basic industrial plants. The opportunity for American management skills is unlimited.

The Soviet Union and the Communist parties offer hungry people the hope for higher living standards and increased economic security. If we are successfully to meet this challenge, it will not be sufficient simply to argue, however rightly, that Communism means the end of political democracy. We must promote on a world-wide scale not only political freedom, but economic democracy as well.

The sixth and final responsibility of our government is to coordinate all its policies in such a way that a market will be provided for all that we are capable of producing.

What I am urging is government assurance that the purchasing power will always be present to buy all the goods which our workers, farmers and businessmen can produce each year. This is essential if we are to maintain full production and full employment. The more effective the guarantee, the greater will be the confidence in the economic outlook, and the more certainly will pent-up demand be translated into orders. This is a point that deserves particular emphasis.

* * *

IN SO-CALLED normal times, every businessman is forced to take two risks. The first is the normal risk of competition, the test of his ability to compete with other businessmen in his industry in producing quality goods at reasonable prices. This is a proper risk which every businessman who sincerely believes in our system of private enterprise must accept.

The second risk is the possibility that depression lurks just around the corner. A depression drives the efficient into bankruptcy along with the inefficient. The constant fear of depression leads businessmen to restrict their production, to curb their plans for expansion, to pile up huge reserves on which they may hope to survive during a period of hard times.

This second risk, in view of all that we know today about the workings of a modern economy, is an unnecessary risk. It can and must be eliminated by intelligent, democratic action.

We will need, first of all, to coordinate and to time the construction of public works.

We shall also need to review carefully our tax and fiscal policies. The tax legislation under which we have operated for the past few years has grown like an old country house, with a wing added here, a barn there and a toolshed somewhere else. It needs a thorough overhauling if our tax program is to contribute to full production and full employment.

A modern tax program should also provide higher incentives for the development of new enterprise. New businesses should be allowed to balance losses in their early years against the profits they may make after they have turned the corner.

Most economists agree that the basic tax rates in any given period should reflect current economic conditions. In a period of rising prices, taxes should be high. In a period in which underproduction is threatened, taxes should be reduced so that purchasing power and incentives will be increased.

I would like to see the President with the advice of his Economic Council given authority, within specific limits, to move taxes up and down to meet the current needs of our economy. The President's power to do so should, of course, operate under clearly established legislative authority and standards. This would enable us promptly to increase or decrease the total flow of purchasing power as our economy tends toward inflation or deflation. I believe that we have sufficient economic knowledge to enable an agency of this kind to fill an important role in leveling out the business cycle.

It would be a mistake, however, to assume that government can solve all our economic problems under a private enterprise system. Government expenditures, even though carefully coordinated, cannot make up for sweeping failures on the part of business, labor and farm leaders to carry out their proper economic functions in a private enterprise system. As long as we maintain our private enterprise system—and surely we would be foolish to abandon it—the biggest impact on our economy will come from the decisions of individual businessmen, workers and farmers, in establishing wages, prices and profits and planning the expansion of our industrial facilities.

If we are to arrive at a rational solution to our economic future, we shall need responsible labor leadership. We shall need an end to featherbedding practices and a determination on the part of the individual workers that a full day's work will be provided in return for a full day's pay.

But our businessmen will carry the heaviest responsibility of all. This is so because a private enterprise economy is a business economy. It would be unfair to expect businessmen to follow business practices which are unprofitable. Profits are the lifeblood of business.

But if our businessmen are to carry out their responsibilities, not only to themselves but to our economy as a whole, their approach to profit-making must be a long-range approach.

There are only three ways in which wages can be raised. A business which is making more than adequate profit can pay a higher wage, maintain its present price level and still maintain a reasonable profit. A business which is paying substandard wages and making no more than a normal profit can and should raise its wages by raising its price. Where wages are substandard, there is every reason why this step should be taken. If employers cannot meet a minimum wage standard, they should not be in business. None of us as consumers has a right to be subsidized by substandard wages.

Finally, wages can be increased, prices either kept stable or reduced, and profits either maintained or increased through an increase in labor productivity. It is this latter approach on which we must largely depend for an increase in our standard of living. During the twenty years before the war, labor output per man-hour increased 4 percent annually.

The increase in labor output per man-hour results largely from improved machinery and facilities. If management is to have the incentive to invest its profits to improve the efficiency of its plants, it has a right to expect part of the proceeds from increased labor productivity as an increase in its profit. But just as clearly, a substantial proportion of the increase in labor output per man-hour should be set aside for increased wages.

If management fails to accept this view or if labor fails to present its case, we will lack the increased purchasing power necessary to buy the increased output of goods. This is exactly what led to the disastrous depression of 1929.

An all-important area in which businessmen under a private enterprise system must make the key decisions is in the establishment of prices. Some prices are set too high because businessmen fail to appreciate the opportunities for increased volume and increased profits which may result from lower prices. In every section of American business we have seen instances where a lower price has resulted in such an increase in volume that a generous increase in profits has been forthcoming.

What I am urging in this essential field of private decisions is more enterprise, more imagination in labor-management relations, improved business methods and a clearer understanding of the long-range profit opportunities based on increased volume.

Government has an important responsibility if we are to maintain the markets and the purchasing power on which full production must depend. But the responsibility of our businessmen, our workers and our farmers, in setting wages, prices and profits, is even greater.

If, for any reason, we fail in this area of private decisions, the government's role in our economy will surely increase. If monopolistic price-fixing continues to flourish, there will be an increased demand for government control. If labor-management disputes develop into widespread disruptions in our economic life, there will be further demands.

And once government in peacetime is forced to invade the territory which should be set aside for private decisions, government controls will spread as one control leads to another. This we must make every effort to avoid.

=== 3

A FRESH LOOK AT ECONOMIC GROWTH

As the American economy continued to lag, Congressman Bowles in a major address in the House of Representatives urges vigorous private and public action to encourage faster growth. June 29, 1959.

MR. SPEAKER, I have asked for the floor this afternoon to speak on what I believe to be the primary issue facing the American people. I refer to the persistent failure of our national economy in recent years to live up to its vast capacity for sustained growth, with high employment and without inflation.

Our success in meeting this challenge will determine, not only the nature of our own society in the years immediately ahead, but our capacity for leadership itself in a world of revolutionary change.

We are now recovering from our third recession in ten years. The first occurred in 1949, the second in 1953-54, the third in 1957-58.

The production lost in recent years has been lost for good, and the total is substantial. Had our growth since the Korean War continued at the previous post-World War II rate of 4 percent annually, we would have produced $170 billion worth of goods and services more than we actually did produce.

If we had achieved the 5 percent rate of increase which the Rockefeller Report in 1958 asserted was both feasible and necessary, our added post-Korea production would have exceeded $400 billion.

This is a colossal sum. It is nearly equal to a full year's national income. It is one and one-half times our national debt of $285 billion.

Why have we failed since the Korean War to live up to our economic potential? What has gone wrong?

The causes are many and complicated. Honest men may differ on both their nature and their cure. I will hazard the guess that historians will charge much of the lag to our failure to understand the dynamics of the private enterprise system to which we give such strong verbal support.

Our mistakes have not been in our failure to use the federal government's power over our economy. Our difficulties stem largely from the fact that we have used the power for the wrong purposes, for the wrong reasons, in the wrong ways.

Instead of using the agencies and power of our government to encourage growth and high employment, we have often used them inadvertently to inhibit growth on the false assumption that sustained growth, high employment and price stability are incompatible.

Although we all agree that most prices are too high, the cost-of-living indexes have been steady for well over a year. Indeed, according to the Department of Labor, we are now in the longest sustained point of price stability in nineteen years.

What has gone up are the prices of common stocks and real estate. These have increased by tens and tens of billions of dollars.

If this continues, Mr. Speaker, these so-called values will eventually collapse, as they have collapsed in the past. When this occurs, it will be the millions of small investors, many of whom were frightened into the market by irresponsible talk about inflation, who will be hurt most grievously.

The failure of our economy to grow at a sustained high rate profoundly affects almost every question that comes before us in this Congress. In good conscience we cannot shirk our responsibilities in dealing with it. In that spirit let us re-examine the clearest statement of national economic policy ever put together by Congress. I refer to the Employment Act of 1946.

This legislation was written in a spirit of postwar cooperation and confidence. It was ushered through the Congress by a bipartisan team and supported by overwhelming majorities in both parties.

It was addressed explicitly to the general welfare. It called upon the President to transmit to the Congress "an economic report setting forth the levels of employment, production, and purchasing power obtaining in the United States and such levels needed to carry out the policy declared."

In his Economic Report last January, President Eisenhower referred to this responsibility. However, he has never followed the precedent established by the earlier Economic Reports which set national goals adjusted annually, and prescribed the means of reaching these goals.

On this issue as on many others, the ball has been passed to Congress. If we duck this responsibility by failing to clarify our national goals, we will continue to fall short of our opportunities.

It is also essential that we reach some kind of consensus in this House on the causes of our present slow growth. Once this consensus has been established, we can devise a course of action which will put us back again on the high road to sustained and increasing high production with stable prices.

In this connection, I offer the following comments.

First. I hope the studies and report of the Joint Economic Committee can include a documented, statistical picture of what our economy, public and private, would look like with maximum use of our men, machines and capital.

Second. I hope this report will give us some specific estimates of our real potential in terms of the purchasing power needed to help assure industry of ever wider markets, of the kinds and amounts of capital needed for the continued modernization and expansion of our industrial plant, and of the size and variety of social services which could be available to us in the richest nation on earth.

Third. I hope that the report will indicate the over-all expansionist effect that our economy at full capacity would have upon our federal, state and local revenues.

Fourth. I hope the Ways and Means Committee, in analyzing our present tax system and recommending improvements, will consider ways to provide an increased share of our tax revenues to state and local governments and whatever special tax incentives may be required for industrial expansion and growth.

Since at least two dollars of gross national product each year are created for every dollar of capital investment, such an effort will stimulate our entire economy.

Fifth. I hope that serious attention will be paid to existing tax loopholes, such as excessive business expense-account deductions. Some observers believe that we are losing in various ways as much as four billion dollars a year.

Sixth. I hope that various proposals for dealing with the problem of "administered" prices in semimonopolistic industries will be considered. These proposals should be taken seriously. Should present monopoly legislation be broadened? Would a special "excess margin" tax be practical and effective?

Seventh. In this connection I hope that the House will have an opportunity to consider the proposal for public fact-finding hearings on prospective price or wage increases of a magnitude which threatens our national economic stability.

Eighth. Although our major agricultural problem lies in policies affecting production, the possibility of greatly increased food consumption should not be overlooked.

Our agricultural abundance can become a far more powerful instrument for aiding economic development and alleviating the hunger of tens of millions of people in less fortunate lands. It is both unwise, uneconomic and immoral to allow them to remain idle.

There is also need for much of our "surplus" foods right here in America. An expanded school lunch program and a food stamp plan continue to offer two practical opportunities to convert our eight billion dollars' worth of food now in storage into a live domestic asset.

Ninth. In the report of the Joint Economic Committee, I hope a thorough analysis will be made of interest rates and their effects upon industrial and farm production, construction, purchasing power, unemployment and government revenues at all levels.

Tenth. Finally, may I add a few comments on a closely related subject with which I believe Congress must sooner or later come to grips.

For years the Communists have been telling the world that above all else America fears the economic effects of disarmament.

If the flow of armament orders from the Pentagon should cease, the Kremlin asserts, American industries would go bankrupt and American workers would starve. The collapse of capitalism and the triumph of Communism would then become inevitable.

Karl Marx to the contrary, I believe the transition to a peacetime economy could be made much more smoothly than most of us assume.

Within eighteen months after the end of World War II, we switched some 45 percent of American industry from wartime to peacetime production and absorbed nearly ten million men from our armed services into our civilian economy.

To be sure, we had the advantage then of a heavy backlog of war-accumulated demands for housing, schools and consumer durables. But today the percentage of our economy devoted to defense production is only one-fifth of what it was in 1945. As for our backlog of unfilled needs, every mayor, city planner, educator, highway engineer, hospital superintendent and sociologist knows that it is enormous.

The Senate Disarmament Committee under the chairmanship of Senator Humphrey has conducted pioneering hearings on the economic implications of disarmament. I am convinced that further study of this subject would be reassuring to the American people and proof to the world that it is the Soviet Union and not the United States that stands in the way of a realistic reduction of cold war tensions.

In closing let me consider the enormous stake we have as a nation and as individuals in finding practical answers to the questions which I have posed.

What effect, for instance, would high employment and an accelerated rate of economic growth in the next fiscal year have upon federal revenues and the federal budget?

A sustained expansion rate of 4 percent through the fiscal year 1961 would give us eighteen to twenty billion dollars more production over and beyond the increases that may be expected in fiscal 1960.

This would provide several billion dollars more in federal tax income. With a drop in interest costs and federal relief payments, we would then have ample revenues with which to meet our full responsibilities in construction, defense, education, medical research and welfare, while balancing the budget and cutting taxes all at the same time.

In the following years, if we provide a wise policy direction that will assure continued rapid expansion without inflation, we could move further to reduce taxes and to start a long-postponed and effective reduction of the national debt.

Mr. Speaker, this is not daydreaming. This is the hard, factual arithmetic of sustained economic growth.

There will be groups which, each in its own way and for its own reasons, will oppose any effort to do what is so clearly required of us if we are to assure the security of our nation and the well-being of our people.

They will condemn every proposal for dams, schools or housing as likely to unbalance the budget and bring on a disastrous inflation. They will oppose every effort to get at the cause of our dilemma as useless or ill timed.

It would be folly to allow this timid view of America's future to intimidate a majority in this House into political impotence. I submit that the sustained expansion of our American economy at an accelerated rate without inflation is the No. 1 challenge on the agenda of this Congress.

4

STEEL PRICES AND THE
NATIONAL ECONOMY

*The following letter to President Eisenhower was sent during
the fourth week of the prolonged steel strike in August,
1959. In it Congressman Bowles suggests that, for the long-term
good of both the economy and the steel industry, the
price of steel should be lowered rather than raised.*

DEAR MR. PRESIDENT:

As wartime Price Administrator and Director of Economic Stabilization, I was deeply involved on a week-to-week basis with the complex
interrelationship of prices, wages and profits in the steel industry.
Over the years since then, I have been increasingly disturbed in watch-
ing the operations of this key industry which has such widespread
influence on employment and manufacturing costs throughout our
economy.

In these fourteen years, the steel industry has been shut down six
times by labor-management differences. One hundred ninety days of
production have been lost. As a result, an estimated 45 million tons
of steel production that might have been produced were not produced
and, of course, the losses in wages and profits run into hundreds of
millions of dollars.

The present impasse is now moving into its fourth week. Unless some agreement can be reached soon, the implications for our economy as a whole are decidedly disturbing.

We are now emerging from our third recession in ten years. This series of setbacks has slowed our average annual rate of growth to the lowest levels in several decades.

Continued loss of steel production and steelworker purchasing power will curtail our prosperity still further. Moreover, as steel stocks dwindle, almost every industry in America will become affected. Bitterness between the workers and management, which already is distressingly great, will become greater.

If a labor-management settlement is followed by a price rise, the adverse effect on our economy as a whole will be increased still further. Already the price of steel has risen from the OPA ceiling of $54 a ton in 1945 to $155 in 1959. This is four times the increase in the wholesale price level in this fourteen-year period.

Of the 9 percent rise in average wholesale prices since 1953, 7 percent has been directly due to increases in steel and steel-using products.

If it had not been for a drop in the wholesale prices of farm products, which have gone down 9 percent since 1953, the inflationary pressures generated primarily by the steel industry would have been even more evident. This means that sagging food prices have been balancing skyrocketing steel prices.

When asked to explain its repeated and extensive price increases, the steel industry has invariably pointed out that hourly wage rates have also tripled. Continued repetition of this explanation has led many people to assume that the blame for high prices belongs exclusively to labor. This, however, leaves out a critically important point—the relation between hourly wage rates and labor productivity.

Corporate profits are determined by many things. To the degree that labor cost is a factor, it is not the price of labor per hour but the cost of labor per ton of steel produced that is important. Although this precise figure is one of the world's best-kept secrets, the external evidence indicates that the increase in wage rates has to a considerable extent been offset by the increases in labor productivity.

The situation which now confronts us is urgent. Further drift will slow down our economy and endanger both jobs and profits at a critical point in our general recovery.

Viewed strictly as a contest between management and labor, it seems clear that steel wages, in view of recent increases in labor productivity, could and should be increased with no increase in prices. Operating at high capacity, the steel industry could continue to set record profits.

Yet I believe the public interest can best be served by a cut in steel prices with no change in wage rates. The evidence seems clear that the steel industry could take this important step and still maintain record profits.

Naturally, such a proposal is not being pursued enthusiastically by either management or labor. However, there are times when we must all look beyond special group interests in the broader public interest. I deeply believe that we have now arrived at such a point in regard to the steel industry.

A reduction of ten dollars per ton in steel prices could be reflected this fall in lower prices of automobiles, washing machines, refrigerators and other home appliances. It could reduce the cost of our highway program, industrial construction, machine tools and other essential items.

It could also help restore to our economy as a whole the vitality which can only come when our productive facilities are being used to capacity and when our people are fully employed. In regard to the steel industry itself, it could serve to increase sales, assure steadier and larger employment and improve our competitive position in regard to steel imports.

In recent months we have heard much about the danger of inflation, but in my opinion too little about economic growth. I submit that both problems are closely interrelated and that both could be partially met by a reduction in steel prices.

For this reason I respectfully suggest that you call on the steel industry to take this bold, creative action for the long-term good of our country and our economy.

5

THE WATERSHED OF THE SIXTIES

*As the postwar era ends, Mr. Bowles sees new pressures
evolving in our society and urges us to abandon worn-out
political labels in meeting them. An address to the Yale Law
Forum in New Haven, Connecticut, November 21, 1961.*

WE ARE approaching a watershed in regard to the world,
our economy and relations with other nations. We are at the end of
the postwar period, poised uncertainly before the opening of a new
era in the history of man.

I believe that the political, economic and social confusions which
are evident within our own society are part of the ferment that pre-
cedes great national decisions.

Three powerful political forces are at work in our society, no one
of which is likely to succumb to old slogans or to fit easily into familiar political pigeonholes. Bit by bit each of us is being pressed to
come to grips with these forces, to rethink our attitudes toward public questions, to abandon sterile concepts and to stake out new positions.

The first of these forces is the massive impact of the interrelated
postwar world on our American society, and our search for a more
realistic response.

For the past fifteen years many of us have been assuring each other
that the global pressures which we have been striving to meet are

temporary, that if we were wise and courageous the so-called world emergency would somehow subside, and that this would leave us happily undisturbed, with nothing to do but enjoy our material comforts.

This dangerously parochial view is due partly to the pull of our isolationist past and partly to the distorted view of world affairs that developed as a result of the specially favored position from which we tackled international problems following the war.

The American economy alone was physically intact, strengthened by heavy wartime investment, and raring to go. American military power was firmly based in a monopoly of nuclear weapons.

As a result, American power relative to that of other nations was overwhelming. As we looked around the world, there was almost nothing we could not do if we had the will to do it.

In the last few years this situation has been profoundly altered. As we enter the decade of the sixties, a vital new Europe is creating the first integrated society since the Romans, the Soviet Union has emerged with industrial and military power second only to our own, and China under a tough and embittered Communist government has been developing some alarmingly expansionist notions in regard to its neighbors.

Simultaneously, Asia, Africa and Latin America have awakened to the exciting fact that illiteracy, poverty and ill health may gradually be eliminated and that new opportunities can be created for their people.

The result is a world of infinite potential and of profound uncertainties. Is it then surprising that the more timid among us should be anxious to withdraw from it, or to ignore it, or to retreat into intellectual bomb shelters in the hope that when they come out the world will have somehow returned to the more orderly pattern of their fathers' day?

Let us turn, then, to the second force which I believe will help shape the political patterns of the 1960's, namely, the evolving pressures within our own economy. As we attempt to cope with these pressures, we again find that many old concepts begin to sound hollow if not irrelevant.

Working at its most effective and dynamic best our capitalistic system has been based on able management, small-unit profits and a vigorous sales effort to achieve the largest possible volumes, with profits increasing as volume expands.

In certain industries we now see this formula hopelessly compromised by price and wage manipulation which has little relevance to economic realities. In some industries we see prices arbitrarily set to provide for substantial profits with 25 percent or more of productive capacity lying idle. In others we face featherbedding practices in the labor movement which slow down production and raise costs and prices correspondingly.

Taking a broad view, it is clear that we have been drifting into a situation in which powerful vested interests find it possible to protect their own economic interests with several million people unemployed and an important fraction of our people ill-nourished, ill-housed and poorly educated.

What is required is a searching re-examination to determine why many areas of our economy remain stagnant, why our rate of growth has lagged behind that of most industrial countries, why 20 percent of all American families are still living on less than $2,000 a year, and why unemployment stubbornly persists in many centers of population at a time that calls for all the production that we can get.

Among the various questions about our domestic economy which are waiting to be asked and answered are the following:

How can we reorganize our housing industry to build more and better homes each year at lower prices?

How can we speed up the rebuilding of our cities so that our slums may be wiped out in the decade of the sixties?

How can we make the best medical attention available to those who are in greatest need?

Above all, how can we strengthen our public educational system to insure that all bright American boys and girls can enter college?

Our search for better answers should not be confined to local, state and federal governments. It should enlist the best minds in our labor unions, our universities, our business and farm organizations.

Our economy is the essential instrument with which we must achieve greater opportunity and security for all citizens, assure an adequate defense system and provide the resources with which to ease the growing pains of new nations that are striving to relieve their poverty through democratic institutions.

Only a confident, dynamic America can meet this challenge. Yet built-in obstacles to expanding production have kept us on dead center. The third force with which we must contend in this period of political reorientation is found in the rapidly growing demands of our Negro citizens for full citizenship in what we believe to be the greatest democracy on earth.

For generations the struggle against racial discrimination was largely spearheaded by white Americans whose consciences told them that discrimination against any group was a violation of their moral creed. Now the lead is being taken by Negro Americans who are calling upon Negro fellow citizens to demand their rights under our Constitution. The response grows month by month.

Moreover, these voices are now heard, not only in our own country, but increasingly throughout the world. As long as we deny full democratic rights to those Americans whose ancestors came from Africa, we cannot expect the representatives of the Asian and African nations to accept our protestation of democratic faith.

These, then, are the three challenges which face the American people in the decade of the sixties: our relations with the world, our ability to improve the performance of our economy and our efforts to eliminate discrimination against any American on the grounds of race, creed or religion.

Out of our conflicting reactions to these questions new political patterns will almost certainly emerge in the 1960's.

Since the old political tags of "liberal," "conservative," "radical" or "reactionary" are rapidly losing their relevance, the sooner a new orientation develops, the better it will be for all of us. The slogans which moved us in the 1930's are leaving an increasing number of Americans uninspired and apathetic.

I do not suggest that the lines of political argument and action that will divide us in the 1960's will be totally unconnected with the past. Liberalism in any age calls for belief in certain universal values which must be reframed by each generation in response to the realities of its own experience and objectives.

In the new days as in the old, conservative thinkers may be expected to draw more vigorously from the past and to approach the future with greater misgivings.

The more extreme among them will demand that we withdraw from the United Nations and from our alliances, that we slash our governmental budgets, slow down our efforts to rebuild our cities and improve our education, and that we urge American Negroes to be patient for yet a little while.

In effect they will be saying, "Stop the world, we want to get off." But the world will not stop and not even the most timid of us can get off.

No other period in history provides such awesome dangers as does our fast-changing world of today; nor does any other period offer such exhilarating opportunities for the individual to grow, for his dignity to become a reality and for human energies to be released for the common good.

Thus we may hope to hear the liberal-minded people of tomorrow call for a stronger world partnership between ourselves and other non-Communist nations, increased concern for freedom and well-being of other people, added determination not merely to stand up to Soviet threats, but to create a better society here at home in which men are free to do what they are capable of doing, no matter what their race, their creed or their color.

As the true meaning of democracy is debated in the new framework, as new differences are crystallized and new political postures chosen, we must hope that the advantage will continue to lie with those who place above all else the rights and responsibilities of man. It is the task of such people to redefine the potentials of democratic faith in the framework of today's dangerous, exciting and promising world.

RESPONSIBLE STATE GOVERNMENTS: KEY TO DECENTRALIZATION

We have lagged in adjusting the machinery of our state governments to the growing needs of our society.

As a result the federal government has on many occasions been forced by public pressures to deal with problems which might better have been handled in our state capitols. Much of the growth of centralized power in Washington can be traced directly to our failure to keep state governmental techniques abreast of our times.

March 9, 1950

═══ 6

THE GOVERNOR'S JOB AS SEEN
BY A GOVERNOR

Reviewing his first six months in office, Mr. Bowles, as
Governor of Connecticut, sizes up the obligations, pitfalls,
and opportunities of his new job. New York Times Magazine,
July 24, 1949.

LAST November, somewhat to the surprise of my party, the
pollsters and myself, I became Governor of Connecticut. I won by
the second slimmest margin in the modern history of Connecticut
elections—2,225 votes.

Connecticut Republicans, like those across the country, had been
serenely confident. Connecticut is a "land of steady habits" and there
had been only eleven Democratic governors in the last hundred years.

I had run for Governor, not because I thought that any Democrat
had a chance in 1948—least of all in Connecticut—but for several
reasons which seemed to me important.

Connecticut, like most other states, faced some serious problems.
There was a critical shortage of schools and teachers which our towns
couldn't solve unaided. Our housing shortage was even more acute
than that of other states—and we have more than our share of slums.
There was pressing need for modern mental hospitals to replace antiquated firetraps built two generations or more ago. There was need

for broadened labor legislation to meet growing unemployment and need for increased old age assistance.

I felt that such problems could and should be solved by *state* action. Too great centralization of government in Washington can be dangerous. Yet, if a state government fails to house its people properly, or give good education to its children, or take care of its aged, the federal government must eventually step in, either of necessity or by default.

I believe that one extremely important way to prevent too great centralization of government in Washington is to improve the effectiveness of our state governments generally.

It was my hope that if Connecticut and other states could set high enough standards of responsibility and efficiency in handling their problems, there would be less need to turn to Washington.

When the shock of my election wore off, and I took a clear look ahead, I saw two immediate jobs. First, I had to prepare a legislative program to carry out the platform on which I had been elected. Second, I had to prepare a state budget.

I expected rough sledding on both jobs. For while the Connecticut Senate had a comfortable Democratic majority, the House of Representatives was overwhelmingly Republican.

Aside from these two responsibilities, I knew simply that it was my job to administer the state government as competently as I could and, the legislature permitting, make whatever organizational changes would permit improved administrative efficiency. The last six months, however, have taught me that a governor's life involves many other duties, responsibilities, headaches and satisfactions.

One of the most rewarding phases of a governor's job is to see a constant flow of people from all over the state. A governor's office, in fact, looks like, and very often sounds like, a nonstop New England town meeting.

This part of a governor's job has convinced me even more thoroughly that state government fills a place no Washington agency could take. In a state government, particularly in a small state like Connecticut, you live and work in close contact with those whose attitudes eventually decide public policies.

When they think you are right, and especially when they think you are wrong, they manage to get their views to you very quickly. It is direct-action democracy—straight to the point and no holds barred.

In addition, I function as head of my political party, as does every governor. I must be accessible at all times to my party's legislators, and my party's town chairmen and other state and local party officials, and help make political decisions.

Every morning that the legislature convened I saw its Democratic leaders and discussed with them their legislative strategy for the day. (The Republicans were invited, too, but they appeared only on rare occasions.) At any moment during the session my door could be, and was, thrown open by committee chairmen with a fresh legislative crisis on labor, education, housing or other bills to which they needed a quick answer.

All of these extra and special gubernatorial duties are absorbing, fascinating and necessary. They do, however, pile up a tremendous load when added to a governor's basic jobs.

The task of improving administration I knew from the start would not be easy. Connecticut's 108 agencies result in an administrative machine that would startle even Rube Goldberg. There are over eight hundred agency heads or commissioners directly responsible, in theory at least, to me. If I should muster the courage to call a "cabinet meeting," all eight hundred presumably would have to be present. Many of these agencies have "just growed," like Topsy. Some are frank political creations.

Many a Connecticut citizen interested in good government, Republican as well as Democrat, has tried to straighten out this costly, incredible state machinery. Governor Wilbur Cross attempted it in the thirties and made a little headway. I decided to try again.

One of my first acts was to ask the legislature for government reorganization via a state "Hoover Committee." It consented, with some helpful prodding from taxpayer groups concerned with government economy. Recommendations are to be made by that committee early next year. If we are lucky, Connecticut's government may begin to have a more streamlined look by 1951.

Another curious administrative handicap was to find that my sixteen chief commissioners were all Republicans, appointed by Republicans, and in some cases openly committed against my general program and policies. While many of them are able men, I sometimes wonder if this is not like trying to run General Motors with a board of directors provided by Chrysler.

My biggest and certainly my thorniest job was to develop and see through a legislative program. In my inaugural message, I laid down a program on which I had been working almost since Election Day.

The Democratic Senate and party were firmly behind the program, and so were many strong independent groups of citizens. With our Democratic majority in the Senate I knew we could count on legislative approval there. But the Republican-controlled House was another matter, and one it proved impossible to control.

The reason lies in what is called by progressive Republicans as well as Democrats the "rotten borough system." Under this system, every town, however small, which was incorporated before 1850 can send two representatives to the House. Since in Connecticut almost all the small towns have been overwhelmingly Republican since the Civil War, and since they vastly outnumber the cities, the House always has a guaranteed, built-in Republican majority.

Although two-thirds of the representatives in the House are Republican, they represent only one-third of the people. Connecticut's five biggest cities have roughly 35 percent of our population. But instead of electing 35 percent of our representatives to the Lower House, they elect less than 3 percent.

Now I am personally very fond of small towns. In fact, I chose to live in the small town of Essex, with a population of only 3,100. Yet I cannot agree that the ten representatives of these five largest cities, with a combined population of 656,000, should be outvoted, as they usually are, by the twelve representatives of our six smallest towns, with a *total* population of 2,523 men, women and children.

Regardless of what he may say or do during the legislative session, no Republican legislative leader in the Connecticut House of Representatives is ever forced to consider even the remote possibility of being beaten at the polls. This situation does not make for imaginative, responsible democracy.

I believe that it is time for sober reflection on the part of our state governments in this over-all democratic process. The present necessity of looking to Washington for the solution of our governmental problems can, over a period of time, result in a dangerous overcentralization of governmental power.

If we are to assume that public problems must be met, there is a strong case for meeting as many of them as possible through our states. Yet the states will be unable to act effectively and adequately unless their democratic machinery enables them to reflect the will and intent of their citizens.

In Connecticut we are striving to provide such machinery.

THE CHALLENGE OF OUR SCHOOLS

*Connecticut's critical postwar shortage of schools posed severe
problems of financing and politics. Governor Bowles presented
this message to a special "school" session of the state
legislature which he called in November, 1949. Nearly
two-thirds of Connecticut's children are now studying in schools
built under the legislation which was passed a few weeks later.*

WE ARE gathered here today in a special session of the Connecticut General Assembly for the specific purpose of considering actions vitally affecting the future of public education in our state.

There is probably no single subject of greater importance, not only to Connecticut, but to the entire nation and the world. If we fail to take proper action now to improve our educational system, we will jeopardize the future of our democratic form of government.

Clearly, our children will be called upon to deal with a parade of problems no less complicated and probably far more difficult than those which our generation has been struggling to solve during the last thirty years, without distinguished success.

When we talk, therefore, about improving our educational system, we are really talking about the kind of preparation we can give our children now to meet the challenging problems of the future. We are assembled to discuss and decide the most profitable kind of investment that any community, any state or any nation can make in behalf of its own future welfare.

But there are those who argue that an educational system which was good enough for our generation surely must be good enough for our children. Such an attitude, it seems to me, has no basis in logic. The children of today cannot tomorrow meet the problems of an atomic age equipped with the Model-T education which our fathers obtained in the little red schoolhouse.

Nevertheless, we now face the threat of a serious decline in the quality of our public education. Not only are we failing to move ahead, but, even more serious, we stand in grave jeopardy of losing ground.

As I have stressed over and over again, we must strengthen our teacher-training, our teacher recruitment and the curriculum of our educational system from kindergarten through our universities.

In addition, we must face up to the mounting shortage of adequate school building facilities. An excellent education *can* be provided in a bad school and a bad education can come out of a good school. Nevertheless, a greatly expanded program of school-building is an urgent essential step toward maintaining and improving the quality of our Connecticut education, and this is the subject of this special message to you today.

The general problem of state aid for school-building is admittedly complex. A series of questions must be considered before a final answer is found. Let me review these questions here.

Question 1 is the extent of the need for modernizing and expanding our school-building facilities. On this point there can be no valid basis for disagreement.

The recent report of the local school boards points up sharply the inadequacy of our existing school facilities. It tells us that nearly one-fourth of our present schools were built in the nineteenth century; that there are still fifty-five one-room schoolhouses in use; that in the decade of the 1930's we did very little to maintain or expand our school buildings, and in the last ten years we have built even fewer schools. At the same time our school population is rapidly expanding.

The report further shows that while the situation will grow steadily worse, our children even now are obliged to accept substandard educational facilities. A large number of our cities and towns have been forced to hold some classes outside of regular classrooms, and in many schools classes are being held in the basement, town meeting places, and even barns and shower rooms. These are established facts.

Looking to the future, the report summarizes the amount of school-building which, in the opinion of the local school board members, will be required in the next two years, and also over the next ten years. The figures run into sizable totals. They demonstrate the need for a large school-building program which must begin, not next year, or the year after, but now.

The second question is whether state aid for this purpose is necessary. Although only a few towns have actually reached their legal debt limit, a far larger number are rapidly approaching or have already reached their *practical* economic debt limit. We know, moreover, that many local governments have already been forced to raise property taxes to the economic limit.

Our towns and cities in most instances face, not only a substantial educational building program, but other large capital requirements, such as improved or expanded water and sewage facilities, fire and police protection facilities, public buildings and the like. These general conditions are revealed in the detailed findings of local school boards.

Specifically, the school boards in 116 cities and towns state that their communities must have state aid if they are to go ahead with necessary school buildings. An additional seventeen towns imply that such aid is necessary. Only seven say positively that no aid will be required. Thus the evidence is overwhelmingly clear that unless the State of Connecticut follows the example of many other states, and lends a financial hand to local communities for school-building programs, these schools will not be built.

The third question then is: Are all our cities and towns in equal need of assistance? The answer is obvious: The financial ability of our cities and towns to meet their needs varies widely. We have some very wealthy towns and some very poor towns, and many other towns in between. Each community's ability to pay must be judged mainly by its basic taxable wealth compared to its size.

In our democratic society every child should have an equal opportunity for a good education, whether he comes from a rich town or a poor town, a rich city or a poor city. Our goal, therefore, must be to equalize the educational opportunities of all Connecticut children. To achieve this goal, we must use state aid to help equalize the financial ability of various communities to meet their pressing obligations to their children.

Let me turn now to the fourth question. If there is need for state aid to help towns build schools, can the State of Connecticut actually afford such aid at this time?

Much of the answer to this question can be found in the following facts. Our ability to invest in education is directly related to our income. The total income of the people of Connecticut has increased tremendously in the last ten years. Yet, although we are faced with a clear-cut emergency in education, we are today investing a substantially smaller *proportion* of our total income in education than we were ten years ago, when we were far less prosperous.

There can be little doubt that the people of Connecticut are able financially to increase our investment in such an important enterprise as education.

The fifth question is this: How much state aid should be granted and how should these funds be raised? My own judgment is that on the basis of an equalization method state aid to cities and towns should average somewhere between one-quarter and one-half of the total school-building costs, though with aid in specific cases running above and below this average.

Some have proposed that we should provide the necessary funds by slashing our expenditures for other purposes. Any of you who takes this stand has a responsibility to state explicitly where you would cut our present state service, and to what extent.

Would you, for instance, cut our expenditures for the State Police? Would you cut our expenditures for welfare payments to our old people and to our unfortunates? And, if so, in what amounts? Would you cut our state health programs? Our already understaffed mental hospitals? Our programs of unemployment compensation and workmen's compensation? Our National Guard? Our aid to dependent children?

Some of you who recognize the tightness of our budget, and the fact that no drastic expenditure cuts could be made without jeopardizing important state services, have proposed that we meet our present school-building needs through a tax increase.

This is an honest and forthright position. But I must state that I am in disagreement with it. I believe that increasing taxes at this time of economic slack would mean imposing a serious deterrent to the improvement in business and employment throughout the state.

Moreover, I believe that a tax increase is unnecessary. Unless our revenue picture becomes far darker than the Budget Director now anticipates, I believe that with cautious management and prudent legislation we can keep our income and expenditures in balance.*

There is an important alternative way of meeting the problem. I refer to the installment plan method of paying the state's share of locally built schools.

When a business expands its plant, it typically borrows money and pays it back over a period of years during the useful life of the plant. When a family buys a home, they typically finance that home by a mortgage which is amortized over a number of years. This is also the way we in Connecticut are now building our teachers colleges, our vocational schools and the additions to the University of Connecticut. This is the way we can raise the $25 million of state funds needed annually for school construction.

It seems to me that this session comes down to a test of the sincerity of each individual legislator and each political party. Do we or do we not want to strengthen our educational system? If we do, then are we or are we not willing to take the necessary steps to carry out this objective?

The question is sharp and clear and impossible of honest misunderstanding. For nearly a year we have been talking about building schools. At every hand we have been protesting our belief that action should be forthcoming. We have now reached what, in colloquial terms, might be called the "put up or shut up" phase of the discussion.

We all carry a very heavy responsibility as we enter this session. Part of my responsibility is to state to you clearly where I stand on these critical issues and to give you the best facts that I can secure.

This I have done. What happens now is in your hands.

---

* During Governor Bowles' administration, Connecticut was one of three states that balanced its budget without a tax increase.

═══ 8

MEETING CONNECTICUT'S
HOUSING SHORTAGE

*Home-hungry veterans were a sharp political issue in 1948-49.
How the Connecticut government developed an effective
low-cost home-building and ownership program, in an effort
rarely attempted by a state government, is reported in this
article. Seventy thousand men, women, and children are now
living in houses built under this special program. From
"Two Thirds of a Nation," a symposium, published in
November, 1950.*

Do OUR state governments have a role to play in public
housing? This question deserves careful consideration, not only by
those interested in housing, but by everyone concerned with our growing dependence on our central government.

By and large it is federal-municipal programs, not state programs,
which are now clearing our slums, building low-cost homes, stimulating private construction and tackling the thorny problem of middle-
income housing.

In slum clearance, in redevelopment, in housing research, in mortgage loan programs to home builders and buyers, the federal government provides assistance of a size, kind and quality that few state
governments under our present tax systems can afford to duplicate.

But my experience as Governor of Connecticut has convinced me that a responsible, well-run state government can initiate, finance and carry through a substantial housing program that is both a necessary and valuable supplement to federal and local programs.

For instance, a competent and vigorous state government can finance excellent moderate-income housing through its borrowing power, without cost to the taxpayers. It can test on a small scale new types of housing programs and financing methods that would be impractical for the federal government to attempt.

Through direct day-to-day contacts that are impossible for a distant federal government, it can also coordinate the activities and raise the standards of performance of Local Housing Authorities. And it can encourage further slum clearance, redevelopment and low-rent housing, both by providing funds to supplement federal grants and by prodding local officials and stimulating community action.

Moreover, the question goes far beyond housing itself to the heart of our concept of democratic government, and particularly to the relation of state and federal powers. To ask the federal government plus city governments to carry the entire load on public housing is to overlook what I believe can be one of the most important roles of our state governments, and at the same time to encourage even greater dependence on Washington.

After listening to over two years of stormy legislative and political debate on housing in Connecticut, I have no illusions that a state housing program is all clear sailing. Opponents to public housing are just as determined and vociferous in state capitols and within state political parties as they are in Washington, D.C.

Yet as I watch 2,500 excited Connecticut families move into the first of ten thousand clean, decent, state-financed homes, I can only say, with feeling, that the contribution that a state housing program can make to the creation of dynamic democratic communities is well worth a few political and legislative headaches.

The American people are firmly and properly convinced that good housing, at a fair price or rental, is fundamental to the health of our free society. When such housing cannot be financed through private means, they feel that their government has a responsibility operating within our private enterprise system to devise plans to fill the gap.

Connecticut's housing situation after the war was typical of industrial states throughout the nation. Largely because of the heavy influx of war workers to man Connecticut's specialized war industries, our population increased by about 300,000 in ten years. With the exception of 5,000 temporary Lanham Act homes, virtually no homes had been built during the war.

As a result some 37,000 families in our small state were living doubled up with relatives and friends, and another 42,000 were living in what the experts described as "substandard" homes, in other words, slums.

At the same time it became apparent that private enterprise in Connecticut could finance only about 7,000 to 8,000 homes a year. After the elimination of the federal Veteran's Emergency Housing Program in 1946, these homes were built only for the higher income brackets, at sale prices well above $15,000, and at rents of more than $90 a month.

Indignant veterans appealed to the nearest governmental body they could find, which was their state legislature. Their demand for speedy, effective action in supplementing privately financed contractors with a really adequate state housing program for lower- and middle-income groups became a major issue in my campaign for Governor in the fall of 1948.

Following my inaugural I asked the legislature to authorize a state bond issue with which to build 13,000 homes. My proposal was finally agreed upon with the provision that half of them would be for rental and half for sale to families of moderate means.

A key provision of the plan was the financing of much of the program through one-year notes to be issued by the state government and renewed each year. At present the interest rate on these notes is less than 1 percent compared to the usual 2.6 percent on fifty-year loans. The use of this low-cost, short-term financing enabled us to bring shelter rents down to an average of $43. This figure will be adjusted upward or downward each year to fit the current interest rate, with no risk to the State.

However, some risk of loss is involved in regard to the homes built for sale. If the interest rate should rise substantially a deficit would be created which the State would pay. In view of the desperate nature of our housing shortage it was agreed that this risk should be taken.*

---

* Interest rates did rise and a deficit did accumulate. Yet this appears a small price to pay for the easing of a severe housing shortage.

Before presenting this broad program to the General Assembly I discussed it at length with architects, contractors, building material distributors and labor leaders from all over the state. From all of them I have received assurances that every effort would be made to give the state maximum cooperation in building high-grade homes at the lowest possible cost.

I was particularly gratified by the assurance of labor leaders, representing building trade councils all over Connecticut, that no feather-bedding and make-work practices of any kind would be tolerated. This promise has been kept.

Through our housing efforts in Connecticut we have established a kind of shared responsibility between state and local governments, and between government and private enterprise. We have persuaded even the most skeptical, I believe, that a well-planned, government-financed housing program is a tremendous stimulus to private building activity as well as to home equipment and furniture suppliers.

Private enterprise handles almost every phase of the state program. Local housing authorities use private architects. They turn over construction to private building contractors who buy the building materials from private sources and employ labor working under the usual conditions of private business.

All the financing, including the processing of state mortgage loans for the home ownership phase of the program, is done through private banks and private lending agencies.

Our estimates show that the entire program of 13,000 new houses will increase the number of homes built in Connecticut in 1950 by as much as 75 percent over previous yearly records. These homes would not have been built without the efforts of the state government.

A decent home for every American family is part of the challenge of modern democracy. In carrying their fair share of the load, state governments will not only speed the day when such housing is fully available; they will also demonstrate that our traditional federal-state system is as effective in fact as in theory, and that our citizens need not *always* go to Washington to "get things done."

9

A PROPOSED STATE MEDICAL CARE PROGRAM

How a state government can plan and support an insurance program to help its people meet the costs of "catastrophic illness" is outlined by Governor Bowles in a radio address, August 28, 1950.

WE AMERICANS have been growing healthier year by year. Since 1900 we have added nearly twenty years to the expected life span of a newborn baby. We have dealt heavy blows to such diseases as tuberculosis, pneumonia, and diphtheria, which used to be massive killers.

We are now making great advances against cancer, infantile paralysis, heart trouble, and similar ailments.

In Connecticut our health record has been particularly good. We have excellent doctors and good hospitals; our people live healthier and longer lives than in almost any other section of the United States.

Yet there are three questions in regard to medical care which I believe deserve greater consideration.

First, what can we do to detect more serious illnesses before they get started?

Second, how can we provide more training for doctors here in Connecticut?

Third, how can we deal with the devastating cost of long-drawn-out "catastrophic" illnesses which have put so many families in a state of permanent indebtedness?

Let us start with the first question: the early identification of a serious illness. Doctors agree that if they can diagnose a serious disease in its early stages they can save the lives of thousands of people who otherwise would have no chance. That is why we are all urged to go to the doctor annually for a complete check-up.

Some of us fail to heed this advice because of personal indifference or laziness; we can never seem to find the time. But there are many thousands of others who feel that they can't afford it.

To meet this problem I have suggested that we set up twenty or thirty diagnostic clinics throughout the state which would be controlled and operated by the doctors themselves. Through these clinics, many of which could be moved from town to town, all Connecticut citizens could be given complete annual or semiannual health examinations at a low cost.

The expense could be handled through a state-wide insurance system, with the state government making a direct financial contribution to ease the burden of the lower-income families.

Several doctors have told me that regular health examinations organized through a system of this kind may save several thousand lives each year here in Connecticut. The gain already made against tuberculosis through mass X-ray examinations shows what can be done on a broader scale.

The second problem is the need to expand our present health resources so that all our people may enjoy the high quality of health service which modern medicine is capable of providing. In the years ahead we must build more hospitals, equip them well, and train more doctors, nurses, and other health specialists.

I am particularly concerned about the need to enlarge our medical school facilities. Although the Yale University Medical School is one of the finest in the United States, its physical limitations allow only sixty-five young men and women to be graduated each year. That is no more than were graduated twenty-five years ago.

A new Connecticut University Medical School, based on our excellent Hartford Hospital, could train each year for the medical profession many Connecticut young men and women who are now denied an opportunity to become doctors.

Now the third problem to which I believe an answer must be found is the most crucial of all: the extremely high cost of medical care for a lingering illness, a cost that runs far beyond the income capacity of many Connecticut families.

There are valid reasons why high-quality medical care now costs so much. Modern hospitals are expensive to build, equip, and operate. A doctor's training takes seven or eight years. Many essential new drugs are costly to produce and dispense.

These high costs hit many thousands of our citizens with a devastating effect. Some have written me heart-breaking letters.

Let us consider a typical case that came to my attention a few days ago: The father in this particular family is forty-seven years old and earns $65 a week—which is now about average for all Connecticut families. By hard work and careful budgeting he and his wife had put aside $3,100 in savings over a period of years. It gave them a comfortable feeling to know that this money would be available to help send their highly talented son and daughter to college.

However, three years ago the mother's father, who lived with them, came down with a serious heart ailment. The illness was long and required extensive medical and hospital care totaling more than $4,000. As a result, their $3,100 in savings dwindled rapidly away; now college for the two children has become impossible.

This case is not unusual. I am sure you know of similar tragic cases in your own town, as I do in mine.

The voluntary health insurance programs such as Blue Cross are helping to ease the problem. But they cannot reach all of our citizens by any means; nor can they cover all types of cases.

To cope with this situation I propose a special Connecticut insurance plan that would *supplement* the present voluntary programs.

To finance this program each of us would make a small contribution to a common fund through our annual taxes. This common fund would *not* be used to pay the cost of ordinary illnesses. It would be used solely for those long, serious, and costly illnesses that most families cannot hope to pay for as part of their normal family expenses.

Let me explain more specifically how my proposal would work: A line would be drawn for each family, depending on its income, below which all medical costs would be paid for directly in the normal way, but above which the family would receive help from the central insurance fund.

An illness that cost no more than 10 percent of a family's annual income, for instance, would be paid for directly by the patient or his family. The insurance fund would be drawn on only when the total costs of family illness in a single year exceeded that 10 percent figure.

Here's how this plan would assist the family that I recently described. As you will remember, the father was earning $65 a week, or $3,380 a year. An ordinary illness or illnesses costing up to $338 —in other words, 10 percent of $3,380—would be paid for out of the regular income, savings, or other family resources.

But the grandfather's lingering heart illness resulted in hospital and doctors' bills totaling more than $4,000. To pay these extra heavy costs the family could call on the state insurance fund.

After carefully checking the facts the fund would pay the difference between the $4,000 total cost of the illness and $338, representing 10 percent of the family income, which would be paid for directly by them. In this case the cost to the fund would be $3,662.

This state-wide program would be available to everyone on a sliding-scale basis dependent on individual incomes. For instance, a member of a family with an annual income of $25,000 would be expected to pay the first 10 percent, or $2,500, for the cost of any illness or illnesses in a given year.

There are many possible variations on this proposal. I am sure that it can be improved by full debate and professional consideration, particularly through the advice of the voluntary health insurance agencies which have had so much experience.

However, we cannot afford to allow the complexities of the problem to become obstacles to action. As medical costs rise the situation will become increasingly serious. A workable plan must be devised to lessen the terrible financial load on those low- and moderate-income families who are suddenly struck with what some doctors call a "catastrophic illness."

Let me emphasize that a proposal of this kind does not call for government control of medicine or what some extremists call "socialized medicine." On the contrary, the program should be operated by a board of trustees of which a majority might be professional people —doctors, hospital superintendents, and the like.

It would not disturb in any way the free choice of doctors and patients or the relationship between them. It would permit high standards of medical care to be preserved and improved. It would be a *Connecticut* program using private health resources—doctors, nurses, hospitals, and druggists—with no connection whatsoever with the federal government in Washington.

The advantages would be great, not only for the tens of thousands of Connecticut families who have to face the prospects of high medical costs, but for the doctors, druggists, nurses, and hospital superintendents who now find it difficult in many cases to collect for the essential services which they have provided.

The three problems I have mentioned have worried me for a long time—just as I know they have worried many of you. Others may have better answers than those which I have proposed. All I ask is that we face up to the need and work together to find the most practical, efficient, and least expensive way to handle it.

We in Connecticut, with our great wealth and excellent record of health services, are in an unusually good position to show the way for others. We have a responsibility, here as elsewhere, to find effective answers to our problems on a state-wide basis without recourse to our federal government.

Our federal system provides forty-eight "state government laboratories" in which new methods for meeting social needs can be originated and perfected on a modest scale.

In this tradition some of our far Western states created much of our present wages-and-hours legislation. Connecticut contributed in a major way to our present nation-wide agricultural extension and research program.

Now I am proposing that Connecticut again lead the way in developing a state health program that will meet the needs of our people for adequate medical care, for more doctors and nurses, for more hospitals and clinics under the direction of the professional people themselves.

In any such effort we must carefully preserve the freedom of doctors and patients alike from governmental interference. We must vigilantly guard our high medical standards.

But we cannot use our traditional fear of government cooperative efforts as an excuse to sit back and do nothing.

We must expand our present medical resources to prevent and to cure sickness. At the same time we must bring good medical care within the financial reach of every Connecticut family.

It is our task to work together—private medicine, government, and all other groups—in finding ways to achieve these goals through programs that are workable, economical, and in keeping with our American way of doing things.

One of the reasons why the national health program now under discussion in Washington has been so strongly opposed by the medical profession is that the profession had little part in shaping it.

For this reason I am particularly anxious to hear from Connecticut doctors, nurses, medical educators, and professional societies about my proposals for a *Connecticut* approach to a nation-wide problem.

May I add that I have already discussed this challenge in a series of private meetings with an informal committee of outstanding Connecticut doctors and surgeons, including many of the top medical experts in the state. As a follow-up to these conversations I have appointed a special Governor's Committee on Health Resources.

The Committee has been provided with ample funds from my contingency fund for staff and research. I understand their first reports and recommendations will be ready in a few weeks.*

* This promising project died when Governor Bowles left office in January, 1951.

10

TOWARD A MODERN
STATE GOVERNMENT

*In a special session in April, 1950, Governor Bowles urges
a reluctant legislature to accept the recommendation of
the "Little Hoover Commission," which he had appointed to
study the antiquated and inefficient Connecticut state
government procedures. Though most of them were rejected
by a strongly rural Republican House of Representatives, the
recommendations were adopted ten years later, virtually in full,
under the governorship of Abraham Ribicoff, with the help of
the first Democratic State Assembly in a hundred years.*

FOR 170 years, in both our federal and state governments,
the system of checks and balances has been the rock upon which our
democracy has been built. It has proved its practical strength in the
face of many crises any one of which might have destroyed a weaker
form of government.

If we are to make this tested principle serve us as well in the future
as it has in the past, we should work constantly to strengthen each
of the three divisions, legislative, executive and judicial. We should
see that each is kept close to the people, and responsible to their
needs and desires. We should provide each with the machinery necessary to resolve quickly and in a democratic manner the conflicts and
problems of our modern society.

Considerable progress has been made in keeping the machinery of our federal government in good working order. The techniques and methods of our federal Congress and courts have been steadily improved, and the executive branch of the federal government has been reorganized on many occasions. This constant re-examination of the operation of our federal government has enabled us to keep the delicate balance of power among its three great departments.

But the framers of the Constitution established another fundamental balance in our system of government—a division of power and responsibilities between the central government and the *states*. I think it is fair to say that here we have been much less successful in maintaining the essential fundamental balance.

We have lagged in adjusting the machinery of our state governments to the growing needs of our society.

As a result, the federal government on many occasions has been forced by public pressure to deal with problems which might better have been handled in our state capitols. Much of the growth of centralized power in Washington can be traced directly to our failure to keep state governmental techniques abreast of our times.

Let us review the situation in our own State of Connecticut. Our State Constitution, and the governmental structure which stems from it, was developed in 1818—more than 130 years ago. It was built to fit the needs of a different and far simpler era, when industrialization had not yet reached our farms, our villages and towns; when there were no railroads, no airplanes, radios or automobiles, no huge industrial plants, no crowded cities, no problems of mass unemployment or atomic wars.

Our early Connecticut state government was a simple affair with only four small departments. Fifty years ago, 80 percent of our present 202 departments and agencies still did not exist. As late as 1930 the governorship and the heads of many state departments were considered part-time jobs. The methods and needs of our machine age have gradually replaced those of a slow-moving, horse-drawn economy.

Meanwhile the tasks of state government have grown steadily greater, in good times and bad, through Republican and Democratic administrations alike and more often than not with little regard for costs or efficiency.

It has been obvious for generations that the growth of government responsibilities in Connecticut, as in the other states, requires a tightening up of administrative machinery, that part-time government is wasteful and ineffective, and that reforms are long past due.

On several occasions, proposals have been made for a sweeping reorganization of our state government in the interests of increased democracy and increased efficiency. In 1902, Governor George P. McLean, a Republican, and in 1936, Governor Wilbur Cross, a Democrat, made courageous but fruitless fights to modernize our State Constitution.

The reasons why these and other efforts were not more effective can be simply stated: We have consistently underestimated the number and power of those individuals and organizations which have a heavy stake in bad government. The vested interests which were affected by the proposed changes were very much on the job, while the people who would benefit from them were very much asleep.

In my Inaugural Message on January 5, 1949, I recommended that you and I—the executive and the legislature—join together in an all-out effort to bring our Connecticut government thoroughly up to date; to make whatever changes might be necessary to improve our services to the people of our state, to eliminate waste and to cut our operating costs wherever possible.

On March 31, 1949, we agreed to the appointment of a five-man State Organization Commission to study each branch of our state government, to compare our governmental operation to that of other well-run states, and to present a complete set of recommendations. The findings of this Commission are now before us.

The substance of these findings can be stated simply: In the judgment of the Commission, the machinery of our state government, based upon a 132-year-old Constitution, is woefully and dangerously antiquated. An administrative jungle has grown up which defies responsible control by the legislature, the governor, the courts or the people, and causes widespread waste, inefficiency and frustration.

It seems clear that only the perseverance, ability and sense of public service of our thousands of state employees and scores of volunteer board and commission members have kept our state government from bogging down completely in inept and stumbling bureaucracy.

The Commission's recommendations go straight to the fundamentals. The solutions suggested have been drawn in part from the administrative experience of large and successful business enterprises; from the principles of good management endorsed by the Hoover Commission; from the experiences of states which have already put through reorganization plans; and, finally, from the practical experience of the Commission members themselves who know Connecticut, its traditions and its peculiar problems.

The recommendations fall into several different groups.

First, it is proposed that the financial structure of our state be completely revamped so that we may know at all times the exact status of our revenues and our expenses. Today some five different agencies, representing almost as many different attitudes and viewpoints, have divided responsibility for our general budgetary and fiscal operation.

Second, the report calls for a businesslike consolidation into eighteen departments of the 202 agencies and commissions which make up the executive branch of our government.

Third, the Organization Commission recommends the elimination of our wasteful county system which has been a fifth governmental wheel for several generations. The taxpayer has paid a heavy price for this outworn county system in duplication, higher costs and unnecessary political jobs.

Fourth, the Commission calls for an honest program of home rule for our cities and towns. Under our present system the local governments are, in effect, wards of the state government, unable to take positive action on many problems without the consent of the General Assembly. The best government is that government which is closest to the people. As the Commission points out, this concept calls for greatly increased home rule and decentralization.

Fifth, the Commission calls for a revamping of our court system, with full-time minor court judges and a consolidation of our superior and common pleas courts. This step should do much to improve our whole court setup and to remove the last vestiges of politics, wherever they may exist.

Sixth, the Commission proposes that the General Assembly should be well staffed, well organized and properly paid for its long hours and conscientious work.

Seventh, the Commission recommends the adoption of a simplified and clarified State Constitution, with full safeguards for our traditional civil liberties.

These proposals will provide Connecticut for the first time in recent history with a modern system of government. By strengthening each of the three basic divisions of our government, they will bring new vitality to our democracy. These proposals will enable us to improve substantially the services which we now provide for our people. In addition, they will enable us to make substantial savings, which the Commission estimates at a very minimum of twelve million dollars for each biennium.

The Commission Report is disappointing in only one respect. I know that many of you will share my regret over the inability of the five members of the Commission to agree on a method of revising our badly antiquated system of representation in the legislature.

The principles upon which the members of our Senate and House of Representatives are elected were laid down in the original Constitution of 1818. Under this system the members of the Senate were elected on the basis of equal representation. The members of the House, on the other hand, were elected to represent, not equal numbers of constituents, but specific cities and towns.

In 1818, this was not unreasonable. In the Connecticut of those early days the modest differences in size between our largest and smallest towns were relatively unimportant. Today the spread is vastly greater and the situation correspondingly different. As a result, this antiquated method of choosing the House of Representatives discriminates sharply against some two-thirds of our people.

At present, one-third of our people elect two-thirds of our House of Representatives. This Connecticut situation is cited throughout the United States as a textbook example of an antiquated and undemocratic form of representative government.

The Commission worked long and earnestly in an effort to provide an alternative system on which the five members could agree. Unfortunately, they were unable to reconcile their differences, and suggested that this issue should be postponed to a later date. This unequal system of citizen representation remains, however, a roadblock to the achievement of full-fledged democracy in Connecticut. Sooner or later, that roadblock must be removed.

In Connecticut, as elsewhere, political apathy is disappearing. In the atomic age our people are deeply concerned with the operation of their government and, more than at any time in our history, determined that it shall represent their true interests.

Let me make my own position perfectly clear. With the single exception of this question of representation, I accept this report with enthusiasm. I endorse it wholeheartedly. I urge you, the Connecticut General Assembly, with all the earnestness at my command, to take the action necessary to put it into law.

FREE MEN AND FREE MINDS

Today the struggle for individual liberty is the crucial political conflict of our times. What America thinks about liberty and, even more important, what America does about liberty, affects the policies of every government and the people of every nation. More than at any other time in our history, we in America cannot be confused about what liberty is, but must seek broad, deep agreement on what liberty means and how we may secure it.

May 28, 1950

11

THE ENDLESS SEARCH FOR LIBERTY

In this article in the New York Times Magazine *(May 28, 1950) Governor Bowles asserts that it is the responsibility of this generation to prove that the "Rights of Man" can successfully be translated from the eighteenth to the twentieth century.*

IN 1864 Lincoln said, "The world has never had a good definition of liberty, and the American people, just now, are much in need of one. We all declare for liberty; but in using the same word we do not all mean the same thing."

We still do not all mean the same thing. Yet today the struggle for individual liberty is the crucial political conflict of our times. What America thinks about liberty and, even more important, what America does about liberty, affects the policies of every government and the people of every nation. More than at any other time in our history, we in America cannot be confused about what liberty is, but must seek broad, deep agreement on what liberty means and how we may secure it.

"Liberty" is, clearly, a many-faceted word; liberty itself is of many kinds. To call liberty indivisible is neither honest nor realistic.

There is obviously, and first, political liberty: the liberty to go to the polls to choose our own Congressmen, President, Governors,

Prime Ministers and tax collectors; to approve or to disapprove government policies.

There are civil liberties: the liberty to speak our minds freely; to assemble in peaceful groups; to have equal access to public services; to move freely about in our own country; the right to a fair trial; freedom from unwarranted search, seizure or exile.

There are personal liberties: the liberty to choose our own religion; to marry whom we will and to bring up our children according to our own concepts; to become, if we wish, vegetarians, hermits or jitterbugs.

There are certain human liberties: the liberty for every one of us, regardless of race, religion, national origin or economic status, to develop freely, consistently with human dignity and to the full extent of our abilities. This is a relatively new concept, which I shall discuss more fully later.

Then there are economic liberties: the liberty to work where we will; to choose our job or start a business; to invent or market a new product; to charge whatever price or wage we can get; to take a job or quit; to own and sell property—all limited only by our capacity, intelligence and willingness to work.

Most civilizations have granted some of these liberties. None until our day has even pretended to grant them all. Most frequently, in past civilizations, all or most of these liberties were granted to one favored class and denied for the most part to all other classes.

The test for a modern democratic society is not only how many of these separate liberties exist in actual practice, but how many are available to how many people. Since its founding, America, on this test, has scored higher than any other country or civilization in history. More than that, today we are extending more liberties to more people than any other country on earth.

Since all liberties are dependent on political liberty, let us take it up first.

Our country was founded on the fundamental principle of political liberty for its citizens. For the last 150 years we have been working to establish this basic liberty in fact as well as in theory. When the United States was first established, only a minority of our adult citizens were allowed to vote or hold public office. Negroes, women and, in some states, those who owned no property were allowed no voice in the running of their government.

Today, with the unhappy exception of several million Negroes in our remaining poll-tax states, every American citizen over twenty-one years of age has been given the ballot.

What about civil liberty? This, too, was a fundamental liberty established in our Declaration of Independence, in our Constitution and in our Bill of Rights.

Compared to most countries, and above all to the totalitarian countries, America has set an enviable record. But we know, in all honesty, that ours is far from a perfect record.

The Negroes of our South have never had civil liberty as America conceives it for whites. And today we see the spectacle of a few demagogues, in and out of Congress, leading a vicious onslaught on the civil liberties of any individual whose thinking does not jibe with their own. The theory that we can strengthen our own freedom and defeat world Communism by borrowing one of its ugliest features—i.e., the suppression of civil liberty—is a dangerous doctrine indeed.

But even in these sore spots there is reason for optimism. Any fair-minded observer must agree that progress toward increased civil liberties for Negro citizens has been far greater since the war than in any similar period in our history. As far as our present orgy of character assassination is concerned, there are already signs that our traditional American sense of fair play and good judgment is beginning to reassert itself.

Although the question of civil liberties has caused many differences throughout our history, the problem of economic liberty is even more controversial, and more susceptible to misunderstanding.

Early America provided an ideal of economic liberty, unique in the history of civilization. We, a new people and new nation, found ourselves in a vast country of untapped resources, of untold wealth, of boundless unclaimed land and unlimited economic opportunity to anyone with an ax, a pick or a plow.

But our nostalgic enthusiasm for this red-blooded era should not obscure the fact that the Industrial Revolution, unprecedented in history, put our original concepts of economic liberty to a crucial test. It brought, of course, a vast increase in national wealth, in labor-saving equipment and in the productive power of workers. But as more and more Americans crowded into our cities to become wage earners in factories and mills, our old ideal of personal economic independence began to vanish into thin air for a majority of our people.

Inevitably, we used democracy's greatest instrument, political liberty, to regain some of the economic liberties which the Industrial Revolution took from us. We began to do so long before 1929. As far back as the Populist movement of the 1890's, the "Square Deal" of Theodore Roosevelt, and the "New Freedom" of Woodrow Wilson, we were making attempts to re-establish a balance between the expanding industrial machine and our shrinking economic freedoms.

After the great debacle of 1929, it was inevitable that we should use our political liberty to put our people back to work, to set up unemployment insurance, to prevent uncontrolled economic disaster in the future, to free our farmers from catastrophic drops in income and to prevent American families from going hungry in the midst of plenty.

At the same time another striking development was taking place that had profound effect on our thinking about liberty. No one who has studied history can be anything but amazed at the startling change in society's attitude toward human rights and liberty in the last 150 years.

I mean in particular our increasing emphasis on the rights of each man, woman or child, regardless of his race, his religion, his economic status, to develop freely, with dignity and to the full extent of his abilities.

In part, this concept grew from the same roots as our political liberty, and can be expressed in the same words used in our Declaration of Independence—"that all men are created equal, that they are endowed by their Creator with certain inherent and unalienable rights, that among these are life, liberty and the pursuit of happiness."

In part, too, this is the concept of our great religions: that even the least of us, the meek, the poor, the overburdened, are valued in the eyes of God.

In part, also, it has grown from our greater knowledge of the human mind and personality, our greater understanding of the effect of environment, of economic, social and psychological forces, on the development of the individual.

One of the earliest and most crucial battles for increased human rights was the movement to establish public education for all American children. No more than a hundred years ago some of our most respected citizens were still arguing that education for the "masses" was unreasonable, unnecessary and positively dangerous.

Thanks to our political liberty to make our government serve the will of the majority, public education was gradually adopted throughout the United States. Today our concept of public education is still expanding, and eventually may include college for all qualified students.

Another chapter in this long struggle for broader human rights has been waged to provide more liberty for more of our people from the burden of human illness. We became determined that the mentally ill, the blind, the crippled, the tubercular and the other diseased and handicapped should no longer be condemned as useless and beyond salvation.

We used our political liberty to provide medical research, rehabilitation, public health and hospital services for these people through our city, state and federal government. Eventually, I believe, we will reach agreement on a practical way to make modern preventive medical care available to all our citizens, regardless of income.

Another example of our developing public conscience is our increasing effort to provide a decent minimum of security, dignity and comfort—in short, more human liberty—for our old people, who were formerly cast aside by a tough industrial society. Still another is the development of programs to clear our slums so that more of our citizens may have the freedom to live and bring up their families in decent modern homes.

What we are working toward is not equality of material wealth, but equality of opportunity to live and to work and to move ahead in line with our capacity and interests; the right to a good education and good health for ourselves and our children; the right to a basic minimum of security; these in addition to the growing political and civil liberties which have always been the basis of our American liberal tradition.

It is the task of our generation to prove that the "Rights of Man" can be successfully translated from the eighteenth to the twentieth century.

12

CALL FOR A NEW IMMIGRATION POLICY

In an article in Survey *magazine in November, 1951, Mr.
Bowles castigates our "shortsighted and discriminatory"
immigration policy and appeals for an approach based on equal
rights for qualified applicants, regardless of national origins.*

AMERICA badly needs a new policy on immigration. Our
present policy is a product of the age of Harding and Coolidge, when
we were naïvely determined to isolate ourselves from the world, its
problems and its people. Its principles are outdated, discriminatory
and in clear violation of the democratic concepts on which our country has been built.

From the signing of the Declaration of Independence until 1921
America offered a generous welcome to immigrants from all over the
world. As a result, some forty million men, women and children
crossed the oceans to create new lives of freedom and opportunity
in the United States.

This flow of newcomers to America was one of the greatest migra-
tions in recorded history. In the first ten years of the twentieth century immigration averaged one million men, women and children each
year—or more than one percent of our total population at that time.
By 1910 40 percent of all people living in the United States were
either born abroad themselves or had a foreign-born parent or parents.

Today part of America's strength lies in the fact that through the years we have thus borrowed generously from the people of Europe, and indeed of all the world. Some of our greatest scholars, scientists, public servants, business and labor leaders are the sons or grandsons of the immigrants of fifty years ago.

In 1921 the first restrictive legislation was passed. This legislation set a top quota of 350,000 immigrants annually, exclusive of newcomers from the Western Hemisphere who were specifically exempt.

The effect of this limitation was to reduce annual immigration to about one-third the average number who had entered our country in the years before the First World War. The national quotas set by this legislation also discriminated sharply against potential newcomers from Eastern and Southern Europe.

But the 1921 Act was only a curtain raiser. In 1924 new legislation was passed which cut its total quotas to less than half, and discriminated even more harshly against Southern and Eastern Europeans. This legislation, which was further modified in 1929, still forms the basis of our immigration policy.

The first objective of this thirty-year immigration policy has obviously been to reduce the number of immigrants coming to our shores. That objective has been achieved with a vengeance. Although our population has increased by one-third since 1914, the quotas set under the 1924 Act allow only one-sixth as many immigrants to come to America each year as came on the average in the fourteen years immediately preceding World War I.

The reduction of immigration on such a drastic basis was demonstrably wrong when our present policy was established in 1924. Such an extreme is even more misguided now in the midst of a world struggle of tremendous proportions. Our ability to succeed in this struggle depends upon the strength, convictions and abilities of our people.

Who will question the fact that we are immeasurably stronger, not only in terms of economic power, but also in spiritual values, because of the millions who came to America from abroad in the last hundred years?

The second objective of our present mistaken immigration policy has been an attempt to legislate what kind of people make the "best" American citizens. In line with this objective our immigration laws insist that the Browns and the Schwartzes are more desirable Americans than the Lavellis and the Petrofskys.

This concept of nationality "class," this effort to place millions of Americans in the role of inferior citizens, runs counter to our democratic principles. It is not only undemocratic, it is ridiculous.

Where is there any evidence that Americans who are descended from Southern or Eastern Europeans have contributed less to the building of our country than Americans descended from Western and Northern Europeans?

Actually, the states in which Polish, Italian, Greek and other immigrants from Southern and Eastern Europe largely have settled— New York, Massachusetts, Rhode Island, Connecticut, New Jersey, Pennsylvania, Ohio and Michigan—are now among the most prosperous in the Union. They lead in progressive legislation.

The following comparisons indicate the shocking amount of discrimination which the 1924 Act established as part of our policy:

Immigration from Italy in 1914, the year immediately before the First World War, totaled 296,000. The 1921 Act lowered it to 42,000 annually. The present Italian immigration ceiling, set in the 1924 Act, slashed this to only 5,000.

In 1914, 174,000 Polish immigrants reached the U.S.A. The 1921 Act reduced their quota to 30,000 a year; the 1924 Act to 6,000. Greece, which sent 46,000 people to our country in 1907, now has an annual quota of only 307.

In contrast, the 1921 Act set a top limit of 77,000 on immigration from Great Britain and Northern Ireland—only slightly under the all-time record from these countries in a single year. Even when the total immigration ceiling was cut in half under the 1924 Act, Great Britain's quota was reduced only to 65,000. Under this law the annual German quota is substantially more than total quotas from all Southern European countries, including Italy and Greece plus Poland.

Although the "Displaced Persons" legislation, passed by Congress in 1948 under spur of the war, allowed many refugees who were in particularly dire straits to come to the U.S.A. at once, it did not modify our basic policy. The 330,000 immigrants who have been admitted under this law are almost all chargeable against the future quotas of the countries in which they lived.

This means that unless the present law is changed, immigration from many Southern and Eastern European countries will be shut off for many years in the future, with the exception of a relatively small number of specialized cases which do not come under the quota restrictions.

We can also eliminate from this law the ugly discrimination against people from Southern and Eastern Europe. National quotas should be scrapped and all applicants placed on an equal basis in regard to race, color, religion and national origin.

In the early stages of the new immigration act most nationality quotas were quickly filled, with growing waiting lists in Southern and Eastern European countries. But in the 1930's, under the influence of the depression, immigration fell off, and in the 1940's the war brought about additional reductions. From 1930 to 1946 the British used only 5 percent of their substantial annual quotas and the Irish used only 3 percent. The average for all countries was only 23 percent. Let us validate this backlog of unfulfilled quotas and pool them without regard to nationality.

I suggest an annual immigration ceiling of four-tenths of one percent of our population from all countries not in the Western Hemisphere, with no nationality quotas. This might be higher than advocates of an ingrown America would welcome. But I am confident that a majority of Americans would accept it as a moderate proportion.

What kind of people would come to the U.S.A. under such legislation? Would they be competent to make their own way, strong, law-abiding and loyal? What about the danger of Communists, Fascists and other undesirables?

For generations, every European town, village and city has had its scores, hundreds and thousands who looked upon the U.S.A. as a dreamland in which someday they hoped to live. The far smaller number who had the actual courage and perseverance to take their families across thousands of miles of ocean to new homes in a distant country were, by and large, the strongest, ablest and the most determined.

Today all over America millions of men and women only a generation or two or three removed from their mother countries are contributing in a hundred different ways to the healthy growth of our economic, social and political system. While some of our older families may have tended to coast on their illustrious past and to take democracy for granted, many of these comparative newcomers have been introducing new life and vitality into our whole American society.

The addition each year of some additional thousands of new Americans from overseas, carefully selected on the basis of health, character and ability, would add further to our national reservoir of skill, imagination and competence. And because these new citizens were chosen without regard for nationality, race or religion, they would demonstrate to the world that in the U.S.A. democracy, now as in earlier decades, is more than a slogan.

As far as Communists and Fascists and other "undesirables" are concerned, our United States Immigration Service has developed great skill in weeding them out. Up to January 1, 1951, of the 250,000 men and women brought in under the Displaced Persons Act, only three have been deported for cause.

Let us accept the challenge of our foolishly restrictive and discriminatory immigration laws. Action is long overdue.

13

PORTRAIT OF AN AMERICAN TOWN:
ESSEX, CONNECTICUT

*Before an Indian social welfare audience in early 1952, Mr.
Bowles draws a vivid portrait of small-town U.S.A. The
address was later published and widely distributed in many
languages throughout India.*

I HAVE always felt that one country cannot really understand
another unless each comes to know how the other people live, what
they think and feel and hope for.

To me, the most interesting and productive time I have spent in
India has been while traveling around the villages, the smaller towns
and bigger cities, visiting neighborhoods and trying to see how people
live, what they think about and how they bring up their children.

Because I am anxious to have you understand my country I would
like to tell you about the little town of Essex where I live in the State
of Connecticut.

Connecticut is a small state with only two million people in the
northeastern part of the United States. It is also one of our oldest
states, settled in 1635. This seems very youthful to you, but it is very
old in my country.

Connecticut was settled by people from England. They were mostly
farmers who came to escape the religious persecutions they had suf-

fered at home. They came to worship God as they wished to do and to try to live their lives as they saw fit, free from autocracy and dictatorship.

Much of the Connecticut land that they tilled was poor and rocky, and the winters were severe. So in the mid-nineteenth century, when they began to hear of the wonderful new land in the American West, where you could plow for a mile in almost any direction, with fertile soil and an easier climate, whole villages and towns picked up and left for the West.

Connecticut was repopulated again in the late nineteenth century by a new rush of emigrants from Europe. Today New Haven, the state's second biggest city, is 65 percent "Italian"—that is, 65 percent of the people were either born in Italy or their parents and grandparents were born there. New Britain is some 60 percent "Polish," and Hartford, the state's capital, is 40 to 50 percent "Irish."

Connecticut has almost no natural resources except its people. It has no mining and no oil. Yet, mainly because the people are so highly skilled, Connecticut has the highest per capita income in the United States. In our hundreds of factories, in all kinds of manufacturing work, those skills are put to constructive work for high wages.

A hundred years ago only 15 percent of Connecticut was forest; the rest was farm land. Although the state is now far more densely populated, with many large cities, nearly 70 percent of the land has returned to forest which now covers most of the old farms.

There are two large universities in the state—Yale University and the University of Connecticut—with a total student body of some twelve thousand. There are also seven smaller colleges and four special colleges for teacher-training.

We have a good public school system, but not as good as we think it should be; we are constantly trying to improve it. We are also trying to make it easier for more of our Connecticut children to go to college. Our laws require every boy and girl to stay in school until the age of sixteen; about 30 percent of them, after graduating from our secondary or "high schools," now go on to the universities.

We are also constantly trying to improve our housing and our hospitals, and here again we are making good progress. In every possible way we are trying to build the basis for a more productive and dignified life for all our people.

The town in which I live, Essex, has some 3,500 people. It is on

the banks of the beautiful Connecticut River. The people of Essex
are occupied in many different ways. There are five small factories,
the biggest of which has about two hundred people working in it.
Some of our people work in a factory only two to six months of the
year, then farm for another four or five months, and fish for another
month. There is a great amount of fish in the river every spring and
usually the fish bring a good price.

There are no very wealthy people in Essex, nor are there any really
poor people. Of the seven hundred families there, I can think of only
fifteen or twenty that have even one servant. As far as I know, only
one family has two servants.

You see, servants in America get such high wages that most of us
can't afford them. That is one reason why we have all these electrical
gadgets that some of my Indian friends tease us about. We have in-
vented the gadgets to take the place of the servants.

The government of our little town may be described as "direct democracy." If there is a need for a new fire engine, or a new street or
school, a notice is posted in the town hall that there will be a town
meeting on such and such a night to decide the question.

Anyone in town of voting age who has an interest in the outcome
comes to the meeting. They elect a moderator who acts as chairman of
the meeting and then the whole town acts like an assembly or a legislature, each person having a single vote. When we go home that night,
we have made a democratic decision in regard to the sidewalk or the
fire engine or school or whatever it may be.

To govern itself, Essex has not only its town meeting but three principal town officials, called selectmen, elected by the people. The first
two selectmen are members of the majority party; the third selectman
is a member of the minority party. It is his task to keep a careful watch
on the majority members so that all our interests are being honestly
and efficiently cared for.

I would say that the greatest concern of most people in our town is
their family and the life centering around the church. There are some
twelve different churches in the town, of Catholic, Protestant and
Jewish faiths. The church and the home are the two most important
institutions for most people.

Foreigners from overseas who visit our small American towns may
consider some of my fellow citizens limited in their outlook. It is true
that we have often become so involved in our own problems that

some of us haven't thought enough about the problems of the world. But this is now changing very rapidly. The people of Essex, as elsewhere in America, are waking up to the challenge of this complicated interrelated new world we all live in. They are trying, just as you are trying here, to find better answers to the problems that belong to us all.

Whenever I have returned home from India, I have had half a dozen invitations to speak on the subject of India—what the Indian people are thinking, what you are like, how you live and all about you. Every week there are now meetings on all kinds of subjects which simply were not of public interest even ten or fifteen years ago.

If you should ask me what my Essex fellow citizens want more than anything else in the world, I would say world peace—a chance to look forward to a future free of hatred, free of bitterness, free of the conflict of which we have seen so much during our lifetimes.

If you went to our Essex churches on Sunday, you would hear the sermons over and over again pleading for peace and understanding between people of all races and religions. You would see the people bowing their heads in prayers for world peace.

These neighbors of mine are reasonable people, and they think peace is simply a matter of everyone being reasonable. And in a sense they are right. If everybody were reasonable and understanding, if everybody tried to see the other person's point of view a little better, if we had no Iron Curtain to shut off one country from another, peace would be more attainable.

If you knew my fellow citizens as I do, you would find that few of them have any real bitterness against anybody. You would find them thinking and saying much the same sort of things that you say and think here in India. They hope above all else that some way can be found to break down the barriers that bar us from true world understanding.

I hope that many people from India can go to America and see our typical towns, like my town, and talk to typical people, such as my Essex neighbors.

I am also hopeful that many more Americans may come to India and see the life of India—the family life, the life in the neighborhoods and villages—and so to get to understand better the people of India, and all that you have to teach the world, as I have come to know you.

14

WHAT NEGROES CAN LEARN
FROM GANDHI

*In late 1957 an extraordinary bus boycott, embodying Mahatma
Gandhi's principles of civic disobedience, was successfully
led by Martin Luther King in Montgomery, Alabama. In an
article from the* Saturday Evening Post *of March 1, 1958,
Mr. Bowles summarizes Gandhi's techniques and their relevance
to America's racial dilemma.*

"NOW let's practice it again," the Negro preacher said to the
members of his congregation. "I'm a white man and I insult you, I
shove you, maybe I hit you. What do you do?"

Their answer was ready: "I keep my temper. I do not budge. I do
not strike back. I turn the other cheek."

It was a December evening in 1956. After a year of walking to work
and of riding in hundreds of cars organized in general pools the 42,000
Negroes of Montgomery, Alabama, had established their constitutional
right to ride in nonsegregated buses.

With the beginning of the next workday the new bus rules would go
into effect. Now they were patiently going through demonstration ses-
sions in their churches, pretending the pews were bus seats, learning
how to apply their Christian principles to this most explosive of all
problems in human relations.

"Now remember," their ministers advised them, "don't crow. Don't lord it over the white riders. Show patience and respect. Do unto them as you would have them do unto you."

In the following weeks, white extremists fired shots, hurled bombs and subjected the Negroes and their leaders to a barrage of threats and insults. But they stood their ground, firm and dignified, without arrogance or bitterness.

When their victory was finally won, many white citizens who had been active in organizing resistance to bus desegregation said grudgingly, "We didn't know the Negroes had the stuff to do what they've just done. We never thought we'd come to respect them, but we have."

How had this practical, latter-day demonstration of the Sermon on the Mount been achieved? What were the techniques which made it possible?

The Montgomery program had deep spiritual roots, not only in Christianity, but in the ancient religions of Asia. Martin Luther King, the twenty-seven-year-old Negro minister who more than any other individual was responsible for its success, says frankly that he borrowed his techniques directly from Gandhi, who used them brilliantly to bring freedom to millions of Indians.

Gandhi in turn was stimulated by the views of the Russian writer, Tolstoy, and by the American, Thoreau, who was sentenced to serve in a Massachusetts prison because of his "peaceful protest" against the Fugitive Slave Law. It was from Thoreau's essay "Civil Disobedience" that Gandhi borrowed the phrase used widely to describe his program.

Many Americans who consider themselves hard-headed may discount the happenings in Montgomery as a special situation and scoff at the suggestion that such techniques could, in fact, ease the explosive racial antagonism that plagues so many American communities. But one thing is sure: their skepticism is no greater than that of Gandhi's contemporaries a few years before his final triumph.

There are suggestive parallels between the Montgomery boycott and the beginning of Gandhi's struggle. The movement in Montgomery started from an incident which blossomed into a crusade.

A quiet Negro seamstress, Mrs. Rosa Parks, had been forced many times to give her bus seat to a white person. But one day, for some reason that she herself does not fully understand, she suddenly decided not to move. When the driver threatened to call the police, she said, "Then you just call them."

Mrs. Parks was arrested. Negro religious leaders called for a one-day city-wide boycott of the buses. When white extremists reacted vigorously, the protest grew until it covered the entire city bus system and involved almost every Negro family in Montgomery.

The Gandhian movement which ultimately freed India from foreign rule started in much the same way; in his case the spark which set it off was struck on a train in remote, race-conscious South Africa in 1893.

Gandhi, then a young lawyer of twenty-three, had come to South Africa to represent an Indian citizen in a legal case. The night of his first train ride in South Africa, he was ordered to leave the compartment reserved for whites. When he refused to do so, he was pushed off the train at the next station stop.

As he stood shivering there in the cold dawn, his overcoat and baggage still on the train now fast disappearing down the tracks, Gandhi asked himself the fateful question, "Should I stay here in South Africa and fight for my rights and those of other underprivileged people or should I give up and go back to India?"

"I came to the conclusion," he recounts, "that to run back to India would be cowardly." The "golden rule," he decided, "is to dare to do the right at any cost."

When he later took the stagecoach for Pretoria, he was addressed as "Sammie," ordered to sit outside on a dirty sackcloth and beaten by a burly white man. When he arrived in Pretoria, the hotels refused to give him a room. It was an American Negro who befriended him and somehow found him lodgings.

The next day Gandhi invited the Indians of Pretoria to a meeting at which he proposed that they stand up and fight the discrimination against them and that the fight be conducted with new, constructive methods.

The end they must seek, Gandhi said, was a community of true neighbors. Therefore the means must be those of persuasion and not of violence. Members of the Indian minority must forego hatred. They must respect their white neighbors as fellow human beings even while opposing their unjust discriminatory laws.

They must prepare themselves to endure blows and prison without flinching and without resort to counterblows or insults. They must persuade, not only through words, but through their lives. Their words must become flesh.

"Let us begin," he suggested, "by considering the grievances held against us by the white people. Let us see if the reasons or rationalizations which the whites give for discriminating against us are justified."

Many of the Indian merchants who came to hear him were known for slick dealings and sharp bargaining. Gandhi proposed that they stick rigidly to the truth and that they show a new concern for their responsibility to the community.

"We can't blame the whites," he continued, "for all our troubles, nor can we by ourselves end all the poverty in which our people are trapped. But we can begin to clean up our homes, to teach illiterate Indian adults to read and to provide free schools for the children of the poor."

By trial and error, Gandhi devised a political-action program with dramatic new dimensions. Instead of working just through the law—by appealing for an end to restrictive legislation in parliament and by seeking court or electoral victories—Gandhi showed the Indians how to combine peaceful resistance to discriminatory laws with constructive community service.

He led tens of thousands of Indians in a peaceful march across the state, deliberately violating the segregation laws. Hundreds were struck down by the police and thousands went to prison.

Eventually, Prime Minister Smuts decided that there was no practical alternative but to reach a fair settlement with Gandhi. "You can't put twenty thousand Indians in jail," he said.

* * *

IN 1915, Gandhi returned to India to apply his energies and his new techniques of nonviolent action to the struggle for independence. In India, as in Africa, his program went far beyond the struggle against British domination. His goal was to build an India that could govern itself. Therefore he spent as much time training his countrymen in constructive work in the villages as in the effort to achieve national independence.

His thirteen-point program for Indian development included the end of untouchability within Hinduism, the establishment of Hindu-Moslem unity and brotherhood, and improved methods of agriculture, diet, education and public health in the 500,000 villages where most Indians lived.

Gandhi's political genius enabled him to select and dramatize issues which the people understood. In 1930 his famous salt march focused the whole independence fight on a simple demand of the Indian villager: an end to the hated British tax on salt and their prohibition of homemade salt.

When Gandhi announced that he would walk two hundred miles to the shores of the Arabian Sea and make salt out of God's ocean in defiance of man's largest empire, India was electrified. Millions of peasants gathered along the roads to cheer him as he strode quickly by.

On the night of April 5 he reached the sea. "God willing," he said, "we will commence civil disobedience at 6:30 tomorrow morning." At sunrise he held his usual prayer meeting and at the appointed time reached down to raise his first handful of salt from the salt beach.

As the news was flashed across the country, the excitement became intense, reaching into the most remote villages. Nehru and nearly 100,000 others were arrested.

Then Gandhi announced that he would lead a nonviolent march of protest on the nearby government salt depot. Although he, too, was promptly arrested, the raid was carried out by 2,500 Indians pledged not to raise their hand or voice against the police.

Although hundreds were struck down, there was no resort to counterviolence. When Gandhi in his cell heard that even the fierce Pathan Moslems from the northwest frontier had maintained their self-discipline, he was overjoyed. Indians everywhere began to stand a little straighter and for the first time to feel that they, as individuals, had rights, responsibilities and a future.

For thirty years Gandhi, with brilliant political timing and a resolute belief in ultimate victory, applied his revolutionary new techniques of peaceful political action to the creation of a free and socially awakened India.

Independence finally came, on August 15, 1947. What a strange and magnificent climax to an anticolonial revolution! Four hundred million people had won their right to rule themselves. Miraculously, they had won it without bloodshed or rancor. Because the British yielded gracefully, the basis was laid for a new relationship of equality and mutual respect within the British Commonwealth.

No thoughtful person can deny the practical effectiveness of the Gandhian approach in India or even in Montgomery, Alabama.

But can it work in Little Rock, Chicago, Levittown and New Orleans? Can it free Americans—north, south, east and west—from the suffocating burden of racial prejudice and fear accumulated in three hundred years of largely unconscious compromise with Christian principles?

The prime conditions for the success of Gandhi's way of fighting injustice was that it took place within a legal system administered by people who professed a democratic creed and who permitted a large measure of free speech and a free press.

Moreover, as a trained lawyer, Gandhi never lost his respect for the majesty of law. He called for the acceptance of the state's right to make and enforce laws, while offering up his person and his freedom in protest until those laws which violated democratic principles were changed. His appeal was from man-made discriminatory laws to a higher natural law, to the moral law.

This is precisely the approach that enabled the brilliantly led, well-organized Negro citizens of Montgomery to abolish segregation on the city buses. Under the leadership and inspiration of the Reverend Martin Luther King and his associates they began their mass meetings with prayers "for those that oppose us," and they regularly pledged themselves to use "only the weapons of love and nonviolence." They said they were "walking with God." They named their movement the Montgomery Improvement Association.

Like Gandhi, Dr. King also stressed that he and his associates were working for the advancement of the whites in Montgomery as well as for that of the colored people.

"Let us examine the reasons given by white men for segregation," Dr. King said. "Let us see which reflect conditions we can do something about, and take action ourselves."

And then Dr. King frankly listed the illegitimacy rate among Negroes, their crime rate, their purchase of cars beyond their means, their lower health standards. And the Montgomery Improvement Association works day and night to remove these legacies of slavery, segregation and enforced second-class citizenship.

Already Montgomery city and welfare records are beginning to reflect the change—a drop in Negro drinking, juvenile delinquency and divorce.

When this combination program of nonviolent opposition to segregation and community service spreads beyond Montgomery, the road is likely to be a rocky one. Gandhi himself demonstrated that there is no easy, effortless path to the attainment of our Christian objective of equal dignity for all men.

By turning the other cheek the Indians at first only enraged the British. Nehru once said that he had never seen men with more hate in their eyes than the soldiers who beat him with their long, steel-tipped rods, while he stood quietly, not lifting a finger in his own defense. No human being likes to have his conscience so severely tested.

What counted, however, was the end result. As the Indians proved their capacity for peaceful resistance, they eventually won the respect of the British. Equally important, they came to respect themselves. "We cast off our fear," said Nehru, "and walked like men."

It is difficult to judge the prospects for such a program on a nation-wide scale here in America. Gandhi was not only a spiritual leader of depth, dedication and courage, but also a political genius. In America much will depend on the ability of Negro leaders to develop similar conviction and skill under pressure. Even more will depend on the number, raw courage and dedication of their followers.

Only one thing is certain: If we are to achieve racial harmony in America, a great moral force of some kind must be created that will awaken our national conscience.

Sooner or later the South and also the North, East and West will respond with the only Christian answer possible, for Christ came to show the fatherhood of God and the brotherhood of man, and He knows neither Gentile nor Jew, Greek nor barbarian, black nor white.

══ 15

NEGRO RIGHTS: THE TIME
FOR ACTION IS HERE

*Racial tensions, erupting in northern suburbs as well as the
South, suggest another look at this "moral cancer" of our
society in all parts of the United States. From the* New York
Times, *January 17, 1960, and the* New Republic, *July 6, 1959.*

THE PRIMARY reason to bring an end to racial discrimination in America is not the Communist challenge. Nor is it our need to
make friends and influence people abroad. The primary reason purely
and simply is because racial discrimination is wrong.

Racial discrimination is a moral cancer within our society. It is a living, continuing, ever-present denial of our religious and democratic
faith. It is a constant drain upon our national conscience.

The issue is not primarily that of living at peace with the rest of
mankind. Until we can remove this blight on our national conscience,
we can have no hope of living at peace with ourselves.

Whatever happens between races in our country—whether in Little
Rock, Montgomery, Levittown or Chicago—is a part of us and is
something we all share as Americans.

What American community—whether east or south or north or
west—can probe its inmost self and judge itself blameless?

Which of us does not daily pass areas of housing and schools and recreation where colored people are excluded? Which of us does not take part, however inadvertently, in the tragic economics of discrimination?

Let us not forget that American Negroes now live in the North. There are five times as many in Detroit as in New Orleans, six times as many in Los Angeles as in Miami.

Yet many Northerners still smugly look at racial discrimination as a sectional problem, condemning what they consider to be the slow pace of integration in the South, while remaining indifferent or nearly so to the discrimination all around them.

Of the thirty-nine states outside the South, only nineteen have established Fair Employment Practices Commissions and three of these are without enforcement powers.

In twenty other non-Southern states there has been no legislative action on employment discrimination at all. Only nine states outside the South have adopted antidiscrimination legislation affecting publicly assisted housing. In thirty other non-Southern states no official action to end housing discrimination has occurred.

Some cities, such as New Haven and Pittsburgh, are now taking far-reaching steps to rebuild themselves, including the slum clearance and human rehabilitation essential to the easing of racial tensions. But in many Northern cities the professed equal protection of the laws still hides extensive segregation in fact—by residential exclusion and by the natural selection of poverty. In very few major Northern cities do more than 20 percent of the Negro students attend school with white children.

Almost any Northern community that honestly examines its own racial relations will realize how far it is from living up to its professed ideals. And once we see what is missing in our own cities and states, we will be less inclined to feel that it is enough to denounce the foolhardy actions of white extremists south of the Mason-Dixon line. Nothing will speak more persuasively to the South than a better example among the too ready critics in the North.

Fortunately for all of us the Constitution is color-blind. The Fourteenth Amendment *does* require the end of racial discrimination in all parts of our public life. The Universal Declaration of Human Rights, endorsed overwhelmingly by the people of the world, affirms this as one of the first principles of world order.

The Supreme Court has ordered desegregation with "all deliberate speed," and Negro litigants will see that this is complied with; the new Negro, arising in the South and elsewhere, will supply all the litigants necessary, no matter what pressures are organized to stop him. Regardless of what party is in power, the observance of the law ultimately will prevail.

And of course law itself is a powerful teacher. The end of segregation in the armed forces, in the nation's capital and on interstate trains did more to convince many skeptics that integration in these areas made sense than any amount of talk could have done.

There appears to be a temptation, however, to rest on the oars of lawyers and judges and say that this has become purely a matter of law and order. President Eisenhower seemed to reflect this view when he stressed that he has told no one, not even his wife, whether he thinks the Supreme Court desegregation decision was right or wrong.

But court orders alone will not change the minds and hearts of people. Our objective is not a reluctant and grudging acceptance of the inevitable force of the law. Our hope is that recognition of historical necessity will encourage an increasing effort to bring elements in each community into harmony.

If school integration were merely a legal issue between those who believe in upholding the law and those who seek to circumvent it, then there would have been no issue until the Supreme Court acted in 1954. But this turns the problem upside down. The Court acted because the Constitutional guarantee of equality involves the deepest political principles of this nation and because there was a moral issue presented which went to the heart of our Bill of Rights and our Christian civilization.

The law does not get its sanction merely because it is the law. It wins support because it embodies the moral purpose of society, and the task of political leaders, and of all who want to establish equal rights, is not only that of invoking and carrying out court decisions, but also of convincing people that they are right.

Our dilemma, then, is a moral and a national dilemma. In this perspective an awareness of world *opinion* may assist us in doing those things which we ought to do anyway. But world *experience* may, I think, be of even greater help to us in at least three ways.

First, it can reduce our excessive self-consciousness on this issue. For the sin of racial prejudice is not ours alone. It is a universal sin. It cuts across the cultures of the earth, it touches all men.

Second, we can take heart from the understanding and admiration with which Asians and Africans have responded to the untiring efforts and skill of our Negro and white lawyers who have successfully fought to implement the Supreme Court's school desegregation decision.

Third, world experience can also teach us that the keys to progress lie not in laws alone, but also in the hearts of men. All of us—white and Negro alike—can learn from the practical experience of other peoples if only we have the humility both to acknowledge our imperfections and to seek assistance.

The greatest opportunity for constructive action lies right in our own neighborhoods in our day-to-day relations with our fellow citizens.

If our growing concern about discrimination can be channeled into community programs on a national scale, spectacular progress can be achieved in the coming years.

A citizens "check list" for communities both north and south of the Mason-Dixon line might include the following questions:

How many Negroes are in the police force? The fire department? City hall? The school system?

Do Negroes have a full opportunity to get such jobs? And if so are they promoted solely on merit and services?

What kind of housing, both public and private, is available to Negroes? What kind of medical and hospital care?

Is there any direct or indirect discrimination in public housing and entertainment facilities?

What about private enterprise jobs? Do Negro workers have jobs which use their skill to the fullest?

Is vocational, professional training freely available to Negroes?

Are the police and the courts as fair to them as to other sections of the population?

An objective study by nongovernmental groups in each city, under the leadership of the mayor and prominent citizens, will do much to bring community agreement on the answers to such questions, and from those facts can flow constructive democratic action.

Gunnar Myrdal's monumental study of the problem, *An American Dilemma,* provides an important clue to such action. This is the immensely hopeful fact that the very rights which the white people are most ready to grant—equality of opportunity in jobs, equal and adequate social security and housing, and equality before the law—are the very rights which the Negroes are most anxious to secure.

That we still have time is a supreme tribute to the extraordinary qualities of endurance and patience of our Negro fellow citizens themselves. It was 185 years ago that we declared in our Declaration of Independence that all men were created free and equal. It was ninety years later that we succeeded in freeing the slaves. It took another ninety years before we decided that compulsory segregation of Negro and white children in our schools was unconstitutional.

Today most Americans know in their hearts that the time for explanations is over, and that the time for action is here. We know that real equality of opportunity among all races and creeds can no longer be denied. Let us move, therefore, to the high ground of action required by our courts and our conscience.

THE MORAL GAP

Before a Smith College graduating class of which his daughter was a member, Mr. Bowles decries the failure of his generation to create an adequate moral framework for modern American society. Commencement Address, Smith College, June 5, 1960.

I BELIEVE that history will be more tolerant toward your parents' generation than many of you have been. Although we were totally untrained, your parents and I, for the kind of world we have had to live in and even help manage, I believe that our record will stand up well under scrutiny.

My generation, for instance, broke with 130 years of tradition to put isolationism behind us in world affairs. It took action, born of economic and social distress, to give new depth and meaning to our national unity. It pioneered in the postwar world with the bold, creative concepts of the Marshall Plan, NATO, Point Four and the Mutual Security Program.

Many of our more timid members view some of our technological achievements with considerable alarm. Our cows, they say, give too much milk, and our new machines produce too much steel.

Unquestionably we have been inadequate to many of the tasks which demanded attention, including the obvious one of putting the world's hungry children in touch with the extra milk.

Nevertheless, on behalf of your parents and the rest of our generation, I hope you will not be too severe on us. We rose, unevenly and fitfully it is true, but nevertheless we rose, to tasks which were historic; may we have the will and capacity to rise to the additional tasks that will confront us in the years ahead.

Yet this is an occasion for frank and honest analysis. In perhaps the most crucial area of all our performance over the years has been weak. In our efforts to deal with a vast agenda of new and unfamiliar problems, we have neglected to cultivate the human values which are most basic to the health and vigor of our American society.

We have not only condoned the slick operator and cynical manipulator; in a backhanded sort of way, we have *glorified* them. We have adopted the semantics of materialism and manipulation to explain some of our most admirable actions. It is as though we felt it necessary to justify decency by proving that the real reasons for our actions are not so decent as they might seem.

For instance, we argue that the time has come to grant our Negro citizens first-class citizenship, not because they have been waiting for 180 years since the Declaration of Independence asserted that "all men are created equal," but because the colored majority of mankind in Asia and Africa is said to be breathing down our necks.

In order to win public support for urgently needed scholarships for our colleges and universities, we call the legislation the "National Defense Education Act"—and fit it out with reassuring anti-Communist disclaimers and loyalty oaths.

Instead of proudly presenting our foreign aid program for what it is —an earnest effort to help new nations ease poverty, illiteracy and disease so that they can remain free within their own cultures—we explain that our real purpose is to buy friends and supporters in the United Nations, or to keep restless people from asking hard questions, or to fill empty bellies on the cynical assumption that well-fed foreigners will more easily tolerate the injustices and harassments of the feudal societies in which they live—and thus join us in support of the status quo.

Even when we set out to do the wrong thing in world affairs—like hiking the tariffs on British bicycles or foreign clothespins—we explain that we are acting in the interests of "national defense."

Through our fears and frustrations of this disorderly new world, we have come to act as though our chief national purpose is not to maintain and extend our basic American commitment to human dignity, but to thwart the Russians in whatever they decide to do.

And while we strive to outfox the Communists abroad, we concentrate on keeping up with the Joneses at home. Politicians, journalists, businessmen—even college professors—increasingly give the most cynical reasons for their most high-minded activities.

We smile with a knowing self-assurance as we explain that scandals in high places and the misuse of positions of national trust simply go to prove that politics is politics.

Northern office-seekers assure their Southern colleagues that they vote for Negro rights only because of the political pressures back home.

Businessmen contributing to boys' summer camp funds and hospital-building drives rush to cover up their decent motivations by pointing out that it is good publicity for their business, and after all, isn't it tax-deductible?

This brings me to my central point: At the very moment in history when the true nature of the world contest is coming into focus, we find ourselves faced with a crisis in values. The moral standards in which we prefer to believe are marked by our immoral tolerance of tax evasion and false expense accounts, of fake advertisement, the thumb on the scale, the adulterated product and the exploitation of violence as entertainment.

In our national effort not to seem gullible, not to seem vulnerable to criticism from any quarter, to avoid controversy, and to prove that we are realists who do not go off half-cocked, we have developed a moral gap between the beliefs to which we subscribe and our actual day-to-day performance. This moral gap can become an increasing danger to our survival as a free society.

There is a real question, at best, whether an open society can endure indefinitely against the military, technological and psychological requirements of twentieth-century nuclear terror.

Already there are many among us who feel more secure under the appalling but familiar dangers of the nuclear stalemate than under the prospect of any relaxation in tensions. It is simpler for them to march off in a straight line in one direction, even if the obvious destination is Armageddon.

Such people seem determined to prove again the prophecy of

William Butler Yeats: "The best lack conviction, while the worst are full of passionate intensity." They are unhappy about complexities, about shades of gray, about difficult choices, about the necessity to pursue various alternative policies at once, about the requirements in the modern world for balance, dexterity and nerve.

They are good people to keep out of the control rooms in this age of push-button war. In the days of limited mayhem by means of bayonets and machine guns they were dangerous enough; in today's nuclear world they have the cataclysmic touch.

The constructive leadership of America is now challenged, not simply to stand up to the Russians, but to understand the nature of a revolutionary world, to explore the forces at work in Communist societies and to put itself in touch with the aspirations of the people in between—the men and women and children of Asia, Africa and Latin America who see our planet as more than an arena for an increasingly reckless Soviet-American conflict.

As we move to meet this challenge, we may be reminded of the words of Woodrow Wilson who once told a graduating class at Annapolis:

There have been other nations as rich as we; there have been other nations as powerful; there have been other nations as spirited; but I hope we shall never forget that we created this nation, not to serve ourselves, but to serve mankind. . . . No other nation was ever born into the world with the purpose of serving the rest of the world just as much as it served itself.

By recapturing that vision, at all levels of American society, we may regain the quiet wisdom of that ancient faith which has come down to us through the ages in Romans 5:3-4: "We glory in tribulations; knowing that tribulation worketh patience; and patience, experience; and experience, hope."

POSTSCRIPT

"DEMOCRACY," Thomas Jefferson once said, "is the only form of government which is not eternally at open or secret war with the rights of mankind." Yet democracy has never been challenged so profoundly as at this moment.

This challenge lies partly in the threat of antidemocratic ideology, but even more in the decline of our own traditional vision, ideals and sense of individual commitment.

We can recapture our common purpose only by returning to first principles. The truths which our Declaration once held to be "self-evident" are still among the great truths of all time: "That all men are created equal, that they are endowed by their Creator with certain unalienable rights, that among these are life, liberty and the pursuit of happiness."

It is the task of our generation to pursue these universal truths in a new world setting with all the spirit and dedication of our forefathers. I believe that each of us carries his share of personal responsibility for the ultimate outcome.

Both at home and abroad we must learn to act with charity, not self-interest; with compassion, not violence; with love, not hate. We must assert, not deny, our positive faith in ourselves, our future and our common brotherhood.

Only by so doing can we create an America that is strong not only in the material power necessary for the common defense, but also in its moral commitment to the essential rights and dignity of all men, which alone can provide the basis for a lasting peace. The outcome, I believe, now hangs in the balance.

Washington, D.C., August 17, 1962

ABOUT THE AUTHOR

CHESTER BOWLES has been a businessman, writer, public administrator, governor, Congressman, and ambassador. He is now President Kennedy's Special Representative and Adviser on African, Asian, and Latin-American Affairs. No other man in American public life has had greater breadth of experience.

Born in 1901 in Springfield, Massachusetts, Mr. Bowles' first career was as a business executive. With the outbreak of World War II he left business and served under President Roosevelt as Federal Price Administrator, then under President Truman as Director of Economic Stabilization.

After the war, Mr. Bowles served as Special Assistant to Trygve Lie, the Secretary General of the United Nations. In 1948 he was elected Governor of Connecticut, and in 1951 President Truman appointed him United States Ambassador to India and Nepal.

The years from 1953 to 1958 were largely devoted to world-wide travel and to speaking and writing on foreign affairs. He has lectured at most major American universities. He is the author of seven books, five of which were written in this period.

In 1958 Mr. Bowles returned to public office as a Congressman from Connecticut. In the Presidential campaign of 1960, Mr. Bowles served as Chairman of the Platform Committee of the Democratic National Convention and as foreign policy adviser to Senator Kennedy. He was named Under Secretary of State in late 1960, a post he held until he was appointed to his present position.

Mr. and Mrs. Bowles now live in Washington; their permanent home is in Essex, Connecticut. They have five children.